Penguin Books

A Time of Gifts

In December 1933, Patrick Leigh Fermor set out to walk from Rotterdam to Constantinople and *A Time of Gifts* is the enthralling account of his journey as far as Hungary. Patrick Leigh Fermor is one of the finest travel writers of his generation and his books have won widespread praise. Writing of this book, Vincent Cronin said, 'almost every page . . . is distinguished by an image, a metaphor, a flash of humour always original and sometimes incisive as a laser beam' and Peter Levi commented, 'I know of no other account of pre-war Europe which conveys so much so powerfully.'

Patrick Leigh Fermor was born in 1915 of English and Irish descent. After a 'stormy' school career and his year-and-a-half journey on foot to Constantinople, he lived and travelled in the Balkans and the Greek Archipelago. During that time he acquired a deep interest in languages and a love of remote places. He enlisted in the Irish Guards in 1939 , joined the 'I' Corps in 1941, became Liaison officer in Albania, and fought in Greece and Crete to which, during the German occupation, he returned three times (once by parachute). Disguised as a shepherd, he lived for over two years in the mountains organizing the resistance and the capture and evacuation of the German Commander, General Kreipe. He was awarded the DSO in 1944 and the OBE in 1943, and was made Honorary Citizen of Herakleion, Crete. Patrick Leigh Fermor has also written *The Traveller's Tree*, about the West Indies, which won the Heinemann Foundation Prize for Literature in 1950 and the Kemsley Prize in 1951; *A Time to Keep Silence*; *The Violins of Saint Jacques*; *Mani*, winner of the Duff Cooper Memorial Prize and a Book Society Choice, and its companion volume, *Roumeli*; and *Between the Woods and the Water*, the sequel to *A Time of Gifts* and winner of the Thomas Cook Travel Book Award and the Silver Pen Award for 1987. Patrick Leigh Fermor now lives in Greece in a house he designed and built. He is a visiting member of the Athens Academy.

A Time of Gifts, winner of the 1978 W. H. Smith Literary Award, was described by Jan Morris as 'nothing short of a masterpiece'.

PATRICK LEIGH FERMOR

A TIME OF GIFTS

*

On foot to Constantinople:
from the Hook of Holland
to the Middle Danube

PENGUIN BOOKS

PENGUIN BOOKS

Published by the Penguin Group
27 Wrights Lane, London w8 5TZ, England
Viking Penguin Inc., 40 West 23rd Street, New York, New York 10010, USA
Penguin Books Australia Ltd, Ringwood, Victoria, Australia
Penguin Books Canada Ltd, 2801 John Street, Markham, Ontario, Canada L3R 1B4
Penguin Books (NZ) Ltd, 182–190 Wairau Road, Auckland 10, New Zealand

Penguin Books Ltd, Registered Offices: Harmondsworth, Middlesex, England

First published in Great Britain by John Murray 1977
First published in the United States of America by
Harper & Row, Publishers, Inc. 1977
Published in Penguin Books 1979
15 17 19 20 18 16

Printed and bound in Great Britain by
Cox & Wyman Ltd, Reading
Set in Linotype Juliana

Contents

Linque tuas sedes alienaque litora quaere,
o juvenis: major rerum tibi nascitur ordo.
Ne succumbe malis: te noverit ultimus Hister,
Te Boreas gelidus securaque regna Canopi,
quique renascentem Phoebum cernuntque cadentem
major in externas fit qui descendit harenas.

Titus Petronius Arbiter

I struck the board and cry'd 'No more;
    I will abroad'.
What, shall I ever sigh and pine?
My life and lines are free; free as the road,
Loose as the wind.

George Herbert

For now the time of gifts is gone –
O boys that grow, O snows that melt,
O bathos that the years must fill –
Here is dull earth to build upon
Undecorated; we have reached
Twelfth Night or what you will . . . you will.

*Louis MacNeice**

----

* From 'Twelfth Night', in *The Collected Poems*, by kind permission
of Faber & Faber, London, and Oxford University Press, New York.

Introductory Letter to Xan Fielding

DEAR XAN,

As I have only just finished piecing these travels together, the times dealt with are very fresh in my mind and later events seem more recent still; so it is hard to believe that 1942 in Crete, when we first met – both of us black-turbaned, booted and sashed and appropriately silver-and-ivory daggered and cloaked in white goats' hair, and deep in grime – was more than three decades ago. Many meetings and adventures followed that first encounter on the slopes of Mt Kedros, and fortunately our kind of irregular warfare held long spells of inaction in the sheltering mountains: it was usually at eagle-height, with branches or constellations overhead, or dripping winter stalactites, that we lay among the rocks and talked of our lives before the war.

Indeed, indifference to the squalor of caves and speed at the approach of danger might have seemed the likeliest aptitudes for life in occupied Crete. But, unexpectedly in a modern war, it was the obsolete choice of Greek at school which had really deposited us on the limestone. With an insight once thought rare, the army had realized that the Ancient tongue, however imperfectly mastered, was a short-cut to the Modern: hence the sudden sprinkling of many strange figures among the mainland and island crags. Strange, because Greek had long ceased to be compulsory at the schools where it was still taught: it was merely the eager choice – unconsciously prompted, I suspect, by having listened to Kingsley's *Heroes* in childhood – of a perverse and eccentric minority: early hankerings which set a vague but agreeable stamp on all these improvised cave-dwellers.

As it chanced, neither of our school careers had run their course: yours had been cut short by a family mishap and mine by the sack and we had both set off on our own at an earlier age than most of our contemporaries. These first wanderings – impecunious, moss-repellant, frowned on by our respective elders, and utterly congenial – had pursued rather similar lines; and as we reconstructed our pre-war lives for each others' entertainment we soon agreed that the disasters which had set us on the move had not been disasters at all, but wild strokes of good luck.

This book is an attempt to complete and set in order, with as much detail as I can recapture, the earliest of those disjointedly recounted travels. The narrative, which should end at Constantinople, has turned out longer than I expected; I have split it in two, and this first volume breaks off in the middle of an important but arbitrary bridge spanning the Middle Danube. The rest will follow. From the start I wanted to dedicate it to you, which I now do with delight and some of the formality of a bull-fighter throwing his cap to a friend before a corrida. May I take advantage of the occasion by turning this letter into a kind of introduction? I want the narrative, when it begins, to jump in the deep end without too much explanatory delay. But it does need a brief outline of how these travels came about.

We must go back a bit.

In the second year of World War I, soon after I was born, my mother and sister sailed away to India (where my father was a servant of the Indian Government) and I was left behind so that one of us might survive if the ship were sunk by a submarine. I was to be taken out when the oceans were safer, and, failing this, remain in England until the war had reached its quick and victorious end. But the war was long and ships scarce; four years passed; and during the interim, on a temporary footing which perforce grew longer, I remained in the care of a very kind and very simple family. This period of separation was the opposite of the ordeal Kipling describes in Baa Baa Black Sheep. I was allowed to do as I chose in everything. There was no question of disobeying orders: none were given; still less was there ever a stern word or an admonitory smack. This new family, and a background of barns, ricks and teazles, clouded with spinneys and the undulation of ridge and furrow, were the first things I can remember setting eyes on; and I spent these important years, which are said to be such formative ones, more or less as a small farmer's child run wild: they have left a memory of complete and unalloyed bliss.

But when my mother and sister got back at last, I rushed several fields away and fought off their advances in gruff Northamptonshire tones; and they understood that they had a small savage on their hands and not a friendly one; the joy of reunion was tempered by harrowing dismay. But I was secretly attracted to these beautiful strangers nevertheless: they were extravagantly beyond anything in my range of conjecture. I was fascinated by the crocodile pattern of the shoes in which one of them ended and by the sailor-suit of the other, who was four years my senior: the pleated skirt, the three white stripes on the blue collar, the black silk scarf with its white lanyard and whistle and the ribanded cap with the still indecipherable gold letters that spelled out H.M.S. Victory. Between the two, a black pekinese with white feet resembling spats was floundering and leaping in the long grass and giving tongue like a lunatic.

Those marvellously lawless years, it seems, had unfitted me for the faintest shadow of constraint. With tact and charm and skill, backed by my swift treason and by London and *Peter Pan* and *Where the Rainbow Ends* and *Chu Chin Chow*, my mother succeeded in bringing about a complete shift of affection, and in taming me, more or less, for family purposes. But my early educational ventures, when the time came – at a kindergarten, then at a school of my sister's which also took small boys, and finally at a horrible preparatory school near Maidenhead named after a Celtic saint – ended in uniform catastrophe. Harmless in appearance, more presentable by now and of a refreshingly unconstricted address, I would earn excellent opinions at first. But as soon as early influences began to tell, those short-lived virtues must have seemed a cruel Fauntleroy veneer, cynically assumed to mask the Charles Addams fiend that lurked beneath: it coloured with an even darker tint the sum of misdeeds which soon began heaping up. When I catch a glimpse of similar children today, I am transfixed with fellow-feelings, and with dread.

First bewilderment reigned, and then despair. After a particularly bad cropper when I was about ten, I was taken to see two psychiatrists. In a recent biography I read with excitement that the first of these and the most likeable had been consulted by Virginia Woolf; and I thought for a moment that I might have gazed at her across the waiting-room; alas, it was before I was born. The second, more severe in aspect, recommended a co-educational and very advanced school for difficult children near Bury St Edmunds.

Salsham Hall, at Salsham-le-Sallows, was an unclassifiable but engaging manor-house with woods and a rough lake in a wide-skied and many-belfried expanse of Suffolk. It was run by a grey-haired, wild-eyed man called Major Truthful and when I spotted two beards – then very rare – among the mixed and eccentric-looking staff, and the heavy bangles and the amber and the tassels and the homespun, and met my fellow-alumni – about thirty boys and girls from four-year-olds to nearly twenty, all in brown jerkins and sandals: the musical near-genius with occasional fits, the millionaire's nephew who chased motor-cars along country lanes with a stick, the admiral's pretty and slightly kleptomaniac daughter, the pursuivant's son with nightmares and an infectious inherited passion for heraldry, the backward, the somnambulists and the mythomaniacs (by which I mean those with an inventive output more pronounced than the rest, which, as no one believed us, did no harm), and, finally, the small bad hats like me who were merely very naughty – I knew I was going to like it. The nature-worshipping eurythmics in a barn and the country-dances in which the Major led both staff and children, were a shade be-wildering at first, because everybody was naked. Nimbly and gravely, keeping time to a cottage piano and a recorder, we sped through the figures of Gathering Peascods, Sellinger's Round, Pick-ing-up Sticks and Old Mole.

It was midsummer. There were walled gardens close at hand, and giant red and gold gooseberries, and the nets over the loaded currant bushes foiled starlings but not us; and beyond them, the trees and the water descended in dim and beckoning perspectives. I understood the implications of the landscape at once: life under the greenwood tree. To choose a Maid Marion and a band, to get the girls to weave yards of Lincoln green on the therapeutic looms and then to slice and sew them into rough hoods with crenellated collars, cut bows and string them, carry off raspberry-canes for arrows and to take to the woods, was a matter of days. No one stopped us: 'Fay ce que vouldras' was the whole of their law. English schools, the moment they depart from the conventional track, are oases of strangeness and comedy, and it is tempting to linger. But vaguely guessed-at improprieties among the staff or the older children, or both – things of which we knew little in our sylvan haunts – brought about the dissolution of the place and I was soon back 'for a second chance', a forest exile among the snake-belts and the bat-oil of the horrible preparatory school. But, predictably after this heady freedom, not for long.

My mother had to cope with these upheavals. I would turn up in mid-term: once, at our cottage at Dodford, a tiny thatched village under a steep holt full of foxgloves (and, indeed, full of foxes) with a brook for its one street, where she was simultaneously writing plays and, though hard up, learning to fly a Moth biplane at an aerodrome forty miles away; once, at Primrose Hill Studios near Regent's Park, within earshot of the lions in the Zoo at night, where she had persuaded Arthur Rackham, a neighbour in that cloister, to paint amazing scenes – navigable birdsnests in a gale-wind, hobgoblin transactions under extruding roots and mice drinking out of acorns – all over an inside door; and more than once at 213 Piccadilly, which we moved to later, where a break-neck stair climbed to a marvellous Aladdin's cave of a flat over-looking long chains of street-lamps and the acrobatic sky-signs of the Circus. I would be hangdog on the doormat, flanked by a master with a depressing tale to unfold. Though upset, my mother was gifted with too much imagination and humour to let gloom settle for long. Nevertheless, these reverses filled me for the time being with suicidal despair.

But this particular disaster happened to coincide with one of my father's rare leaves from directing the Geological Survey of India. He and my mother had parted by then, and since these furloughs only came round every three years, we scarcely knew each other. All at once, as though at the wave of a wand, I found myself high above Lake Maggiore and then Como, trying to keep up with his giant stride across the gentian-covered mountains. He was an out-and-out naturalist and rightly proud of being an F.R.S.; indeed, he had discovered an Indian mineral which was named after him and a worm with eight hairs on its back; and – brittle trove! – a form-ation of snowflake. (I wondered, much later on, when white specks whirled past in the Alps or the Andes or the Himalayas, whether any of them were his.) That enormously tall and thin frame, dressed in a pepper-and-salt Norfolk jacket and knickerbockers, was festooned with accoutrements. Laden with his field glasses and his butterfly net, I would get my breath while he was tapping at the quartz and the hornblende on the foothills of Monte Rosa with his hammer and clicking open a pocket lens to inspect the fossils and insects of Monte della Croce. His voice at such moments was simultaneously cavernous and enthusiastic. He would carefully embed wild flowers for later classification in a moss-lined vasculum and sometimes halt for a sketch with his water-colours balanced on a rock. What a change, I thought, from those elephants and the jungles full of monkeys and tigers which I imagined, not wholly wrongly, to be his usual means of transport and habitat. At ground level I trailed behind him through half the picture galleries of northern Italy.

Three peaceful years followed. Gilbert and Phyllis Scott-Malden, with three sons and half a dozen boys cramming for Common Entrance under their wing, lived in a large house with a rambling garden in Surrey. (I can't think of them, nor of Mrs Scott-Malden's sister Josephine Wilkinson, who had a strong and separate influence later on, without the utmost gratitude and affection.) He was an excellent classicist and a kind and patient all-round teacher, and she filled out his firm structure with a great love of literature and poetry and painting. I was still an intermittent pest, but calmer existence began and I shot ahead in the subjects I enjoyed: everything, that is, except mathematics, for which my ineptitude seemed akin to imbecility. We made up plays and acted Shakespeare scenes and lay about the grass under a holm-oak with a dish of plums and listened to Mr Scott-Malden reading Gilbert Murray's translation of *The Frogs*; he would switch to the original to explain and give point to the comic passages and the onomatopoeia. We had built a hut in an enormous walnut tree, with rope-ladders climbing half-way, then hand over hand; and I was allowed to sleep in it all my last summer term. In spite of maths, I scraped through Common Entrance in the end and looked forward to Public School life with ill-founded confidence.

*

Copious reading about the Dark and the Middle Ages had floridly coloured my views of the past and the King's School, Canterbury touched off emotions which were sharply opposed to those of Somerset Maugham in the same surroundings; they were closer to Walter Pater's seventy years earlier, and probably identical, I liked to think, with those of Christopher Marlowe earlier still. I couldn't get over the fact that the school had been founded at the very beginning of Anglo-Saxon Christianity – before the sixth century was out, that is: fragments of Thor and Woden had hardly stopped smouldering in the Kentish woods: the oldest part of the buildings was modern by these standards, dating only from a few decades after the Normans landed. There was a wonderfully cobwebbed feeling about this dizzy and intoxicating antiquity – an ambiance both haughty and obscure which turned famous seats of learning, founded eight hundred or a thousand years later, into gaudy mushrooms and seemed to invest these hoarier precincts, together with the wide green expanses beyond them, the huge elms, the Dark Entry, and the ruined arches and the cloisters – and, while I was about it, the booming and jackdaw-crowded pinnacles of the great Angevin cathedral itself, and the ghost of St Thomas à Becket and the Black Prince's bones – with an aura of nearly prehistoric myth.

Although it was a one-sided love in the end, for a time things went well. I liked nearly everybody, from the headmaster and my housemaster down, and prospered erratically at dead and living languages and at history and geography – at everything, once more, except mathematics. I found my mind wandering at games; loved boxing and was good at it; and in summer, having chosen rowing instead of cricket, lay peacefully beside the Stour, well upstream of the rhythmic creaking and the exhortation, reading *Lily Christine* and Gibbon and gossiping with kindred lotus-eaters under the willow-branches. Verse, imitative and bad but published in school magazines nevertheless, poured out like ectoplasm. I wrote and read with intensity, sang, debated, drew and painted: scored minor successes at acting, stage-managing and in painting and designing scenery; and made gifted and enterprising friends. One of these, a year older, was Alan Watts, a brilliant classical scholar who, most remarkably, wrote and published an

authoritative book on Zen Buddhism – years before the sect
became fashionable – while he was still at school. Later, he became
a respected authority on Eastern and Western religions. (In his
autobiography *In My Own Way*, which came out shortly before
his premature death a few years ago, he writes at some length of
my troubles at school – and especially of their abrupt end – in the
warm spirit of a champion; and if he didn't quite get the hang of it
in one or two places, it was not his fault.)

What went wrong? I think I know now. A bookish attempt to
coerce life into a closer resemblance to literature was abetted – it
can only be – by a hangover from early anarchy: translating ideas
as fast as I could into deeds overrode every thought of punishment
or danger; as I seem to have been unusually active and restless, the
result was chaos. It mystified me and puzzled others. 'You're mad!'
prefects and monitors would exclaim, brows knit in glaring scrum-
half bewilderment, as new misdeeds came to light. Many of my
transgressions involved breaking bounds as well as rules – climbing out at night and the like, only half of which were found out.
Frequent gatings joined the mileage of Latin hexameters copied
out as impositions, and lesser troubles filled in the gaps between
more serious bust-ups: absent-mindedness, forgetfulness and confusion about where I ought to be; and constant loss: 'forgetting
my books under the arches' was a recurrent bane. There were some
savage fights; also erratic behaviour which was construed, perhaps
rightly, as showing off: 'anything for a laugh' was the usual term
for this; and, even when I succeeded, 'trying to be funny'. Always
that withering gerund! These strictures were often on monitors'
lips. Aediles and rod-bearing lictors, they were the guardians of an
inflexible code and all breaches were visited by swift and flexible
sanctions which came whistling shoulder-high across panelled
studies and struck with considerable force; but, however spectacular the results, they left the psyche unbruised, and, though
they were disagreeable and, in this case, record-breaking in frequency, clinically and morally speaking, they didn't seem to take.
If these meetings are carried off with enough studied nonchalance,
a dark and baleful fame begins to surround the victim, and it
makes him, in the end, an infliction past bearing. Everything was
going badly and my housemaster's penultimate report, in my third

year, had an ominous ring: '... some attempts at improvement' it went 'but more to avoid detection. He is a dangerous mixture of sophistication and recklessness which makes one anxious about his influence on other boys.'

Catastrophe was staved off for a few months. As I was thought to have done myself some damage skiing in the Berner Oberland just before I was sixteen, I skipped a term and a half, and, on my return, I was temporarily excused games: when everyone trooped off with oblong balls under their arms, I could spin about Kent on a bicycle and look at the Norman churches at Patrixbourne and Barfrestone and explore the remoter parts of Canterbury. This windfall of leisure and freedom soon coincided with a time when all good impressions were wiped out by a last series of misdeeds. A more prophetic eye would have seen that patience on high had at last given out and that any further trouble would be hailed as a release long overdue.

Intramural romances spring up and prosper in places of learning, but some exotic psychological fluke directed my glance beyond the walls and, once more, out of bounds. It was a time when one falls in love hard and often, and my aesthetic notions, entirely formed by Andrew Lang's Coloured Fairy Books, had settled years before on the long-necked, wide-eyed pre-Raphaelite girls in Henry Ford's illustrations, interchangeably kings' daughters, ice-maidens, goose-girls and water spirits, and my latest wanderings had led me, at the end of a green and sweet-smelling cave set dimly with flowers and multicoloured fruit and vegetation – a greengrocer's shop, that is, which she tended for her father – to the vision of just such a being. The effect was instantaneous. She was twenty-four, a ravishing and sonnet-begetting beauty and I can see her now and still hear that melting and deep Kent accent. This sudden incongruous worship may have been a bore but she was too good-natured to show it, and perhaps she was puzzled by the verse which came showering in. I knew that such an association in the town, however innocent, broke a number of taboos too deep-rooted and well-understood to need any explicit veto; nevertheless I headed for the shop beyond the Cattle Market the moment I could escape. But the black clothes we wore, those stiff wing-collars and the wide and speckled straw boaters with their blue and white silk ribands were as conspicuous as broad-arrows. My footsteps were discreetly dogged, my devices known and after a week, I was caught red-handed – holding Nellie's hand, that is to say, which is about as far as this suit was ever pressed; we were sitting in the back-shop on upturned apple-baskets – and my schooldays were over.

Captain Grimes was right. A few months after this setback, the idea of an Army career, which had been floating mistily in the air for some time, began to take firmer shape; and the prospect of entering Sandhurst raised its distant hurdle. But what about the sack? When he was appealed to, my ex-housemaster, a strange and brilliant man, composed and dispatched the necessary letter of recommendation; and, like the Captain's, it was a corking good letter, too. (There were no bitter feelings; there had been disappointment on the side of the school authorities as well as relief; utter dejection on mine. But I felt thankful they had alighted on more avowable grounds for my eclipse than the charge of being an intolerable nuisance. The actual pretext could be made to sound dashing and romantic.)

I had not yet sat for School Cert. – which, because of maths, I would certainly have failed – and as it was indispensable for would-be cadets, I soon found myself in London, seventeen by now, cramming for an exempting examination called the London Certificate. I spent most of the next two years in Lancaster Gate, then in Ladbroke Grove with rooms of my own overlooking tree tops, under the tolerant and friendly aegis of Denys Prideaux. I did Maths, French, English and Geography with him, and Latin, Greek, English and History, often in deck chairs in Kensington Gardens, with Lawrence Goodman. (Unconventional and a poet, he took me to every Shakespeare play that appeared.) During the first year I led a fairly sensible life, had a number of friends, was asked away to stay in the country, followed rustic pursuits, and read more books than I have ever crammed into a similar stretch of time. I passed the London Cert. respectably in most papers, and even without disgrace in the subjects I dreaded.

But a long interregnum still stretched ahead.

One of the early chapters of this book touches at some retrospective length on the way things began to change; how I moved
from the fairly predictable company of fellow army-candidates
into older circles which were simultaneously more worldly, more
bohemian and more raffish: the remainder, more or less, of the
Bright Young People, but ten years and twenty thousand double
whiskies after their heyday, and looking extremely well on the
regime. This new and captivating world seemed brilliant and
rather wicked; I enjoyed being the youngest present, especially
during the dissipated nocturnal ramblings in which every evening
finished: ('Where's that rather noisy boy got to? We may as well
take him too'). I had reached a stage when one changes very fast: a
single year contains a hundred avatars; and while these were
flashing kaleidoscopically by, the idea of my unsuitability for
peace-time soldiering had begun to impinge. More serious still, the
acceptance of two poems and the publication of one of them –
admittedly, only on foxhunting – had fired me with the idea of
authorship.

In the late summer of 1933, with Mr Prideaux's permission, I
rashly moved into a room in an old and slightly leaning house in
Shepherd Market where several friends had already fixed their
quarters. This little backwater of archways and small shops and
Georgian and Victorian pubs had the charm, quite evaporated
now, of a village marooned in the still-intact splendours of May-
fair. I had a vision of myself, as I moved in, settling down to
writing with single-minded and almost Trollopian diligence. Instead, to my ultimate discomfiture but immediate delight, the
house became the scene of wild and continuous parties. We paid
almost nothing for our lodgings to Miss Beatrice Stewart, our
kind-hearted landlady, and always late. She didn't mind this, but
pleaded with us again and again in the small hours to make less
noise. The friend and model of famous painters and sculptors in
the past, she was accustomed to the more decorous Bohemia of
earlier generations. She had sat for Sargent and Sickert and Shannon and Steer and Tonks and Augustus John and her walls were

radiant with mementoes of those years; but the loss of a leg in a
motor accident had cruelly slowed her up. Much later, a friend
told me that she had been the model for Adrian Jones's bronze
figure of Peace in the quadriga on Decimus Burton's Wellington
Arch. Since then, I can never pass the top of Constitution Hill
without thinking of her and gazing up at the winged and wreath-
bearing goddess sailing across the sky. As the pigeon flies, it was
under a minute from her window-sill.

My scheme was not working well. That improvident flight from
the rooms and meals and all that went with them at my tutor's
had reduced my funds to a pound a week and the way things were
shaping, it looked as though opulence from writing might be delayed for a time. I managed somehow, but gloom and perplexity
descended with the start of winter. Fitful streaks of promise and
scrapes and upheavals had marked my progress so far; they still
continued; but now I seemed to be floating towards disintegration
in a tangle of submerged and ill-marked reefs. The outlook grew
steadily darker and more overcast. About lamplighting time at the
end of a wet November day, I was peering morosely at the dog-
eared pages on my writing table and then through the panes
at the streaming reflections of Shepherd Market, thinking as
Night and Day succeeded *Stormy Weather* on the gramophone
in the room below, that *Lazybones* couldn't be far behind;
when, almost with the abruptness of Herbert's lines at the
beginning of these pages, inspiration came. A plan unfolded
with the speed and the completeness of a Japanese paper flower in
a tumbler.

To change scenery; abandon London and England and set out
across Europe like a tramp – or, as I characteristically phrased it
to myself, like a pilgrim or a palmer, an errant scholar, a broken
knight or the hero of *The Cloister and the Hearth*! All of a
sudden, this was not merely the obvious, but the only thing to do.
I would travel on foot, sleep in hayricks in summer, shelter in
barns when it was raining or snowing and only consort with
peasants and tramps. If I lived on bread and cheese and apples,
jogging along on fifty pounds a year like Lord Durham with a few
noughts knocked off, there would even be some cash left over for

paper and pencils and an occasional mug of beer. A new life! Freedom! Something to write about!

Even before I looked at a map, two great rivers had already plotted the itinerary in my mind's eye: the Rhine uncoiled across it, the Alps rose up and then the wolf-harbouring Carpathian watersheds and the cordilleras of the Balkans; and there, at the end of the windings of the Danube, the Black Sea was beginning to spread its mysterious and lopsided shape; and my chief destination was never in a moment's doubt. The levitating skyline of Constantinople pricked its sheaves of thin cylinders and its hemispheres out of the sea-mist; beyond it Mount Athos hovered; and the Greek archipelago was already scattering a paper-chase of islands across the Aegean. (These certainties sprang from reading the books of Robert Byron; dragon-green Byzantium loomed serpent-haunted and gong-tormented; I had even met the author for a moment in a blurred and saxophone-haunted night club as dark as Tartarus.)

I wondered during the first few days whether to enlist a companion; but I knew that the enterprise had to be solitary and the break complete. I wanted to think, write, stay or move on at my own speed and unencumbered, to gaze at things with a changed eye and listen to new tongues that were untainted by a single familiar word. With any luck the humble circumstances of the journey would offer no scope for English or French. Flights of unknown syllables would soon be rushing into purged and attentive ears.

The idea met obstruction at first: why not wait till spring? (London by now was shuddering under veils of December rain.) But when they understood that all was decided, most of the objectors became allies. Warming to the scheme after initial demur, Mr Prideaux undertook to write to India putting my démarche in a favourable light; I determined to announce the *fait accompli* by letter when I was safely on the way, perhaps from Cologne ... Then we planned the dispatch of those weekly pounds – each time, if possible, after they had risen to a monthly total of four – by registered letter to suitably spaced-out *postes restantes*. (Munich would be the first; then I would write and suggest a second.) I next borrowed fifteen pounds off the father of a school friend, partly to buy equipment and partly to have something in hand when I set out. I telephoned to my sister Vanessa, back from India again a few years before, and married and settled in Gloucestershire. My mother was filled with apprehension to begin with; we pored over the atlas, and, bit by bit as we pored, the comic possibilities began to unfold in absurd imaginary scenes until we were falling about with laughter; and by the time I caught the train to London next morning, she was infected with my excitement.

During the last days, my outfit assembled fast. Most of it came from Millet's army surplus store in The Strand: an old Army greatcoat, different layers of jersey, grey flannel shirts, a couple of white linen ones for best, a soft leather windbreaker, puttees, nailed boots, a sleeping bag (to be lost within a month and neither missed nor replaced); notebooks and drawing blocks, rubbers, an aluminium cylinder full of Venus and Golden Sovereign pencils; an old *Oxford Book of English Verse*. (Lost likewise, and, to my surprise – it had been a sort of Bible – not missed much more than the sleeping bag.) The other half of my very conventional travelling library was the Loeb *Horace*, Vol. I, which my mother, after asking what I wanted, had bought and posted in Guildford. (She had written the translation of a short poem by Petronius on the flyleaf, chanced on and copied out, she told me later, from another volume on the same shelf:* 'Leave thy home, O youth, and seek out alien shores . . . Yield not to misfortune: the far-off Danube shall know thee, the cold North-wind and the untroubled kingdom of Canopus and the men who gaze on the new birth of Phoebus or upon his setting . . .' She was an enormous reader, but Petronius was not in her usual line of country and he had only recently entered mine. I was impressed and touched.) Finally I bought a ticket on a small Dutch steamer sailing from Tower Bridge to the Hook of Holland. All this had taken a shark's bite out of my borrowed cash, but there was still a wad of notes left over.

At last, with a touch of headache from an eve-of-departure

---

* Quoted in the original at the beginning of these pages.

party, I got out of bed on the great day, put on my new kit and tramped south-west under a lowering sky. I felt preternaturally light, as though I were already away and floating like a djinn escaped from its flask through the dazzling middle air while Europe unfolded. But the grating hobnails took me no farther than Cliveden Place, where I picked up a rucksack left for me there by Mark Ogilvie-Grant. Inspecting my stuff, he had glanced with pity at the one I had bought. (His – a superior Bergen affair resting on a lumbar semicircle of metal and supported by a triangular frame, had accompanied him – usually, he admitted, slung on a mule – all round Athos with Robert Byron and David Talbot-Rice when *The Station* was being written. Weathered and faded by Macedonian suns, it was rife with *mana*.) Then I bought for ninepence a well-balanced ashplant at the tobacconist's next to the corner of Sloane Square and headed for Victoria Street and Petty France to pick up my new passport. Filling in the form the day before – born in London, 11 February 1915; height 5′ 9¾″; eyes, brown; hair, brown; distinguishing marks, none – I had left the top space empty, not knowing what to write. Profession? 'Well, what shall we say?' the Passport Official had asked, pointing to the void. My mind remained empty. A few years earlier, an American hobo song called *Hallelujah I'm a bum!* had been on many lips; during the last days it had been haunting me like a private *leitmotif* and without realizing I must have been humming the tune as I pondered, for the Official laughed. 'You can't very well put *that*,' he said. After a moment he added: 'I should just write "student" '; so I did. With the stiff new document in my pocket, stamped '8 December 1933', I struck north over the Green Park under a dark massing of cloud. As I crossed Piccadilly and entered the crooked chasm of White Horse Street, there were a few random splashes and, glistening at the end of it, Shepherd Market was prickly with falling drops. I would be just in time for a goodbye luncheon with Miss Stewart and three friends – two fellow lodgers and a girl: then, away. The rain was settling in.

The next move was my first independent act and, as it turned out – with a run of luck – the first sensible one. You know the rest, dear Xan, disjointedly told, so here it is with an attempt at coherence. I hope that mentions of Crete remind you as lucidly as me of the ilex-woods and caves and folds where our earlier adventures were first exchanged.

Kardamyli 1977   P.

HOLLAND

Hook of
Holland
Rotterdam
Dordrecht
Gorinchem Sliedrech Tiel
Nijmegen
Rhine
Goch
Kevelaer
Krefeld

Cologne

Bad Godesberg
Linz
Andernach
Coblenz
Boppard
Rüdesheim
Bingen
Mainz
Oppenheim

Worms
Mannheim
Heidelberg
Spires
Bruchsal
Mühlacker
Pforzheim
Strasbourg
Stuttgart
Göppingen
R. Danu
Ulm
Augsburg
Freiburg
Munich
Rosenh

FRANCE

GERMA

Main

SWITZERLAND

0   50   100 miles

ONE

The Low Countries

'A SPLENDID afternoon to set out!', said one of the friends who was seeing me off, peering at the rain and rolling up the window.

The other two agreed. Sheltering under the Curzon Street arch of Shepherd Market, we had found a taxi at last. In Half Moon Street, all collars were up. A thousand glistening umbrellas were tilted over a thousand bowler hats in Piccadilly; the Jermyn Street shops, distorted by streaming water, had become a submarine arcade; and the clubmen of Pall Mall, with china tea and anchovy toast in mind, were scuttling for sanctuary up the steps of their clubs. Blown askew, the Trafalgar Square fountains twirled like mops, and our taxi, delayed by a horde of Charing Cross commuters reeling and stampeding under a cloudburst, crept into The Strand. The vehicle threaded its way through a flux of traffic. We splashed up Ludgate Hill and the dome of St Paul's sank deeper in its pillared shoulders. The tyres slewed away from the drowning cathedral and a minute later the silhouette of The Monument, descried through veils of rain, seemed so convincingly liquefied out of the perpendicular that the tilting thoroughfare might have been forty fathoms down. The driver, as he swerved wetly into Upper Thames Street, leaned back and said: 'Nice weather for young ducks.'

A smell of fish was there for a moment, then gone. Enjoining haste, the bells of St Magnus the Martyr and St Dunstans-in-the-East were tolling the hour; then sheets of water were rising from our front wheels as the taxi floundered on between The Mint and the Tower of London. Dark complexes of battlements and tree-tops and turrets dimly assembled on one side; then, straight ahead, the pinnacles and the metal parabolas of Tower Bridge were looming. We halted on the bridge just short of the first barbican and the driver indicated the flight of stone steps that descended to Irongate Wharf. We were down them in a moment; and beyond the cobbles and the bollards, with the Dutch tricolour beating damply from

her poop and a ragged fan of smoke streaming over the river, the
Stadthouder Willem rode at anchor. At the end of lengthening
fathoms of chain, the swirling tide had lifted her with a sigh
almost level with the flagstones: gleaming in the rain, and with
full steam-up for departure, she floated in a mewing circus of gulls.
Haste and the weather cut short our farewells and our embraces
and I sped down the gangway clutching my rucksack and my
stick while the others dashed back to the steps – four sodden
trouser-legs and two high heels skipping across the puddles – and
up them to the waiting taxi; and half a minute later there they
were, high overhead on the balustrade of the bridge, craning and
waving from the cast-iron quatrefoils. To shield her hair from the
rain, the high-heel-wearer had a mackintosh over her head like a
coalheaver. I was signalling frantically back as the hawsers were
cast loose and the gangplank shipped. Then they were gone. The
anchor-chain clattered through the ports and the vessel turned
into the current with a wail of her siren. How strange it seemed,
as I took shelter in the little saloon – feeling, suddenly, forlorn;
but only for a moment – to be setting off from the heart of
London! No beetling cliffs, no Arnoldian crash of pebbles. I might
have been leaving for Richmond, or for a supper of shrimps and
whitebait at Gravesend, instead of Byzantium. Only the larger
ships from the Netherlands berthed at Harwich, the steward said:
smaller Dutch craft like the *Stadthouder* always dropped anchor
hereabouts: boats from the Zuider Zee had been unloading eels
between London Bridge and the Tower since the reign of Queen
Elizabeth.

Miraculously, after the pitiless hours of deluge, the rain
stopped. Above the drifts of smoke there was a quickly-fading
glimpse of restless pigeons and a few domes and many steeples and
some bone-white Palladian belfries flying rain-washed against a
sky of gunmetal and silver and tarnished brass. The girders overhead framed the darkening shape of London Bridge; further up,
the teeming water was crossed by the ghosts of Southwark and
Blackfriars. Meanwhile St Catherine's Wharf was sliding offstage
and upstream, then Execution Dock and Wapping Old Stairs and
The Prospect of Whitby and by the time these landmarks were
astern of us, the sun was setting fast and the fissures among the

western cloudbanks were fading from smoky crimson to violet.

In the gulfs spanned by catwalks between the warehouses, night was assembling too, and the tiers of loading-loopholes yawned like caverns. Slung with chains and cables weighted with shot, hoists jutted on hinges from precipices of warehouse wall and the giant white letters of the wharfingers' names, grimed by a century of soot, were growing less decipherable each second. There was a reek of mud, seaweed, slime, salt, smoke and clinkers and nameless jetsam, and the half-sunk barges and the waterlogged palisades unloosed a universal smell of rotting timber. Was there a whiff of spices? It was too late to say: the ship was drawing away from the shore and gathering speed and the details beyond the wider stretch of water and the convolutions of the gulls were growing blurred. Rotherhithe, Millwall, Limehouse Reach, the West India Docks, Deptford and the Isle of Dogs were rushing upstream in smears of darkness. Chimneys and cranes plumed the banks, but the belfries were thinning out. A chaplet of lights twinkled on a hill. It was Greenwich. The Observatory hung in the dark, and the *Stadthouder* was twanging her way inaudibly through the nought meridian.

The reflected shore lights dropped coils and zigzags into the flood which were thrown into disarray every now and then, by the silhouettes of passing vessels' luminous portholes, the funereal shapes of barges singled out by their port and starboard lights and cutters of the river police smacking from wave to wave as purposefully and as fast as pikes. Once we gave way to a liner that towered out of the water like a festive block of flats; from Hong Kong, said the steward, as she glided by; and the different notes of the sirens boomed up and downstream as though mastodons still haunted the Thames marshes.

A gong tinkled and the steward led me back into the saloon. I was the only passenger. 'We don't get many in December,' he said; 'It's very quiet just now.' When he had cleared away, I took a new and handsomely-bound journal out of my rucksack, opened it on the green baize under a pink-shaded lamp and wrote the first entry while the cruets and the wine bottle rattled busily in their stands. Then I went on deck. The lights on either beam had become scarcer but one could pick out the faraway gleam of other

vessels and estuary towns which the distance had shrunk to faint
constellations. There was a scattering of buoys and the scanned
flash of a light-house. Sealed away now beyond a score of watery
loops, London had vanished and a lurid haze was the only hint of
its whereabouts.

I wondered when I would be returning. Excitement ruled out
the thought of sleep; it seemed too important a night. (And in
many ways, so it proved. The ninth of December, 1933, was just
ending and I didn't get back until January 1937 – a whole lifetime
later it seemed then – and I felt like Ulysses, 'plein d'usage et de
raison', and, for better or for worse, utterly changed by my
travels.)

But I must have dozed, in spite of these emotions, for when I
woke the only glimmer in sight was our own reflection on the
waves. The kingdom had slid away westwards and into the dark.
A stiff wind was tearing through the rigging and the mainland of
Europe was less than half the night away.

It was still a couple of hours till dawn when we dropped anchor
in the Hook of Holland. Snow covered everything and the flakes
blew in a slant across the cones of the lamps and confused the
glowing discs that spaced out the untrodden quay. I hadn't
known that Rotterdam was a few miles inland. I was still the only
passenger in the train and this solitary entry, under cover of night
and hushed by snow, completed the illusion that I was slipping
into Rotterdam, and into Europe, through a secret door.

I wandered about the silent lanes in exultation. The beetling
storeys were nearly joining overhead; then the eaves drew away
from each other and frozen canals threaded their way through a
succession of hump-backed bridges. Snow was piling up on the
shoulders of a statue of Erasmus. Trees and masts were dispersed
in clumps and the polygonal tiers of an enormous and elaborate
gothic belfry soared above the steep roofs. As I was gazing, it
slowly tolled five.

The lanes opened on the Boomjes, a long quay lined with trees
and capstans, and this in its turn gave on a wide arm of the Maas
and an infinity of dim ships. Gulls mewed and wheeled overhead
and dipped into the lamplight, scattering their small footprints on

the muffled cobblestones and settled in the rigging of the anchored boats in little explosions of snow. The cafés and seamen's
taverns which lay back from the quay were all closed except one
which showed a promising line of light. A shutter went up and a
stout man in clogs opened a glass door, deposited a tabby on the
snow and, turning back, began lighting a stove inside. The cat
went in again at once; I followed it and the ensuing fried eggs
and coffee, ordered by signs, were the best I had ever eaten. I made
a second long entry in my journal – it was becoming a passion –
and while the landlord polished his glasses and cups and arranged
them in glittering ranks, dawn broke, with the snow still coming
down against the lightening sky. I put on my greatcoat, slung the
rucksack, grasped my stick and headed for the door. The landlord
asked where I was going: I said: 'Constantinople.' His brows went
up and he signalled to me to wait: then he set out two small
glasses and filled them with transparent liquid from a long stone
bottle. We clinked them; he emptied his at one gulp and I did the
same. With his wishes for godspeed in my ears and an internal
bonfire of Bols and a hand smarting from his valedictory shake, I
set off. It was the formal start of my journey.

I hadn't gone far before the open door of the *Groote Kirk* – the
cathedral attached to the enormous belfry – beckoned me inside.
Filled with dim early morning light, the concavity of grey
masonry and whitewash joined in pointed arches high overhead
and the floor diminished along the nave in a chessboard of black
and white flagstones. So compellingly did the vision tally with a
score of half-forgotten Dutch pictures that my mind's eye instantaneously furnished the void with those seventeenth-century
groups which should have been sitting or strolling there: burghers
with pointed corn-coloured beards – and impious spaniels that
refused to stay outside – conferring gravely with their wives and
their children, still as chessmen, in black broadcloth and identical
honeycomb ruffs under the tremendous hatchmented pillars.
Except for this church, the beautiful city was to be bombed to
fragments a few years later. I would have lingered, had I known.

In less than an hour I was crunching steadily along the icy ruts
of a dyke road and the outskirts of Rotterdam had already vanished in the falling snow. Lifted in the air and lined with willow-

trees, the road ran dead straight as far as the eye could see, but not so far as it would have in clear weather, for the escorting willows soon became ghostlike in either direction until they dissolved in the surrounding pallor. A wooden-clogged bicyclist would materialize in a peaked cap with circular black ear pads against frostbite, and sometimes his cigar would leave a floating drift from Java or Sumatra on the air long after the smoker had evaporated. I was pleased by my equipment. The rucksack sat with an easy balance and the upturned collar of my second-hand greatcoat, fastened with a semi-detachable flap which I had just discovered, formed a snug tunnel; and with my old cord breeches, their strapping soft after long use, and the grey puttees and the heavy clouted boots, I was impenetrably greaved and jambed and shod; no chink was left for the blast. I was soon thatched with snow and my ears began to tingle, but I was determined never to stoop to those terrible ear pads.

When the snow stopped, the bright morning light laid bare a wonderful flat geometry of canals and polders and willows, and the sails of innumerable mills were turning in a wind that was also keeping all the clouds on the move – and not only clouds and mills; for soon the skaters on the canals, veiled hitherto by the snowfall, were suddenly scattered as a wind-borne portent came whirling out of the distance and tore through their midst like a winged dragon. It was an ice-yacht – a raft on four rubber-tyred wheels under a taut triangle of sail and manned by three reckless boys. It travelled literally with the speed of the wind while one of them hauled on the sail and another steered with a bar. The third flung all his weight on a brake like a shark's jawbone that sent showers of fragments flying. It screamed past with an uproar of shouts as the teeth bit the ice and a noise like the rending of a hundred calico shirts which multiplied to a thousand as the raft made a sharp right-angle turn into a branch-canal. A minute later, it was a faraway speck and the silent landscape, with its Brueghelish skaters circling as slowly as flies along the canals and the polders, seemed tamer after its passing. Snow had covered the landscape with a sparkling layer and the slaty hue of the ice was only becoming visible as the looping arabesques of the skaters laid it bare. Following the white parallelograms the lines of the willows dwindled as insubstantially as trails of vapour. The breeze that impelled those hastening clouds had met no hindrance for a thousand miles and a traveller moving at a footpace along the hog's back of a dyke above the cloud-shadows and the level champaign was filled with intimations of limitless space.

My spirits, already high, steadily rose as I walked. I could scarcely believe that I was really there; alone, that is, on the move, advancing into Europe, surrounded by all this emptiness and change, with a thousand wonders waiting. Because of this, perhaps, the actual doings of the next few days emerge from the general glow in a disjointed and haphazard way. I halted at a signpost to eat a hunk of bread with a yellow wedge of cheese sliced from a red cannon ball by a village grocer. One arm of the signpost pointed to Amsterdam and Utrecht, the other to Dordrecht, Breda and Antwerp and I obeyed the latter. The way followed a river with too swift a current for ice to form, and brambles and hazel and rushes grew thick along the banks. Leaning over a bridge I watched a string of barges gliding downstream underneath me in the wake of a stertorous tug bound for Rotterdam, and a little later an island as slender as a weaver's shuttle divided the current amidstream. A floating reed-fringed spinney, it looked like; a small castle with a steeply-pitched shingle roof and turrets with conical tops emerged romantically from the mesh of the branches. Belfries of a dizzy height were scattered haphazard across the landscape. They were visible for a very long way, and, in the late afternoon, I singled one of them out for a landmark and a goal.

It was dark when I was close enough to see that the tower, and the town of Dordrecht which gathered at its foot, lay on the other bank of a wide river. I had missed the bridge; but a ferry set me down on the other shore soon after dark. Under the jackdaws of the belfry, a busy amphibian town expanded; it was built of weathered brick and topped by joined gables and crowsteps and snow-laden tiles and fragmented by canals and re-knit by bridges. A multitude of anchored barges loaded with timber formed a flimsy extension of the quays and rocked from end to end when bow-waves from passing vessels stirred them. After supper in a waterfront bar, I fell asleep among the beer mugs and when I woke, I couldn't think where I was. Who were these bargees in peaked caps and jerseys and sea-boots? They were playing a sort of whist in a haze of cheroot-smoke and the dog-eared cards they smacked down were adorned with goblets and swords and staves; the queens wore spiked crowns and the kings and the knaves were slashed and ostrich-plumed like François I and the Emperor Maximilian. My eyes must have closed again, for in the end someone woke me and led me upstairs like a sleep-walker and showed me into a bedroom with a low and slanting ceiling and an eiderdown like a giant meringue. I was soon under it. I noticed an oleograph of Queen Wilhelmina at the bed's head and a print of the Synod of Dort at the foot before I blew the candle out.

The clip-clop of clogs on the cobblestones – a puzzling sound until I looked out of the window – woke me in the morning. The kind old landlady of the place accepted payment for my dinner but none for the room: they had seen I was tired and taken me under their wing. This was the first marvellous instance of a kindness and hospitality that was to occur again and again on these travels.

Except for the snow-covered landscape and the clouds and the tree-bordered flow of the Merwede, the next two days have left little behind them but the names of the towns I slept in. I must have made a late start from Dordrecht: Sliedrecht, my next halting place, is only a few miles on, and Gorinchem, the next after that, is not much more. Some old walls stick in my memory, cobbled streets and a barbican and barges moored along the river, but, clearest of all, the town lock-up. Somebody had told me that humble travellers in Holland could doss down in police stations, and it was true. A constable showed me to a cell without a word, and I slept, rugged up to the ears, on a wooden plank hinged to the wall and secured on two chains under a forest of raffish murals and graffiti. They even gave me a bowl of coffee and quarter of a loaf before I set off. Thank God I had put 'student' in my passport: it was an amulet and an Open Sesame. In European tradition, the word suggested a youthful, needy, and earnest figure, spurred along the highways of the West by a thirst for learning – thus,

notwithstanding high spirits and a proneness to dog-Latin drinking songs, a fit candidate for succour.

During these first three days I was never far from a towpath,
but so many and confused are the waterways that unconsciously I
changed rivers three times: the Noorwede was the first of them,
the Merwede followed, then came the Waal; and at Gorinchem the
Waal was joined by the Maas. In the morning I could see the great
stream of the Maas winding across the plain towards this
rendezvous; it had risen in France under the more famous name of
Meuse and then flowed across the whole of Belgium; a river only
less imposing than the Waal itself, to whose banks I clung for the
remainder of my Dutch journey. The Waal is tremendous; no
wonder, for it is really the Rhine. 'The Rijn', in Holland, Rembrandt's native stream, is a minor northern branch of the main
flow, and it subdivides again and again, loses itself in the delta and
finally enters the North Sea through a drainage-canal; while the
Waal, gorged with Alpine snows and the waters of Lake Constance and the Black Forest and the tribute of a thousand Rhenish
streams, rolls sea-ward in usurped and stately magnificence. Between this tangle of rivers, meanwhile – whose defections and
reunions enclosed islands as big as English shires – the geometric
despotism of canal and polder and windmill held firm; those turning sails were for drainage, not grinding corn.

All the country I had traversed so far was below sea-level and
without this discipline, which everlastingly redressed the balance
between solid and liquid, the whole region would have been wild
sea, or a brackish waste of flood and fen. When one looked down
from a dyke, the infinity of polders and canals and the meander-
ings of the many streams were plain to the eye; from a lower
vantage-point, only the nearest waters were discernible. But, at
ground-level, they all vanished. I was sitting and smoking on a
millstone by a barn near the old town of Zaltbommel, when I was
alerted by the wail of a siren. In the field a quarter of a mile away,
between a church and some woods, serenely though invisibly
afloat on the hidden Maas, a big white ship a-flutter with pennants was apparently mooing its way across solid meadows under
a cloud of gulls.

The Maas advanced and retreated all day long, and towards evening it vanished to the south. Once out of sight, its wide bed climbed the invisible gradients of Brabant and Limburg, bound for a faraway Carolingian hinterland beyond the Ardennes.

Dark fell while I was trudging along a never-ending path beside the Waal. It was lined with skeleton trees; the frozen ice-puddles creaked under my hobnails; and, beyond the branches, the Great Bear and a retinue of winter constellations blazed in a clear cold sky. At last the distant lights of Tiel, poised on the first hill I had seen in Holland, twinkled into being on the other bank. An opportune bridge carried me over and I reached the market-place soon after ten, somnambulant with fatigue after traversing a vast stretch of country. I can't remember under what mountainous eiderdown or in what dank cell I slept the night.

A change came over the country. For the first time, next day, the ground was higher than sea-level and with every step the equipoise of the elements tilted more decisively in favour of dry land. A gentle rolling landscape of water-meadow and ploughland and heath, with the snow melting here and there, stretched away northward through the province of Guelderland and south into Brabant. The roadside calvaries and the twinkle of sanctuary lamps in the churches indicated that I had crossed a religious as well as a cartographic contour-line. There were farm-buildings which elms and chestnut trees and birches snugly encompassed and Hobbema-like avenues of wintry trees which ended at the gates of seemly manor-houses – the abodes, I hoped, of mild jonkheers. They were gabled in semicircles and broken right-angles of weathered brick bordered with white stone. Pigeon-lofts saddled the scales of the roofs and the breeze kept the gilded weather-vanes spinning; and when the leaded windows kindled at lighting-up time, I explored the interiors in my imagination. A deft chiaroscuro illuminated the black and white flagstones; there were massive tables with bulbous legs and Turkey carpets flung over them; convex mirrors distorted the reflections; faded wall-charts hung on the walls; globes and harpsichords and inlaid lutes were elegantly scattered; and Guelderland squires with pale whiskers – or their wives in tight bonnets and goffered ruffs – lifted needle-thin wine-glasses to judge the colour by the light of the branching and globular brass candelabra which were secured on chains to the beams and the coffered ceilings.

Imaginary interiors ... No wonder they took shape in painting terms! Ever since those first hours in Rotterdam a three-dimensional Holland had been springing up all round me and expanding into the distance in conformity with another Holland which was already in existence and in every detail complete. For, if there is a foreign landscape familiar to English eyes by proxy, it is this one; by the time they see the original, a hundred mornings and afternoons in museums and picture galleries and country houses have done their work. These confrontations and recognition-scenes filled the journey with excitement and delight. The nature of the landscape itself, the colour, the light, the sky, the openness, the expanse and the details of the towns and the villages are leagued together in the weaving of a miraculously consoling and healing spell. Melancholy is exorcized, chaos chased away and wellbeing, alacrity of spirit and a thoughtful calm take their place. In my case, the relationship between familiar landscape and reality led to a further train of thought.

A second kind of scenery – the Italian – is almost as well known in England as the Dutch, and for the same gallery-haunting reasons. How familiar, at one remove, are those piazzas and arcades! The towers and the ribbed cupolas give way to the bridged loops of a river, and the rivers coil into umbered distances between castled hills and walled cities; there are shepherds' hovels and caverns; the fleece of woods succeeds them and the panorama dies away in fluted mountains that are dim or gleaming under skies with no more clouds than a decorative wreath of white vapour. But this scenery is a backcloth, merely, for lily-bearing angels who flutter to earth or play violins and lutes at Nativities; martyrdoms are enacted in front of it, miracles take place, and mystic marriages, scenes of torture, crucifixions, funerals and resurrections; processions wend, rival armies close in a deadlock of striped lances, an ascetic greybeard strikes his breast with a stone or writes at a lectern while a lion slumbers at his feet; a sainted stripling is riddled with crossbow bolts and gloved prelates collapse with upcast eyes and swords embedded across their tonsures.

Now, all these transactions strike the eye with a monopolizing impact; for five centuries and more, in many thousands of frames, they have been stealing the scene; and when the strange deeds are absent, recognition is much slower than it is in the Low Countries, where the precedence is reversed. In Holland the landscape is the protagonist, and merely human events – even one so extra-ordinary as Icarus falling head first in the sea because the wax in his artificial wings has melted – are secondary details: next to Brueghel's ploughed field and trees and sailing ship and plough-man, the falling aeronaut is insignificant. So compelling is the identity of picture and reality that all along my path numberless dawdling afternoons in museums were being summoned back to life and set in motion. Every pace confirmed them. Each scene conjured up its echo. The masts and quays and gables of a river port, the backyard with a besom leaning against a brick wall, the chequer-board floors of churches – there they all were, the entire range of Dutch themes, ending in taverns where I expected to find boors carousing, and found them; and in every case, like magic, the painter's name would simultaneously impinge. The willows, the roofs and the bell-towers, the cows grazing self-consciously in the foreground meadows – there was no need to ask whose easels they were waiting for as they munched.

These vague broodings brought me – somewhere between Tiel and Nijmegen, it must have been – to the foot of one of those vertiginous belfries which are so transparent in the distance and so solid close to. I was inside it and up half a dozen ladders in a minute and gazing down through the cobwebbed louvres. The whole kingdom was revealed. The two great rivers loitered across it with their scatterings of ships and their barge-processions and their tributaries. There were the polders and the dykes and the long willow-bordered canals, the heath and arable and pasture dotted with stationary and expectant cattle, windmills and farms and answering belfries, bare rookeries with their wheeling specks just within earshot and a castle or two, half-concealed among a ruffle of woods. The snow had melted here, or fallen more lightly: blue and green and pewter and russet and silver composed the enormous vista of turf and flood and sky. There was a low line of hills to the east, and everywhere the shine of intruding water and even a faint glimmer, faraway to the north, of the Zuider Zee. Filled with strange light, the peaceful and harmonious land slid away to infinity under a rush of clouds.

In the bottom chamber, as I left, an octet of clogged bell-ringers was assembling and spitting on their palms before grasping the sallies, and the clangour of their scales and changes, muted to a soft melancholy by the distance, followed me for the next few miles of nightfall and sharpening chill.

It was dark long before I reached the quays of Nijmegen. Then, for the first time for days, I found myself walking up a slant and down again. Lanes of steps climbed from the crowding ships along the waterfront; between the lamplight and the dark, tall towers and zig-zag façades impended. The quayside lamps strung themselves into the distance beside the dark flow of the Waal and upstream a great iron bridge sailed northwards and away for miles beyond the river. I had supper and after filling in my journal I searched the waterfront for a sailors' doss-house and ended up in a room over a blacksmith's.

I knew it was my last night in Holland and I was astonished how quickly I had crossed it. My heels might have been winged. I was astonished, too, at the impressive, clear beauty of the country and its variety, the amazing light and the sway of its healing and collusive charm. No wonder it had produced so many painters! And the Dutch themselves? Although we were reciprocally tongue-tied, the contact was not quite as slight as these pages must suggest. On foot, unlike other forms of travel, it is impossible to be out of touch; and our exchanges were enough, during this brief journey, to leave a deposit of liking and admiration which has lasted ever since.

Sleep fell so fast and empty of dreams that when I woke at six next morning the night seemed to have rushed by in a few minutes. It was the blacksmith's hammer just under the floor boards which had roused me. I lay as though in a trance, listening to the stop-gap bounces as they alternated with resonant horse-shoe notes on the beak of the anvil and when the rhythmic banging stopped, I could hear panting bellows and the hiss of steam and the fidgeting of enormous hoofs, and soon the smell of singe-

ing horn that rose through the cracks in the floor was followed
by fresh clangs and finally by the grate of a rasp. My host was
shoeing a great blond carthorse with a mane and tail of tousled
flax. He waved when I went into his smithy and mumbled good
morning through a mouthful of horsenails.

It was snowing. A signpost pointed over the bridge to Arnhem,
but I stuck to the south bank and followed the road for the
German border. In a little while it veered away from the river and
after a few miles I espied two figures in the distance: short of the
frontier, they were the last people I saw in Holland. They turned
out to be two nuns of St Vincent de Paul waiting for a country
bus. They were shod in clogs, they had black woollen shawls over
their shoulders and their blue stuff habits, caught in the middle,
billowed in many pleats. Their boxwood rosaries hung in loops
and crucifixes were tucked in their belts like daggers. But their
two umbrellas were of no avail – the slanting snow invaded their
coifs and piled up in the wide triangular wings.

The officials at the Dutch frontier handed back my passport,
duly stamped, and soon I was crossing the last furlongs of No
Man's Land, with the German frontier post growing nearer
through the turning snow. Black, white and red were painted in
spirals round the road barrier and soon I could make out the scarlet flag charged with its white disc and its black swastika. Similar
emblems had been flying over the whole of Germany for the last
ten months. Beyond it were the snow-laden trees and the first
white acres of Westphalia.

TWO

Up the Rhine

NOTHING remains from that first day in Germany but a confused memory of woods and snow and sparse villages in the dim West-phalian landscape and pale sunbeams dulled by clouds. The first landmark is the town of Goch, which I reached by nightfall; and here, in a little tobacconist's shop, the mist begins to clear. Buying cigarettes went without a hitch, but when the shopkeeper said: 'Wollen Sie einen Stocknagel?', I was at sea. From a neat row of them in a drawer, he picked a little curved aluminium plaque about an inch long with a view of the town and its name stamped in relief. It cost a pfennig, he said. Taking my stick, he inserted a tack in the hole at each end of the little medallion and nailed it on. Every town in Germany has its own and when I lost the stick a month later, already barnacled with twenty-seven of these plaques, it flashed like a silver wand.

The town was hung with National Socialist flags and the window of an outfitter's shop next door held a display of Party equipment: swastika arm-bands, daggers for the Hitler Youth, blouses for Hitler Maidens and brown shirts for grown-up S.A. men; swastika buttonholes were arranged in a pattern which read *Heil Hitler* and an androgynous wax-dummy with a pearly smile was dressed up in the full uniform of a *Sturmabteilungsmann*. I could identify the faces in some of the photographs on show; the talk of fellow-gazers revealed the names of the others. 'Look, there's Roehm,' someone said, pointing to the leader of the S.A. clasping the hand which was to purge him next June, 'shaking hands with the Führer!' Baldur von Schirach was taking the salute from a parade of *Hitlerjugend*; Goebbels sat at his desk; and Goering appeared in S.A. costume; in a white uniform; in vol-uminous leather shorts; nursing a lion cub; in tails and a white tie; and in a fur collar and plumed hunting hat, aiming a sporting gun. But those of Hitler as a bare-headed Brownshirt, or in a belted mackintosh or a double-breasted uniform and a peaked cap or patting the head of a flaxen-plaited and gap-toothed little girl offering him a bunch of daises, outnumbered the others. 'Ein sehr schöner Mann!', a woman said. Her companion agreed with a sigh and added that he had wonderful eyes.

The crunch of measured footfalls and the rhythm of a marching song sounded in a side street. Led by a standard bearer, a column of the S.A. marched into the square. The song that kept time to their tread, 'Volk, ans Gewehr!'* – often within earshot during the following weeks – was succeeded by the truculent beat of the *Horst Wessel Lied*: once heard, never forgotten; and when it finished, the singers were halted in a three-sided square, and stood at ease. It was dark now and thick snowflakes began falling across the lamplight. The S.A. men wore breeches and boots and stiff brown ski-caps with the chin-straps lowered like those of motor bicyclists, and belts with a holster and a cross-brace. Their shirts, with a red arm-band on the left sleeve, looked like brown paper; but as they listened to an address by their commander they had a menacing and purposeful look. He stood in the middle of the empty fourth side of the square, and the rasp of his utterance, even robbed of its meaning, struck a chill. Ironic crescendoes were spaced out with due pauses for laughter and each clap of laughter preceded a serious and admonitory drop in key. When his per-oration had died away the speaker clapped his left hand to his belt buckle, his right arm shot out, and a forest of arms answered him in concert with a three-fold 'Heil!' to his clipped introductory 'Sieg!' They fell out and streamed across the square, beating the snow off their caps and readjusting their chin-straps, while the standard-bearer rolled up his scarlet emblem and loped away with the flagpole over his shoulder.

I think the inn where I found refuge was called *Zum Schwar-zen Adler*. It was the prototype of so many I fetched up in after the day's march that I must try to reconstruct it.

The opaque spiralling of the leaded panes hid the snowfall and the cars that churned through the slush outside, and a leather curtain on a semi-circular rod over the doorway kept the room

* 'People, to arms!'

snug from cold blasts. The heavy oak tables were set about with
benches, hearts and lozenges pierced the chair-backs, a massive
china stove soared to the beams overhead, logs were stacked high
and sawdust was scattered on the russet tiles. Pewter-lidded beer-
mugs paraded along the shelves in ascending height. A framed
colour-print on the wall showed Frederick the Great, with cocked
hat askew, on a restless charger. Bismarck, white-clad in a breastplate under an eagle-topped helmet, beetled baggy-eyed next door;
Hindenburg, with hands crossed on sword-hilt, had the torpid solidity of a hippopotamus; and from a fourth frame, Hitler himself
fixed us with a scowl of great malignity. Posters with scarlet
hearts advertised *Kaffee Hag*. Clamped in stiff rods, a dozen newspapers hung in a row; and, right across the walls were painted
jaunty rhymes in bold Gothic black-letter script:

> Wer liebt nicht Wein, Weib und Gesang,
> Der bleibt ein Narr sein Leben lang!*

Beer, caraway seed, beeswax, coffee, pine-logs and melting snow
combined with the smoke of thick, short cigars in a benign aroma
across which every so often the ghost of sauerkraut would float.

I made room between the bretzel-stand, the Maggi sauce-bottle
and my lidded mug on its round eagle-stamped mat and set to
work. I was finishing the day's impressions with a dramatic description of the parade when a dozen S.A. men trooped in and
settled at a long table. They looked less fierce without their horrible caps. One or two, wearing spectacles, might have been clerks
or students. After a while they were singing:

> Im Wald, im grünen Walde
> Da steht ein Försterhaus ...

The words, describing a pretty forester's daughter in the green-

---

* 'Who loves not wine, women and song,
  Remains a fool his whole life long!'
The exploding exclamation marks and the metaphorical slaps on
the back always managed to weave a note of obscure melancholy into
these otherwise charming places. They spoke of wine but it was beer-
mugs, not glasses, that jostled each other on the tables.

wood, bounced along cheerfully and ended in a crashing and sharply syncopated chorus. *Lore, Lore, Lore,* as the song was called, was the rage of Germany that year. It was followed hotfoot by another that was to become equally familiar and obsessive. Like many German songs it described love under the linden trees:

Darum wink, mein Mädel, wink! wink! wink!*

The line that rhymed with it was 'Sitzt ein kleiner Fink, Fink, Fink'. (It took me weeks to learn that *Fink* was a finch; it was perched on one of those linden boughs.) Thumps accentuated the rhythm; the sound would have resembled a rugger club after a match if the singing had been less good. Later on, the volume dwindled and the thumping died away as the singing became softer and harmonies and descants began to weave more complex patterns. Germany has a rich anthology of regional songs, and these, I think, were dreamy celebrations of the forests and plains of Westphalia, long sighs of homesickness musically transposed. It was charming. And the charm made it impossible, at that moment, to connect the singers with organized bullying and the smashing of Jewish shop windows and nocturnal bonfires of books.

The green and intermittently wooded plains of Westphalia unfolded next day with hints of frozen marsh and a hovering threat of more snow. A troop of workmen in Robin Hood caps marched singing down a side lane with their spades martially at the slope: a similar troop, deployed in a row, was digging a turnip field at high speed and almost by numbers. They belonged to the *Arbeitsdienst,* or Labour Corps, a peasant told me. He was shod in those clogs I have always connected with the Dutch; but they were the universal footgear in the German country-side until much further south. (I still remembered a few German phrases I had picked up on winter holidays in Switzerland, so I was never as completely tongue-tied in Germany as I had been in Holland. As I spoke nothing but German during the coming months, these remnants blossomed, quite fast, into an ungrammatical fluency, and it is

* 'So wave, my maiden, wave, wave, wave.'

almost impossible to strike, at any given moment in these pages, the exact degree of my dwindling inarticulacy.)

I halted that evening in the little town of Kevelaer. It is lodged in my memory as a Gothic side-chapel overgrown with ex-votos. A seventeenth-century image of Our Lady of Kevelaer twinkled in her shrine, splendidly dressed for Advent in purple velvet, stiff with gold lace, heavily crowned and with a many-spiked halo behind a face like a little painted Infanta's. Westphalian pilgrims flocked to her chapel at other seasons and minor miracles abounded. Her likeness stamped my second *Stocknagel* next morning.

One signpost pointed to Kleve, where Anne of Cleves came from, and another to Aachen: if I had realized this was Aix-la-Chapelle, and merely the name of Charlemagne's capital in German, I would have headed there at full speed. As it was, I followed the Cologne road across the plain. Unmemorable and featureless, it flowed away until the fringes of the Ruhr hoisted a distant palisade of industrial chimneys along the horizon and barred the sky with a single massed streamer of smoke.

Germany!... I could hardly believe I was there.

For someone born in the second year of World War I, those three syllables were heavily charged. Even as I trudged across it, early subconscious notions, when one first confused Germans with germs and knew that both were bad, still sent up fumes; fumes, moreover, which the ensuing years had expanded into clouds as dark and baleful as the Ruhr smoke along the horizon and still potent enough to unloose over the landscape a mood of – what? Something too evasive to be captured and broken down in a hurry.

I must go back fourteen years, to the first complete event I can remember. I was being led by Margaret, the daughter of the family who were looking after me,* across the fields in Northamptonshire in the late afternoon of 18 June 1919. It was Peace Day, and she was twelve, I think, and I was four. In one of the water-meadows, a throng of villagers had assembled round an enormous bonfire all ready for kindling, and on top of it, ready for burning, were dummies of the Kaiser and the Crown Prince. The

---

* See *Introductory Letter*.

Kaiser wore a real German spiked-helmet and a cloth mask with huge whiskers; Little Willy was equipped with a cardboard monocle and a busby made of a hearthrug, and both had real German boots. Everyone lay on the grass, singing *It's a Long, Long Trail A-winding*, *The Only Girl in the World* and *Keep the Home Fires Burning*; then, *Good-byee, Don't Cryee*, and *K-K-K-Katie*. We were waiting till it was dark enough to light the bonfire. (An irrelevant remembered detail: when it was almost dark, a man called Thatcher Brown said 'Half a mo!' and, putting a ladder against the stack, he climbed up and pulled off the boots, leaving tufts of straw bursting out below the knees. There were pro-testations: 'Too good to waste,' he said.) At last someone set fire to the dry furze at the bottom and up went the flames in a great blaze. Everyone joined hands and danced round it, singing *Mademoiselle from Armentières* and *Pack up Your Troubles in Your Old Kitbag*. The whole field was lit up and when the flames reached the two dummies, irregular volleys of bangs and cracks broke out; they must have been stuffed with fireworks. Squibs and stars showered into the night. Everyone clapped and cheered, shouting: 'There goes Kaiser Bill!' For the children there, hoisted on shoulders like me, it was a moment of ecstasy and terror. Lit by the flames, the figures of the halted dancers threw concentric spokes of shadow across the grass. The two dummies above were beginning to collapse like ghostly scarecrows of red ash. Shouting, waving sparklers and throwing fire-crackers, boys were running in and out of the ring of gazers when the delighted shrieks changed to a new key. Screams broke out, then cries for help. Everyone swarmed to a single spot, and looked down. Margaret joined them, then rushed back. She put her hands over my eyes, and we started running. When we were a little way off, she hoisted me piggy-back, saying 'Don't look back!' She raced on across the dark fields and between the ricks and over the stiles as fast as she could run. But I did look back for a moment, all the same; the abandoned bonfire lit up the crowd which had assembled under the willows. Everything, somehow, spelt disaster and mishap. When we got home, she rushed upstairs, undressed me and put me into her bed and slipped in, hugging me to her flannel nightdress, sobbing and shuddering and refusing to answer questions. It was only after an endless siege that she told me, days later, what had happened. One of the village boys had been dancing about on the grass with his head back and a Roman candle in his mouth. The firework had slipped through his teeth and down his throat. They rushed him in agony, – 'spitting stars', they said – down to the brook. But it was too late . . .

It was a lurid start. A bit later, Margaret took me to watch trucks full of departing German prisoners go by; then to see *The Four Horsemen of the Apocalypse*, which left a confused impression of exploding shells, bodies on barbed wire, and a Prussian officers' orgy in a chateau. Much later on, old copies of *Punch* and *Queen Mary's Gift Book* and albums of war-time cartoons abetted the sinister mystique with a new set of stage properties: atrocity stories, farmhouses on fire, French cathedrals in ruins, Zeppelins and the goose-step; uhlans galloping through the autumn woods, Death's Head Hussars, corsetted officers with Iron Crosses and fencing slashes, monocles and staccato laughs . . . (How different from our own carefree subalterns in similar illustrations! Fox-terriers and Fox's puttees and Anzora hair-cream and Abdullah cigarettes; and Old Bill lighting his pipe under the star-shells!) The German military figures had a certain terrifying glamour, but not the civilians. The bristling paterfamilias, his tightly-buttoned wife, the priggish spectacled children and the odious dachshund reciting the Hymn of Hate among the sausages and the beer-mugs – nothing relieved the alien strangeness of these visions. Later still the villains of books (when they were not Chinese) were always Germans – spymasters or megalomaniac scientists bent on world domination. (When did these visions replace the early nineteenth-century stereotype of picturesque principalities exclusively populated – except for Prussia – by philosophers and composers and bandsmen and peasants and students drinking and singing in harmony? After the Franco-Prussian War, perhaps.) More recently, *All Quiet on the Western Front* had appeared; tales of night life in Berlin came soon after . . . There was not much else until the Nazis came into power.

How did the Germans seem, now I was in the thick of them?

No nation could live up to so melodramatic an image. Anti-climactically but predictably, I very soon found myself liking them. There is an old tradition in Germany of benevolence to the wandering young: the very humility of my status acted as an Open Sesame to kindness and hospitality. Rather surprisingly to me, being English seemed to help; one was a rare bird and an object of curiosity. But, even if there had been less to like, I would have felt warmly towards them: I was abroad at last, far from my familiar habitat and separated by the sea from the tangles of the past; and all this, combined with the wild and growing exhilaration of the journey, shed a golden radiance.

Even the leaden sky and the dull landscape round Krefeld became a region of mystery and enchantment, though this great industrial city itself only survives as a landmark for a night's shelter. But, at the end of the next day, the evening flush of Düsseldorf meant that I was back on the Rhine! There, once again, flowed the great river flanked by embankments, active with barges and spanned by an enormous modern bridge (called, slightly vexingly, the Skagerrakbrücke, after the Battle of Jutland) and looking no narrower than when we had parted. Great boulevards diminished in perspective on the other shore. There were gardens and a castle and an ornamental lake where a nearly static and enforcedly narcissistic game of swans were reflected in holes that had been chopped for them in the ice; but no black one that I can remember, like Thomas Mann's in the same piece of water.

I asked a policeman where the workhouse was. An hour's walk led to a sparsely lit quarter. Warehouses and the factories and silent yards lay deep under the untrodden snow. I rang a bell and a bearded Franciscan in clogs unbarred a door and led the way to a dormitory lined with palliasses on plank beds and filled with an overpowering fug and a scattering of whispers. A street lamp showed that all the beds round the stove were taken. I pulled off my boots and lay down, smoking in self-defence. I hadn't slept in a room with so many people since leaving school. Some of my contemporaries would still be there, at the end of their last term, snug, at this very moment (I thought as I fell asleep), in their green curtained cubicles,* long after their housemaster's rounds

---

* Nunc mihi, mox hujus, sed postmodo nescio cujus.

and lights out with Bell Harry tolling the hours and the night-watchman's voice in the precincts announcing a quiet night.

A long stertorous note and a guttural change of pitch from the next bed woke me with a start. The stove had gone out. Snores the groans and sighs were joining in chorus. Though everyone was fast asleep, there were broken sentences and occasional laughs; random explosions broke out. Someone sang a few bars of song and suddenly broke off. Lying in wait in the rafters all the nightmares of the Rhineland had descended on the sleepers.

It was dark in the yard and still snowing when the monk on duty supplied us with axes and saws. We set to work by lamp-light on a pile of logs and when they were cut, we filed past a second silent monk and he handed each of us a tin bowl of coffee in exchange for our tools. Another distributed slices of black bread and when the bowls had been handed in, my chopping-mate broke the icicles off the spout of the pump and we worked the handle in turn to slosh the sleep from our faces. The doors were then un-barred.

My chopping-mate was a Saxon from Brunswick and he was heading for Aachen, where, after he had drawn blank in Cologne, Duisburg, Essen and Düsseldorf and combed the whole of the Ruhr, he hoped to find work in a pins-and-needles factory. 'Gar kein Glück!' he said. He hunched his shoulders into his lumber-jack's coat and turned the flaps of his cap down over his ears. A few people were about now, stooping like us against the falling flakes. Snow lay on all the ledges and sills and covered the pave-ments with a trackless carpet. A tram clanged by with its lights still on, although daylight was beginning and when we reached the heart of the city, the white inviolate gardens and frozen trees expanded round the equestrian statue of an Elector. What about the government, I asked: were they any help? He said 'Ach Quatsch!' ('All rot!') and shrugged as though it were all too taxing a theme for our one-sided idiom. He had been in trouble, and he had no hopes of a turn for the better ... The sky was loosening and lemon-coloured light was dropping through the gaps in the snow-clouds as we crossed the Skagerrak Bridge and wails downstream announced that a ship of heavy draught was weighing anchor. At the crossroads on the other side we lit the last two cigars from a packet I had bought on the *Stadthouder*. He blew out a long cloud and burst out laughing: 'Man wird mich für einen Grafen halten!', he said: 'They'll take me for a Count!' When he'd gone a few paces, he turned and shouted with a wave: 'Gute Reise, Kamerad!' and struck west for Aachen. I headed south and upstream for Cologne.

After a first faraway glimpse, the two famous steeples grew taller and taller as the miles that separated us fell away. At last they commanded the cloudy plain as the spires of a cathedral should, vanishing when the outskirts of the city interposed themselves, and then, as I gazed at the crowding saints of the three Gothic doorways, sailing up into the evening again at close range. Beyond them indoors, although it was already too dark to see the colours of the glass, I knew I was inside the largest Gothic cathedral in Northern Europe. Except for the little constellation of tapers in the shadows of a side chapel, everything was dim. Women knelt interspersed with nuns and the murmured second half of the *Gegrüsset seist Du, Maria* rose in answering chorus to the priest's initial solo; a discreet clatter of beads kept tally of the accumulating prayers. In churches with open spires like Cologne, one could understand how congregations thought their orisons had a better start than prayers under a dome where the syllables might flutter round for hours. With steeples they follow the uprush of lancets and make an immediate break for it.

Tinsel and stars flashed in all the shops and banners saying *Fröhliche Weihnacht!* were suspended across the streets. Clogged villagers and women in fleece-lined rubber boots slipped about the icy pavements with exclamatory greetings and small screams, spilling their armfuls of parcels. The snow heaped up wherever it could and the sharp air and the lights gave the town an authentic Christmas card feeling. It was the real thing at last! Christmas was only five days away. Renaissance doors pierced walls of ancient brick, upper storeys jutted in salients of carved timber and glass, triangles of crow-steps outlined the steep gables, and eagles and lions and swans swung from convoluted iron brackets along a maze of lanes. As each quarter struck, the saint-encrusted towers

challenged each other through the snow and the rivalry of those
heavy bells left the air shaking.

Beyond the Cathedral and directly beneath the flying-buttresses
of the apse, a street dropped sharply to the quays. Tramp steamers
and tugs and barges and fair-sized ships lay at anchor under the
spans of the bridges, and cafés and bars were raucous with music. I
had been toying with the idea, if I could make the right friends, of
cadging a lift on a barge and sailing upstream in style for a bit.

I made friends all right. It was impossible not to. The first place
was a haunt of seamen and bargees shod in tall sea-boots rolled
down to the knee, with felt linings and thick wooden soles. They
were throwing schnapps down their throats at a brisk rate. Each
swig was followed by a chaser of beer, and I started doing the
same. The girls who drifted in and out were pretty but a rough lot
and there was one bulky terror, bursting out of a sailor's jersey
and wearing a bargeman's cap askew on a nest of candy-floss hair,
called Maggi – which was short for Magda – who greeted every
newcomer with a cry of 'Hallo, Bubi!' and a sharp, cunningly
twisted and very painful pinch on the cheek. I liked the place,
especially after several schnapps, and I was soon firm friends with
two beaming bargemen whose Low German speech, even sober,
would have been blurred beyond the most expert linguist's grasp.
They were called Uli and Peter. 'Don't keep on saying *Sie*,' Uli
insisted, with a troubled brow and an unsteadily admonishing
forefinger: 'Say *Du*.' This advance from the plural to the greater
intimacy of the singular was then celebrated by drinking
Brüderschaft. Glasses in hand, with our right arms crooked
through the other two with the complexity of the three Graces on
a Parisian public fountain, we drank in unison. Then we reversed
the process with our left arms, preparatory to ending with a triune
embrace on both cheeks, a manoeuvre as elaborate as being
knighted or invested with the Golden Fleece. The first half of the
ceremony went without a hitch, but a loss of balance in the
second, while our forearms were still interlocked, landed the three
of us in the sawdust in a sottish heap. Later, in the fickle fashion
of the very drunk, they lurched away into the night, leaving their
newly-created brother dancing with a girl who had joined our

unsteady group: my hobnail boots could do no more damage to her shiny dancing shoes, I thought, than the seaboots that were clumping all round us. She was very pretty except for two missing front teeth. They had been knocked out in a brawl the week before, she told me.

I woke up in a bargemen's lodging house above a cluster of masts and determined to stay another day in this marvellous town.

It had occurred to me that I might learn German quicker by reading Shakespeare in the famous German translation. The young man in the bookshop spoke some English. Was it *really* so good, I asked him. He was enthusiastic: Schlegel and Tieck's version, he said, was *almost* as good as the original; so I bought *Hamlet, Prinz von Dänemark*, in a paperbound pocket edition. He was so helpful that I asked him if there were any way of travelling up the Rhine by barge. He called a friend into consultation who was more fluent in English: I explained I was a student, travelling to Constantinople on foot with not much money, and that I didn't mind how uncomfortable I was. The newcomer asked: student of what? Well – literature: I wanted to write a book. 'So! You are travelling about Europe like Childe Harold?' he said. 'Yes, *yes!* Absolutely like Childe Harold!' Where was I staying? I told them. 'Pfui!' They were horrified, and amused. Both were delightful and, as the upshot of all this, I was asked to stay with one of them. We were to meet in the evening.

The day passed in exploring churches and picture galleries and looking at old buildings, with a borrowed guidebook.

Hans, who was my host, had been a fellow-student at Cologne University with Karl, the bookseller. He told me at dinner that he had fixed up a free lift for me next day on a string of barges heading upstream, all the way to the Black Forest if I wanted. We drank delicious Rhine wine and talked about English literature. The key figures in Germany I gathered, were Shakespeare, Byron, Poe, Galsworthy, Wilde, Maugham, Virginia Woolf, Charles Morgan and, very recently, Rosamund Lehmann. What about Priestley, they asked: *The Good Companions?* – and *The Story of San Michele?*

It was my first venture inside a German house. The interior was composed of Victorian furniture, bobbled curtains, a stove with green china tiles and many books with characteristic German bindings. Han's cheerful landlady, who was the widow of a don at the University, joined us over tea with brandy in it. I answered many earnest questions about England: how lucky and enviable I was, they said, to belong to that fortunate kingdom where all was so just and sensible! The allied occupation of the Rhineland had come to an end less than ten years before, and the British, she said, had left an excellent impression. The life she described revolved round football, boxing matches, fox-hunts and theatricals. The Tommies got drunk, of course, and boxed each other in the street – she lifted her hands in the posture of squaring up – but they scarcely ever set about the locals. As for the colonel who had been billeted on her for years, with his pipe and his fox terriers – what a gentleman! What kindness and tact and humour! 'Ein Gentleman durch und durch!' And his soldier servant – an angel! – had married a German girl. This idyllic world of cheery Tommies and Colonel Brambles sounded almost too good to be true and I basked vicariously in their lustre. But the French, they all agreed, were a different story. There had, it seems, been much friction, bloodshed even, and the ill-feeling still lingered. It sprang mainly from the presence of Senegalese units among the occupying troops; their inclusion had been interpreted as an act of calculated vengeance. The collapse of the Reichsmark was touched on, and Reparations; Hitler cropped up. The professor's widow couldn't bear him: such a mean face! 'So ein gemeines Gesicht!' – and that voice! Both the others were against him too, and the whole Nazi movement: it was no solution to Germany's problems; and wrong ... the conversation slid into a trough of depression. (I divined that it was a theme of constant discussion and that they were all against it, but in different ways and for different reasons. It was a time when friendships and families were breaking up all over Germany.) The conversation revived over German literature: apart from Remarque, the only German book I had read was a translation of *Zarathustra*. Neither of them cared much for Nietzsche, 'But he understood us Germans,' Hans said in an ambiguous tone. The Erasmian pronunciation of Latin cropped up, followed by the

reciting of rival passages from the ancient tongues: innocent showing off all round with no time for any of us to run dry. We grew
excited and noisy, and our hostess was delighted. How her husband would have enjoyed it! The evening ended with a third
round of handshakes. (The first had taken place on arrival and the
second at the beginning of dinner, when the word *Mahlzeit* was
ritually pronounced. German days are scanned by a number of
such formalities.)

The evening ended for me with the crowning delight of a bath,
the first since London. I wondered if the tall copper boiler had been
covertly lit as a result of a lively account of my potentially ver-
minous night in the workhouse ... 'My husband's study,' my
hostess had said with a sigh, when she showed me my room. And
here, under another of those giant meringue eiderdowns, I lay at
last between clean sheets on an enormous leather sofa with a
shaded light beside me beneath row upon row of Greek and Latin
classics. The works of Lessing, Mommsen, Kant, Ranke, Niebuhr
and Gregorovius soared to a ceiling decoratively stencilled with
sphinxes and muses. There were plaster busts of Pericles and
Cicero, a Victorian view of the Bay of Naples behind a massive
desk and round the walls, faded and enlarged, in clearings among
the volumes, huge photographs of Paestum, Syracuse, Agrigento,
Selinunte and Segesta. I began to understand that German middle-
class life held charms that I had never heard of.

The gables of the Rhine-quays were gliding past and, as we
gathered speed and sailed under one of the spans of the first bridge,
the lamps of Cologne all went on simultaneously. In a flash the
fading city soared out of the dark and expanded in a geometrical
infinity of electric bulbs. Diminishing skeletons of yellow dots
leaped into being along the banks and joined hands across the
flood in a sequence of lamp-strung bridges. Cologne was sliding
astern. The spires were the last of the city to survive and as they
too began to dwindle, a dark red sun dropped through bars of
amber into a vague *Abendland* that rolled glimmering away
towards the Ardennes. I watched the twilight scene from the bows
of the leading barge. The new plaque on my stick commemorated
the three Magi – their bones had been brought back from the

crusade by Frederick Barbarossa – and the legend of St Ursula and her suite of eleven thousand virgins.*

The barges were carrying a cargo of cement to Karlsruhe, where they were due to take on timber from the Black Forest and sail downstream again, possibly to Holland. The barges were pretty low in the water already: the cement sacks were lashed under tarpaulin lest a downpour should turn the cargo to stone. Near the stern of the leading barge the funnel puffed out a rank volume of diesel smoke, and, just aft of this hazard swung the brightly painted and beam-like tiller.

The crew were my pals from the bar! I had been the first to realize it. The others grasped the fact more slowly, with anguished cries of recognition as everything gradually and painfully came back to them. Four untidy bunks lined the walls of the cabin and a brazier stood in the middle. Postcards of Anny Ondra, Lilian Harvey, Brigitte Helm and Marlene Dietrich were pinned on the planks of this den; there was Max Schmeling with the gloves up in a bruising crouch, and two chimpanzees astride a giraffe. Uli and Peter and the diesel-engineer were all from Hamburg. We sat on the lower bunks and ate fried potatoes mixed with *Speck*: cold lumps of pork fat which struck me as the worst thing I had ever eaten. I contributed a garlic sausage and a bottle of schnapps – leaving presents from Cologne – and at the sight of the bottle, Uli howled like a beagle in pain. Cologne had been a testing time for them all; they were at grips with a group-hangover; but the bottle was soon empty all the same. Afterwards Peter brought out a very elaborate mouth-organ. We sang *Stille Nacht*, and I learnt the words of *Lore, Lore, Lore* and *Muss i denn, muss i denn zum Städtele 'naus*; they said this had been the wartime equivalent of *Tipperary*; then came a Hamburg song about 'Sankt Pauli und die Reeperbahn'. By pulling down a lock of his hair and holding the end of a pocket comb under his nose to simulate a toothbrush moustache, Uli gave an imitation of Hitler making a speech.

---

* They were all from Britain. They sailed up the Rhine on a bridal convoy, to be martyred here – perhaps by Attila, perhaps by the pagan emperor Maximian – and later were canonized en masse and finally immortalized by Carpaccio.

It was a brilliant starry night but very cold and they said I would freeze to death on the cement sacks; I had planned to curl up in my sleeping bag and lie gazing at the stars. So I settled in one of the bunks, getting up every now and then to smoke a cigarette with whoever was on duty at the tiller.

Each barge had a port and starboard light. When another string of barges came downstream, both flotillas signalled with lanterns and the two long Indian files, would slide past each other, rocking for a minute or two in each other's wakes. At one point we passed a tug trailing nine barges, each of them twice the length of ours; and later on, the bright speck of a steamer twinkled in the distance. It expanded as it advanced until it towered high above us, and then dwindled and vanished. Deep quarries were scooped out of the banks between the starlit villages that floated downstream. There was a faint glimmer of towns and villages across the plain. Even travelling against the current, we were moving more slowly than we should; the engineer didn't like the sound of the engine: if it broke down altogether, our little procession would start floating chaotically backwards and downstream. Files of barges were constantly overtaking us. As dawn broke, amid a shaking of heads, we tied up at the quays of Bonn.

The sky was cloudy and the classical buildings, the public gardens and the leafless trees of the town looked dingy against the snow; but I didn't dare to wander far in case we were suddenly ready to start. My companions were more heavily smeared with diesel-oil each time I returned; the engine lay dismembered across the deck amid spanners and hacksaws in an increasingly irreparable-looking chaos and at nightfall it seemed beyond redemption. We supped near and Uli and Peter and I, leaving the engineer alone with his blow-lamp, trooped off to a Laurel and Hardy film – we'd had our eye on it all day – and rolled about in paroxysms till the curtain came down.

At daybreak, all was well! The engine rang with a brisk new note. The country sped downstream at a great pace and the Siebengebirge and the Siegfried-haunted Drachenfels began to climb into the sparkling morning and the saw-teeth of their peaks shed alternate spokes of shadow and sunlight across the water. We sailed between tree-tufted islands. The Rhine crinkled round us where the current ran faster and the bows of vessels creased the surface with wide arrows and each propeller trailed its own long groove between their expanding lines. Among the little tricolours fluttering from every poop the Dutch red-white-and-blue was almost as frequent as the German black-white-and-red. A few flags showing the same colours as the Dutch but with the stripes perpendicular instead of horizontal, flew from French vessels of shallow draught from the quays of Strasbourg. The rarest colours of all were the black-yellow-and-red of Belgium. These boats, manned by Walloons from Liège, had joined the great river *via* the Meuse, just below Gorinchem. (What a long way off the little town seemed now, both in time and distance!) A stiff punctilio ruled all this going and coming. Long before crossing or overtaking each other, the appropriate flags were flourished a prescribed number of times from either vessel; and each exchange was followed by long siren blasts. Note answered note; and these salutations and responses and reciprocally fluttering colours spread a charming atmosphere of ceremony over the watery traffic like the doffing of hats between grandees. Sometimes a *Schleppzug* – a string of barges – lay so heavy under its cargo that the coiling bow-wave hid the vessels in turn as though they were sinking one after the other and then emerging for a few seconds as the wave dropped, only to vanish with the next curl of water; and so all along the line. Seagulls still skimmed and swooped and hovered on beating wings for thrown morsels or alighted on the bulwarks and stood there pensively for a minute or two. I watched all this from a nest among the sacks with a mug of Uli's coffee in one hand and a slice of bread in the other.

How exhilarating to be away from the plain! With every minute that passed the mountains climbed with greater resolution. Bridges linked the little towns from bank to bank and the water scurried round the piers on either side as we threaded upstream. Shuttered for the winter, hotels rose above the town roofs and piers for passenger steamers jutted into the stream. Unfabled as yet, Bad Godesberg slipped past. Castles crumbled on pinnacles. They loomed on their spikes like the turrets of the Green Knight before Sir Gawain; and one of them – so my unfolding river map told me – might have been built by Roland. Charlemagne was associated with the next. Standing among tall trees, the palaces of electors and princes and pleasure-loving archbishops reflected the sunlight from many windows. The castle of the Princes of Wied moved out of the wings, floated to the centre and then drifted slowly off-stage again. Was this where the short-reigned Mpret of Albania grew up? Were any of these castles, I wondered, abodes of those romantic-sounding noblemen, Rheingrafen and Wildgrafen – Rhine-Counts or Counts of the Forest, or the Wilderness or of Deer? If I had had to be German, I thought, I wouldn't have minded being a Wildgrave; or a Rhinegrave ... A shout from the cabin broke into these thoughts: Uli handed up a tin plate of delicious baked beans garnished with some more frightful *Speck*, which was quickly hidden and sent to join the Rheingold when no one was looking.

On the concertina-folds of my map these annotated shores resembled a historical traffic-block. We were chugging along Caesar's *limes* with the Franks. 'Caesar threw a bridge across the Rhine . . .' Yes, but where?* Later emperors moved the frontier eastward into the mountains far beyond the left bank, where, so they said, the Hercynian forest, home of unicorns, was too dense for a cohort to deploy, let alone a legion. (Look what happened to the legions of Quintilius Varus a hundred miles north-east! Those were vague regions, utterly unlike the shores of the brilliant Rhine: the *Frigund* of German myth, a thicket that still continued after sixty days of travel and the haunt, when the unicorns trotted away into fable, of wolves and elks and reindeers and the aurochs. The Dark Ages, when they reached them, found no lights to extinguish, for none had ever shone there.) Westward the map indicated the outlines of Lothair's kingdom after the Carolingian break-up. Later fragmentations were illustrated heraldically by a jostle of crossed swords and crosiers and shields with closed crowns and coronets and mitres on top, and electoral caps turned up with ermine. Sometimes the hats of cardinals were levitated above their twin pyramids of tassels and an unwieldy growth of crests sprang from the helmets of robber knights. Each of these emblems symbolized a piece in a jigsaw of minute but

---

* Just about here! I've looked it up a minute ago in the *Gallic War*.

hardy sovereign fiefs that had owed homage only to the Holy Roman Emperor; each of them exacted toll from the wretched ships that sailed under their battlements; and when Napoleon's advance exorcized the lingering ghost of the realm of Charlemagne, they survived, and still survive, in a confetti of mediatizations. On the terrace of one waterside schloss a strolling descendant in a Norfolk jacket was lighting his mid-morning cigar.

The amazing procession went on all day.

The walled town of Andernach was bearing down on us. The engineer snored in his bunk, Peter was smoking at the tiller and I lolled in the sun on the cabin roof while Uli sent flourishes and grace-notes cascading from his mouth-organ. Two or three bridges and half a dozen castles later, after a final hour or so of snow-covered slopes, we were losing speed under the lee of the Ehrenbreitstein. This colossal and extremely business-like modern fort was a cliff of masonry bristling with casemates and slotted with gun-embrasures. The town of Coblenz rose from the other shore with a noble sweep.

We slanted in towards the quay on the west bank; gradually, to prevent the barges bumping into each other or piling up as we lost speed. The whole manoeuvre was for my sake as the others had to hasten on. It was a sad parting: 'Du kommst nicht mit?', they cried. When we were going slow enough, and close enough to the embankment, I jumped ashore. We waved to each other as they steered amidstream again, and Uli unloosened a succession of piercing shrieks from the siren and then a long blast of valediction that echoed amazingly along the cliffs of Coblenz. Then they straightened out and slid under a bridge of boats and sped south.

A point like a flat-iron jutted into the river and a plinth on its tip lifted a colossal bronze statue of Kaiser Wilhelm I many yards into the air among the sparrows and the gulls. This projection of rock and masonry had once been an isolated southern settlement of the Teutonic Knights – to my surprise: I had always imagined these warriors hacking away at Muscovites in a non-stop snow-storm on the shores of the Baltic or the Masurian lakes. The Thirty Years War raged through the place. Metternich was born a few doors away. But a hoarier, more cosmic chronology had singled it out. Two great rivers, rushing blind down their converging canyons, collide under the tip of the flat-iron and the tangled flux of the current ruffles and dwindles downstream till the Rhine's great silted volume subdues the clearer flow of the newcomer. The Moselle! I knew that this loop of water, swerving under its bridges and out of sight, was the last stretch of a long valley of the utmost significance and beauty. A seagull, flying upstream, would look down for scores of miles on tiered and winding vineyards, and swoop, if he chose, through the great black Roman gates of Trier and then over the amphitheatre and across the frontier into Lorraine. Skimming through the weather-vanes of the old Merovingian city of Metz, he would settle among the rocks of the Vosges where the stream begins. I was tempted, for a moment, to follow it: but its path pointed due west; I'd never get to Constantinople that way. Ausonius, if I had read him then, might have tipped the scales.

Coblenz is on a slant. Every street tilted and I was always look-ing across towers and chimney-pots and down on the two corridors of mountain that conducted the streams to their meeting. It was a buoyant place under a clear sky, everything in the air whispered that the plains were far behind and the sunlight sent a flicker and a flash of reflections glancing up from the snow; and two more invisible lines had been crossed and important ones: the accent had changed and wine cellars had taken the place of beer-halls. Instead of those grey mastodontic mugs, wine-glasses glittered on the oak. (It was under a vista of old casks in a Weinstube that I settled with my diary till bedtime.) The plain bowls of these wine-glasses were poised on slender glass stalks, or on diminishing pagodas of little globes, and both kinds of stem were coloured: a deep green for Mosel and, for Rhenish, a brown smoky gold that was almost amber. When horny hands lifted them, each flashed forth its coloured message in the lamplight. It is impossible, drinking by the glass in those charmingly named inns and wine-cellars, not to drink too much. Deceptively and treacherously, those innocent-looking goblets hold nearly half a bottle and simply by sipping one could explore the two great rivers below and the Danube and all Swabia, and Franconia too by proxy, and the vales of

Imhof and the faraway slopes of Würzburg; journeying in time from year to year, with draughts as cool as a deep well, limpidly varying from dark gold to pale silver and smelling of glades and meadows and flowers. Gothic inscriptions still flaunted across the walls, but they were harmless here, and free of the gloom imposed by those boisterous and pace-forcing black-letter hortations in the beer-halls of the north. And the style was better: less emphatic, more lucid and laconic; and both consoling and profound in content; or so it seemed as the hours passed. *Glaub, was wahr ist,** enjoined a message across an antlered wall, *Lieb, was rar ist; Trink, was klar ist.* I only realized as I stumbled to bed how pliantly I had obeyed.

It was the shortest day of the year and signs of the season were becoming hourly more marked. Every other person in the streets was heading for home with a tall and newly felled fir-sapling across his shoulder, and it was under a mesh of Christmas decorations that I was sucked into the Liebfrauenkirche next day. The romanesque nave was packed and an anthem of great choral splendour rose from the gothic choir stalls, while the cauliflowering incense followed the plainsong across the slopes of the sunbeams. A Dominican in horn-rimmed spectacles delivered a vigorous sermon. A number of Brownshirts – I'd forgotten all about them for the moment – was scattered among the congregation, with eyes lowered and their caps in their hands. They looked rather odd. They should have been out in the forest, dancing round Odin and Thor, or Loki perhaps.

Coblenz and its great fortress dropped behind and the mountains took another pace forward. Serried vineyards now covered the banks of the river, climbing as high as they could find a foothold. Carefully buttressed with masonry, shelf rose on shelf in fluid and looping sweeps. Pruned to the bone, the dark vine-shoots stuck out of the snow in rows of skeleton fists which shrank to quincunxes of black commas along the snow-covered contour-lines of the vineyards as they climbed, until the steep waves of salients and re-entrants faltered at last and expired overhead among the

---

* 'Believe what is true; love what is rare; drink what is clear.'

wild bare rocks. On the mountains that overhung these flowing
ledges, scarcely a peak had been left without a castle. At Stolzenfels, where I stopped for something to eat, a neo-Gothic keep
climbed into the sky on a staircase of vineyards, and another castle
echoed it from Oberlahnstein on the other shore. Then another
rose up, and another, and yet another: ruin on ruin, and vineyard
on vineyard ... They seemed to revolve as they moved downstream, and then to impend. Finally a loop of the river would carry
them away until the dimness of the evening blurred them all and
the lights of the shore began to twinkle among their darkening
reflections. Soon after dark, I halted at Boppard. It was lodged a
little way up the mountain-side so that next morning a fresh
length of the river uncoiled southward while the Sunday morning
bells were answering our own chimes upstream and down.

When the cliffs above were too steep for snow, spinneys frilled
the ledges of shale, and fans of brushwood split the sunbeams into
an infinity of threads. Higher still, the gap-toothed and unfailing
towers – choked with trees and lashed together with ivy – thrust
angles into the air which followed up the impulse of the crags on
which they were perched; and, most fittingly, their names all
ended in the German word for 'angle' or 'rock' or 'crag' or 'keep':
Hoheneck, Reichenstein, Stolzenfels, Falkenburg ... Each turn of
the river brought into view a new set of stage wings and sometimes a troop of islands which the perpetual rush of the river had
worn thin and moulded into the swerve of the current. They
seemed to float there under a tangle of bare twigs and a load of
monastic or secular ruins. A few of these eyots were sockets for
towers which could bar the river by slinging chains to either bank
and holding up ships for toll or loot or ransom. Dark tales
abound.*

Fragmentary walls, pierced by old gateways, girdled most of the

---

* One of them concerns a mid-stream toll-tower outside Bingen,
where I slept: the Mäuseturm. It is the legendary scene of the death
of Hatto, Archbishop of Mainz, in the tenth century. He was devoured by mice in the tower, the legend says, in retribution for his
tyranny; the story inspired Southey's poem. Rodents play a great part
in German legend, e.g. The Pied Piper of Hamelin.

little towns. I halted in many of them for a glass of wine out of
one of those goblets with coloured stems with a slice of black
bread and butter, sipping and munching by the stove while, every
few minutes, my dripping boots shed another slab of hobnail-im-
pacted snow several inches thick. The river, meanwhile, was nar-
rowing fast and the mountains were advancing and tilting more
steeply until there was barely space for the road. A huge answering buttress loomed on the other bank and on its summit, helped
by the innkeeper's explanation, I could just discern the semblance
of the Lorelei who gave the rock its name. The river, after nar-
rowing with such suddenness, sinks to a great depth here and
churns perilously enough to give colour to the stories of ships and
sailors beckoned to destruction. The siren of a barge unloosed a
long echo; and the road, scanned by brief halts, brought me into
Bingen at dusk.

The only customer, I unslung my rucksack in a little Gasthof.
Standing on chairs, the innkeeper's pretty daughters, who were
aged from five to fifteen, were helping their father decorate a
Christmas tree; hanging witch-balls, looping tinsel, fixing candles
to the branches, and crowning the tip with a wonderful star. They
asked me to help and when it was almost done, their father, a tall,
thoughtful-looking man, uncorked a slim bottle from the
Rüdesheim vineyard just over the river. We drank it together
and had nearly finished a second by the time the last touches to
the tree were complete. Then the family assembled round it and
sang. The candles were the only light and the solemn and charming ceremony was made memorable by the candle-lit faces of the
girls – and by their beautiful and clear voices. I was rather surprised that they didn't sing *Stille Nacht*: it had been much in the
air the last few days; but it is a Lutheran hymn and I think this
bank of the Rhine was mostly Catholic. Two of the carols they
sang have stuck in my memory: *O Du Heilige* and *Es ist ein Ros
entsprungen*: both were entrancing, and especially the second,
which, they told me, was very old. In the end I went to church
with them and stayed the night. When all the inhabitants of
Bingen were exchanging greetings with each other outside the
church in the small hours, a few flakes began falling. Next morning the household embraced each other, shook hands again and

wished every one a happy Christmas. The smallest of the daughters gave me a tangerine and a packet of cigarettes wrapped beautifully in tinsel and silver paper. I wished I'd had something to hand her, neatly done up in a holly-patterned ribbon – I thought later of my aluminium pencil-case containing a new Venus or Royal Sovereign wound in tissue paper, but too late. The time of gifts.*

The Rhine soon takes a sharp turn eastwards, and the walls of the valley recede again. I crossed the river to Rüdesheim, drank a glass of Hock under the famous vineyard and pushed on. The snow lay deep and crisp and even. On the march under the light fall of flakes, I wondered if I had been right to leave Bingen. My kind benefactors had asked me to stay, several times; but they had been expecting relations and, after their hospitality, I felt, in spite of their insistence, that a strange face at their family feast might be too much. So here I was on a sunny Christmas morning, plunging on through a layer of new snow. No vessels were moving on the Rhine, hardly a car passed, nobody was out of doors and, in the little towns, nothing stirred. Everyone was inside. Feeling lonely and beginning to regret my flight, I wondered what my family and my friends were doing, and skinned and ate the tangerine rather pensively. The flung peel, fallen short on the icy margin, became the target for a sudden assembly of Rhine gulls. Watching them swoop, I unpacked and lit one of my Christmas cigarettes, and felt better.

In the inn where I halted at midday – *where was it?* Geisenheim? Winkel? Östrich? Hattenheim? – a long table was splendidly spread for a feast and a lit Christmas tree twinkled at one end. About thirty people were settling down with a lot of jovial noise when some soft-hearted soul must have spotted the solitary figure in the empty bar. Unreluctantly, I was drawn into the feast; and here, in my memory, as the bottles of Johannisberger and Markobrunner mount up, things begin to grow blurred.

A thirsty and boisterous rump at the end of the table was still drinking at sunset. Then came a packed motorcar, a short journey, and a large room full of faces and the Rhine twinkling far below.

---

* See page 7.

Perhaps we were in a castle . . . some time later, the scene changes: there is another jaunt, through the dark this time, with the lights multiplying and the snow under the tyres turning to slush; then more faces float to the surface and music and dancing and glasses being filled and emptied and spilled.

I woke up dizzily next morning on someone's sofa. Beyond the lace curtains and some distance below, the snow on either side of the tramlines looked unseasonably mashed and sooty for the feast of Stephen.

THREE

Into High Germany

APART from that glimpse of tramlines and slush, the mists of the *Nibelungenlied* might have risen from the Rhine-bed and enveloped the town; and not only Mainz: the same vapours of oblivion have coiled upstream, enveloping Oppenheim, Worms and Mannheim on their way. I spent a night in each of them and only a few scattered fragments remain: a tower or two, a row of gargoyles, some bridges and pinnacles and buttresses and the perspective of an arcade dwindling into the shadows. There is a statue of Luther that can only belong to Worms; but there are cloisters as well and the black-letter pages of a Gutenberg Bible, a picture of St Boniface and a twirl of Jesuit columns. Lamplight shines through shields of crimson glass patterned with gold crescents and outlined in lead; but the arch that framed them has gone. And there are lost faces: a chimney sweep, a walrus moustache, a girl's long fair hair under a tam o'shanter. It is like reconstructing a brontosaur from half an eye socket and a basket full of bones. The cloud lifts at last in the middle of the Ludwigshafen–Mannheim bridge.

After following the Rhine, off and on ever since I had stepped ashore, I was about to leave it for good. The valley had widened after Bingen and opened into the snowy Hessian champaign; the mountains still kept their distance as the river coiled southwards and out of sight. But the Rhine map I unfolded on the balustrade traced its course upstream hundreds of miles and far beyond my range. After Spires and Strasbourg, the Black Forest scowled across the water at the blue line of the Vosges. In hungry winters like this, I had been told, wolves came down from the conifers and trotted through the streets. Freiburg came next, then the Swiss border and the falls of Schaffhausen where the river poured from Lake Constance. Beyond, the map finished in an ultimate and unbroken white chaos of glaciers.

On the far side of the bridge I abandoned the Rhine for its

tributary and after a few miles alongside the Neckar the steep lights of Heidelberg assembled. It was dark by the time I climbed the main street and soon softly-lit panes of coloured glass, under the hanging sign of a Red Ox, were beckoning me indoors. With freezing cheeks and hair caked with snow, I clumped into an entrancing haven of oak beams and carving and alcoves and changing floor levels. A jungle of impedimenta encrusted the interior – mugs and bottles and glasses and antlers – the innocent accumulation of years, not stage props of forced conviviality – and the whole place glowed with a universal patina. It was more like a room in a castle and, except for a cat asleep in front of the stove, quite empty.

This was the moment I longed for every day. Settling at a heavy inn-table, thawing and tingling, with wine, bread, and cheese handy and my papers, books and diary all laid out; writing up the day's doings, hunting for words in the dictionary, drawing, struggling with verses, or merely subsiding in a vacuous and contented trance while the snow thawed off my boots. An elderly woman came downstairs and settled by the stove with her sewing. Spotting my stick and rucksack and the puddle of melting snow, she said, with a smile, 'Wer reitet so spät durch Nacht und Wind?' My German, now fifteen days old, was just up to this: 'Who rides so late through night and wind?' But I was puzzled by *reitet*. (How was I to know that it was the first line of Goethe's famous *Erlkönig*, made more famous still by the music of Schubert?) *What, a foreigner?* I knew what to say at this point, and came in on cue: ... 'Englischer Student ... zu Fuss nach Konstantinopel' . . I'd got it pat by now. 'Konstantinopel?' she said. 'Oh Weh!' O Woe! So far! And in midwinter too. She asked where I would be the day after, on New Year's Eve. Somewhere on the road, I said. 'You can't go wandering about in the snow on Sylvesterabend!' she answered. 'And where are you staying tonight, pray?' I hadn't thought yet. Her husband had come in a little while before and overheard our exchange. 'Stay with us,' he said. 'You must be our guest.'

They were the owner and his wife and their names were Herr and Frau Spengel. Upstairs, on my hostess's orders, I fished out things to be washed – it was my first laundry since London – and

handed them over to the maid: wondering, as I did so, how a
German would get on in Oxford if he turned up at The Mitre on a
snowy December night.

One of the stained-glass armorial shields in the windows bore
the slanting zigzag of Franken. This old stronghold of the Salian
Franks is a part of northern Bavaria now and the Red Ox Inn was
the headquarters of the Franconia student league. All the old inns
of Heidelberg had these regional associations, and the most exalted
of them, the Saxoborussia, was Heidelberg's Bullingdon and the
members were Prussia's and Saxony's haughtiest. They held their
sessions at Seppl's next door, where the walls were crowded with
faded daguerrotypes of slashed and incipiently side-whiskered
scions of the *Hochjunkertum* defiant in high boots and tricoloured
sashes. Their gauntlets grasped basket-hilted sabres. Askew on
those faded pates little caps like collapsed képis were tilted to
display the initial of the Corps embroidered on the crown – a
contorted Gothic cypher and an exclamation mark, all picked out
in gold wire. I pestered Fritz Spengel, the son of my hosts, with
questions about student life: songs, drinking ritual, and above all,
duelling, which wasn't duelling at all of course, but tribal
scarification. Those dashing scars were school ties that could never
be taken off, the emblem and seal of a ten-years' cult of the hu-
manities.* With a sabre from the wall, Fritz demonstrated the
stance and the grip and described how the participants were
gauntleted, gorgeted and goggled until every exposed vein and
artery, and every inch of irreplaceable tissue, were upholstered
from harm. Distance was measured; the sabres crossed at the end
of outstretched arms; only the wrists moved; to flinch spelt disgrace; and the blades clashed by numbers until the razor-sharp
tips sliced gashes deep enough, tended with rubbed-in salt, to last
a lifetime. I had noticed these academic stigmata on the spectacled
faces of doctors and lawyers; brow, cheek or chin, and sometimes
all three, were ripped up by this haphazard surgery in puckered or

---

* Hitler had recently suppressed all this, not out of antipathy to
bloodsports but because these cliques and their exciting customs must
have seemed rivals of the official youth and student movements.

gleaming lines strangely at odds with the wrinkles that middle age had inscribed there. I think Fritz, who was humane, thoughtful and civilized and a few years older than me, looked down on this antique custom, and he answered my question with friendly pity. He knew all too well the dark glamour of the Mensur among foreigners.

The rather sad charm of a university in the vacation pervaded the beautiful town. We explored the academic buildings and the libraries and the museum and wandered round the churches. Formerly a stronghold of the Reform, the town now harbours the rival faiths in peaceful juxtaposition and if it is a Sunday, Gregorian plainsong escapes through the doors of one church and the Lutheran strains of *Ein' feste Burg* from the next.

That afternoon, with Fritz and a friend, I climbed through the woods to look at the ruins of the palace that overhangs the town: an enormous complex of dark red stone which turns pink, russet or purple with the vagaries of the light and the hour. The basic mass is medieval, but the Renaissance bursts out again and again in gateways and courtyards and galleries and expands in the delicate sixteenth-century carving. Troops of statues posture in their scalloped recesses. Siege and explosion had partly wrecked it when the French ravaged the region. When? In the Thirty Years War; one might have guessed ... But who had built it? *Didn't I know? Die Kurfürsten von der Pfalz!* The Electors Palatine ... We were in the old capital of the Palatinate ...

Distant bells, ringing from faraway English class-rooms, were trying to convey a forgotten message; but it was no good. 'Guess what this gate is called!', Fritz said, slapping a red column. 'The Elizabeth, or English Gate! Named after the English princess.' *Of course!* I was there at last! The Winter Queen! Elizabeth, the high-spirited daughter of James I, Electress Palatine and, for a year, Queen of Bohemia! She arrived here as a bride of seventeen and for the five years of her reign, Heidelberg, my companions said, had never seen anything like the masques and the revels and the balls. But soon, when the Palatinate and Bohemia were both lost and her brother's head was cut off and the Commonwealth had reduced her to exile and poverty, she was celebrated as the Queen of Hearts by a galaxy of champions. Her great-niece,

Queen Anne, ended the reigning line of the Stuarts and
Elizabeth's grandson, George I, ascended the throne where her
descendant still sits. My companions knew much more about it
than I did.*

In spite of its beauty, it was a chill, grey prospect at this
moment. Lagged in sacking for the winter, desolate rose trees
pierced the snow-muffled terraces. These were bare of all footprints
but our own and the tiny arrows of a robin. Below the last balustrade, the roofs of the town clustered and beyond it flowed the
Neckar and then the Rhine, and the Haardt Mountains, and the
Palatine Forest rippled away beyond. A sun like an enormous
crimson balloon was about to sink into the pallid landscape. It
recalled, as it does still, the first time I saw this wintry portent. In
a sailor-suit with H.M.S. *Indomitable* on my cap-ribbon, I was
being hurried home to tea across Regent's Park while the keepers
were calling closing time. We lived so close to the zoo that one
could hear the lions roaring at night.

This Palatine sun was the dying wick of 1933; the last vestige of
that ownerless rump of the seasons that stretches from the winter
solstice to the New Year. ' 'Tis the year's midnight . . . the world's
whole sap is sunk.' On the way back we passed a group of youths
sitting on a low wall and kicking their heels as they whistled the
Horst Wessel Lied between their teeth. Fritz said, 'I *think*,
perhaps, I've heard that tune before . . .'

That night at the inn, I noticed that a lint-haired young man at
the next table was fixing me with an icy gleam. Except for pale
blue eyes set flush with his head like a hare's, he might have been
an albino. He suddenly rose with a stumble, came over, and said:
'So? Ein Engländer?' with a sardonic smile. '*Wunderbar!*' Then
his face changed to a mask of hate. Why had we stolen Germany's

---

* There were many reasons for thinking about this castle later on,
not least because of the Palatine Anthology, which was long treasured
there; and for fascinating though nebulous links between the Princess
and the Rosicrucians. She was preoccupied, in the layout of the Palace
gardens, with devices like talking statues, singing fountains, water
organs and the like. She had grown up among the plays of Shakespeare and Ben Jonson and the conceits of Donne and played in
masques where the scenery was designed by Inigo Jones.

colonies? Why shouldn't Germany have a fleet and a proper army? Did I think Germany was going to take orders from a country that was run by the Jews? A catalogue of accusation followed, not very loud, but clearly and intensely articulated. His face, which was almost touching mine, raked me with long blasts of schnapps-breath. 'Adolf Hitler will change all that,' he ended. '*Perhaps you've heard the name?*' Fritz shut his eyes with a bored groan and murmured 'Um Gottes willen!' Then he took him by the elbow with the words, 'Komm, Franzi!' and, rather, surprisingly, my accuser allowed himself to be led to the door. Fritz sat down again, saying: 'I'm so sorry. You see what it's like.' Luckily, none of the other tables had noticed and the hateful moment was soon superseded by feasting and talk and wine and, later, by songs to usher in St Sylvester's Vigil; and by the time the first bells of 1934 were clashing outside, everything had merged in a luminous haze of music and toasts and greetings.

Frau Spengel insisted that it was absurd to set off on New Year's Day; so I spent another twenty-four hours wandering about the town and the castle and reading and writing and talking with this kind and civilized family. (My sojourn at the Red Ox, afterwards, was one of several high points of recollection that failed to succumb to the obliterating moods of war. I often thought of it.)*

'Don't forget your *treuer Wanderstab*,' Frau Spengel said, handing me my gleaming stick as I was loading up for departure on the second of January. Fritz accompanied me to the edge of the town. Ironed linen lay neatly in my rucksack; also a large parcel of Gebäck, special Sylvestrine cakes rather like shortbread, which I munched as I loped along over the snow. All prospects glowed, for

* After writing these words and wondering whether I had spelt the name Spengel right – also to discover what had happened to the family – on a sudden impulse I sent a letter to the Red Ox, addressed 'to the proprietor'. A very nice letter from Fritz's son – he was born in 1939 – tells me that not only my host and hostess are dead, but that Fritz was killed in Norway (where the first battalion of my own regiment at the time was heavily engaged) and buried at Trondheim in 1940, six years after we met. The present Herr Spengel is the sixth generation of the same family to own and run this delightful inn.

the next halt – at Bruchsal, a good stretch further – was already
fixed up. Before leaving London, a friend who had stayed there the
summer before and canoed down the Neckar by *faltboot* with one
of the sons of the house, had given me an introduction to the
mayor. Fritz had telephoned; and by dusk I was sitting with Dr
Arnold and his family drinking tea laced with brandy in one of
the huge baroque rooms of Schloss Bruchsal. I couldn't stop
gazing at my magnificent surroundings. Bruchsal is one of the
most beautiful baroque palaces in the whole of Germany. It was
built in the eighteenth century by the Prince-Bishops of Spires, I
can't remember when their successors stopped living in it; perhaps
when their secular sovereignty was dissolved. But for many
decades it had been the abode of the Burgomasters of Bruchsal. I
stayed here two nights, sleeping in the bedroom of an absent son.
After a long bath, I explored his collection of Tauchnitz editions
and found exactly what I wanted to read in bed – *Leave it to
Psmith* – and soon I wasn't really in a German schloss at all, but in
the corner seat of a first class carriage on the 3.45 from Paddington
to Market Blandings, bound for a different castle.

It was the first time I had seen such architecture. The whole of
next day I loitered about the building; hesitating half-way up
shallow staircases balustraded by magnificent branching designs
of wrought metal; wandering through double doors that led from
state room to state room; and gazing with untutored and marvelling eyes down perspectives crossed by the diminishing slants
of winter sunbeams. Pastoral scenes unfolded in light-hearted
colours across ceilings that were enclosed in a studiously asym-
metrical icing of scrolls and sheaves; shells and garlands and foliage and ribands depicted myths extravagant enough to stop an
unprepared observer dead in his tracks. The sensation of wintry
but glowing interior space, the airiness of the snowy convolutions,
the twirl of the metal foliage and the gilt of the arabesques were
all made more buoyant still by reflections from the real snow that
lay untrodden outside; it came glancing up through the panes,
diffusing a still and muted luminosity: a northern variant (I
thought years later) of the reflected flicker that canals, during
Venetian siestas, send up across the cloud-born apotheoses and

rapes that cover the ceilings. Only statues and skeleton trees
broke the outdoor whiteness, and a colony of rooks.

In England, the Burgomaster, with his white hair and
moustache, his erect bearing and grey tweeds, might have been
colonel of a good line regiment. After dinner he tucked a cigar in a
holder made of a cardboard cone and a quill, changed spectacles
and, hunting through a pile of music on the piano, sat down and
attacked the Waldstein Sonata with authority and verve. The
pleasure was reinforced by the player's enjoyment of his capacity
to wrestle with it. His expression of delight, as he peered at the
notes through a veil of cigar smoke and tumbling ash, was at odds
with the gravity of the music. It was a surprise; so different was it
from an evening spent with his putative English equivalent; and
when the last chord had been struck, he leapt from the stool with
a smile of youthful and almost ecstatic enjoyment amid the good-
humoured applause of his family. A rush of appraisal broke out,
and hot argument about possible alternative interpretations.

There was no doubt about it, I thought next day: I'd taken a
wrong turning. Instead of reaching Pforzheim towards sunset, I
was plodding across open fields with snow and the night both
falling fast. My new goal was a light which soon turned out to be
the window of a farmhouse by the edge of a wood. A dog had
started barking. When I reached the door a man's silhouette appeared in the threshold and told the dog to be quiet and shouted:
'Wer ist da?' Concluding that I was harmless, he let me in.

A dozen faces peered up in surprise, their spoons halted in mid
air, and their features, lit from below by a lantern on the table,
were as gnarled and grained as the board itself. Their clogs were
hidden in the dark underneath, and the rest of the room, except
for the crucifix on the wall, was swallowed by shadow. The spell
was broken by the unexpectedness of the irruption: A *stranger
from Ausland!* Shy, amazed hospitality replaced earlier fears and I
was soon seated among them on the bench and busy with a spoon
as well.

The habit of grasping and speaking German had been outpaced
during the last few days by another change of accent and idiom.
These farmhouse sentences were all but out of reach. But there

was something else here that was enigmatically familiar. Raw knuckles of enormous hands, half clenched still from the grasp of ploughs and spades and bill-hooks, lay loose among the cut onions and the chipped pitchers and a brown loaf broken open. Smoke had blackened the earthenware tureen and the light caught its pewter handle and stressed the furrowed faces, and the bricky cheeks of young and hemp-haired giants ... A small crone in a pleated coif sat at the end of the table, her eyes bright and timid in their hollows of bone and all these puzzled features were flung into relief by a single wick from below. Supper at Emmaus or Bethany? Painted by whom?

Dog-tired from the fields, the family began to stretch and get down the moment the meal was over and to amble bedwards with dragging clogs. A grandson, apologizing because there was no room indoors, slung a pillow and two blankets over his shoulder, took the lantern and led the way across the yard. In the barn the other side, harrows, ploughshares, scythes and sieves loomed for a moment, and beyond, tethered to a manger that ran the length of the barn, horns and tousled brows and liquid eyes gleamed in the lantern's beam. The head of a cart-horse, with a pale mane and tail and ears pricked at our advent, almost touched the rafters.

When I was alone I stretched out on a bed of sliced hay like a crusader on his tomb, snugly wrapped up in greatcoat and blankets, with crossed legs still putteed and clodhoppered. Two owls were within earshot. The composite smell of snow, wood, dust, cobwebs, mangolds, beetroots, fodder, cattlecake and the cows' breath was laced with an ammoniac tang from the plip-plop and the splash that sometimes broke the rhythm of the munching and the click of horns. There was an occasional grate of blocks and halters through their iron rings, a moo from time to time, or a huge horseshoe scraping or clinking on the cobbles. This was more like it!

The eaves were stiff with icicles next morning. Everyone was out of the kitchen and already at work, except the old woman in the coif. She gave me a scalding bowl of coffee and milk with dark brown bread broken in it. Would an offer to pay be putting my foot in it, I wondered; and then tentatively proposed it. There was no offence; but, equally, it was out of the question: 'Nee, nee!' she said, with a light pat of her transparent hand. (It sounded the same as the English 'Nay'.) The smile of her totally dismantled gums had the innocence of an infant's. 'Gar nix!' After farewells, she called me back with a shrill cry and put a foot-long slice of buttered black bread in my hand; I ate my way along this gigantic and delicious butterbrot as I went, and after a furlong, caught sight of all the others. They waved and shouted 'Gute Reise!' They were hacking at the frostbitten grass with mattocks, delving into a field that looked and sounded as hard as iron.

Stick-nail fetishism carried me to Mühlacker, all of two miles off my way, in order to get the local *Stocknagel* hammered on, the seventeenth. It was becoming a fixation.

Of the town of Pforzheim, where I spent the next night, I remember nothing. But the evening after I was in the heart of Stuttgart by lamp-lighting time, sole customer in a café opposite the cubistic mass of the Hotel Graf Zeppelin. Snow and sleet and biting winds had emptied the streets of all but a few scuttling figures, and two cheerless boys doggedly rattling a collection box. Now they had vanished as well and the proprietor and I were the only people in sight in the whole capital of Württemberg. I was writing out the day's doings and vaguely wondering where to find lodging when two cheerful and obviously well-brought up girls came in, and began buying groceries at the counter. They were amusingly dressed in eskimo hoods, furry boots and gauntlets like grizzly bears which they clapped together to dispel the cold. I wished I knew them ... The sleet, turning to hail, rattled on the window like grapeshot. One of the girls, who wore horn-rimmed spectacles, catching sight of my German-English dictionary, daringly said 'How do you do, do, Mister Brown?' (This was the only line of an idiotic and now mercifully forgotten song, repeated ad infinitum like *Lloyd George Knew My Father*; it had swept across the world two years before.) Then she laughed in confusion at her boldness, under a mild reproof from her companion. I jumped up and implored them to have a coffee, or anything ... They suddenly became more reserved: 'Nein, nein, besten Dank, aber wir müssen weg!' I looked crestfallen; and after an exchange of 'Warum nicht?'s, they consented to stay five minutes, but refused coffee.

The line of the song was almost the only English they knew. My first interlocutrix, who had taken her spectacles off, asked how old I was. I said 'Nineteen', though it wouldn't be quite true for another five weeks. 'We too!' they said. 'And what do you do?' 'I'm a student.' 'We too! W*underbar*!' They were called Elizabeth-Charlotte, shortened to Liselotte or Lise – and Annie. Lise was from Donaueschingen, where the Danube rises, in the Black Forest, but she was living in Annie's parents' house in Stuttgart, where they were studying music. Both were pretty. Lise had unruly brown hair and a captivating and lively face, from which a smile was never absent for long; her glance, with her spectacles off, was wide, unfocused and full of trusting charm. Annie's fair hair was plaited and coiled in earphones, a fashion I'd always hated; but it suited her pallor and long neck and gave her the look of a Gothic effigy from the door of an abbey. They told me they were buying things for a young people's party in celebration of the *Dreikönigsfest*. It was Epiphany, the 6th of January, the feast of the Three Kings. After some whispered confabulation, they decided to have pity on me and take me with them. Lise enter-prisingly suggested we could invent a link with her family – 'falls sie fragen, wo wir Sie aufgegabelt haben' ('Just in case they ask where we forked you out from'). Soon, in the comfortable bath-room of Annie's absent parents – he was a bank manager and they were away in Basel on business – I was trying to make myself presentable: combing my hair, putting on the clean shirt and flannel bags I had extracted before leaving my rucksack in charge of the café. I hadn't fixed up anything for the night yet, they said, when I rejoined them: it was unorthodox and would be un-comfortable – but would I like to doss down on the sofa? 'No, no, no!' I cried: far too much of a nuisance for them, after all their kindness; but I didn't insist too long. 'Don't say you're staying here!' Annie said. 'You know how silly people are.' There was a feeling of secrecy and collusion in all this, like plans for a mid-night feast. They were thrilled by their recklessness. So was I.

Collusion looked like breaking down when we got to the party. 'Can I introduce,' Annie began. 'Darf ich Ihnen vorstellen – .' Her brow puckered in alarm; we hadn't exchanged surnames. Lise quickly chimed in with 'Mr Brown, a family friend'. She might have been a captain of hussars, turning the tide of battle by a brilliant swoop. Later a cake was ceremoniously cut, and a girl was crowned with a gold cardboard crown. Songs were sung in honour of Epiphany and the Magi, some in unison, some solo. Asked if there were any English ones (as I had hoped, in order to show Lise and Annie I wasn't a godless barbarian), I sang *We Three Kings of Orient Are*. A later song, celebrating the Neckar Valley and Swabia, was sung in complex harmony. I can't remember the words completely, but it has stuck in my mind ever since. I put it down here as I've never met anyone who knows it.

> Kennt Ihr das Land in deutschen Gauen,
> Das schönste dort am Neckarstrand?
> Die grünen Rebenhügel schauen
> Ins Tal von hoher Felsenwand.
> Es ist das Land, das mich gebar,
> Wo meiner Väter Wiege stand.
> Drum sing ich heut' und immerdar:
> Das schöne Schwaben ist mein Heimatland!

Then someone put *Couchés dans le foin* on the gramophone, and *Sentimental Journey*, and everyone danced.

When I woke up on the sofa – rather late; we had sat up talking and drinking Annie's father's wine before going to bed – I had no idea where I was; it was a frequent phenomenon on this journey. But when I found my hands muffled like a pierrot's in the scarlet silk sleeves of Annie's father's pyjamas, everything came back to me. He must have been a giant (a photograph on the piano of a handsome ski-booted trio in the snow – my host with his arms round his wife and daughter – bore this out). The curtains were still drawn and two dressing-gowned figures were tiptoeing about the shadows. When they realized I was awake at last, greetings were exchanged and the curtains drawn. It only seemed to make the room very few degrees lighter. 'Look!' Lise said, 'no day for walking!' It was true: merciless gusts of rain were thrashing the roofscape outside. Nice weather for young ducks. 'Armer Kerl! – Poor chap!' she said, 'you'll have to be our prisoner till tomorrow.' She put on another log and Annie came in with coffee. Half-way through breakfast, Sunday morning bells began challenging each other from belfry to belfry. We might have been in a submarine among sunk cathedrals. 'O Weh!' Lise cried, 'I ought to be in church!'; then, peering at the streaming panes: 'Too late now.' 'Zum Beichten, perhaps,' Annie said. (*Beichten* is confession.) Lise asked: 'What for?' 'Picking up strangers.' (Lise was Catholic, Annie Protestant; there was a certain amount of sectarian banter.) I urged their claim to every dispensation for sheltering the needy, clothing the naked – a flourish of crimson sleeve supported this – and feeding the hungry. Across the boom of all these bells a marvellous carillon broke out. It is one of the most famous things in Stuttgart. We listened until its complicated pattern faded into silence.

The evening presented a problem in advance. They were ineluctably bidden to a dinner party by a business acquaintance of Annie's father, and though they didn't like him they couldn't plausibly chuck it. But what was to become of me? At last, screwing up their courage, Annie rang his wife up: could they bring a young English friend of Lise's family – informally clad, because he was on a winter walking tour across Europe? (It sounded pretty thin.) There was a twitter of assent from the other end; the receiver was replaced in triumph. She, it seemed, was very nice; he was an industrialist – *steinreich*, rolling – 'You'll get plenty to eat and drink!' – Annie said he was a great admirer of Lise's. 'No, *no!*' Lise cried, 'of Annies!' 'He's awful! You'll see! You must defend us both.'

We were safe till ten o'clock next morning, when the maid's bus got back; she had gone to her Swabian village for the Dreikönigsfest. We drew the curtains to block out the deluge and put on the lights – it was best to treat the dismal scene outside as if it were night – and lolled in dishabille all the morning talking by the fire. I played the gramophone – *St Louis Blues, Stormy Weather, Night and Day* – while the girls ignored their dresses for the dinner party and the submarine morning sped by, until it was time for Annie and me to face the weather outdoors: she for luncheon – a weekly fixture with relations – me to collect my stuff and to buy some eggs for an omelette. Out of doors, even in a momentary lull, the rain was fierce and hostile and the wind was even worse. When Annie got back about five, I was doing a sketch of Lise; an attempt at Annie followed; then I taught them how to play Heads-Bodies-and-Legs. They took to this with a feverish intensity and we played until tolling bells reminded us how late it was. In my case, all that a flat-iron and a brush and comb could achieve had been done. But the girls emerged from their rooms like two marvellous swans. The door bell rang. It was the first sign of the outer world since my invasion, and a bit ominous. 'It's the car! He always sends one. Everything in style!'

Downstairs, a chauffeur in leggings held his cap aloft as he opened the door of a long Mercedes. When we had rustled in he enveloped us in bearskin from the waist down. 'You see?' the girls said, 'High life!'

We soared through the liquid city and up into the wooded hills and alighted at a large villa of concrete and plate glass. Our host was a blond, heavy man with bloodshot eyes and a scar across his forehead. He hailed my companions with gallantry; me, much more guardedly. His dinner-jacket made me feel still more of a ragamuffin. (I cared passionately about these things; but the fact of being called Michael Brown* – we had to stick to it now – induced a consoling sense of disembodiment.) Perhaps to account for my lowly outfit among these jewelled figures, he introduced me to the women as 'der englische Globetrotter', which I didn't like much. Men guests who were unacquainted toured the room in the German way, shaking hands and reciprocally announcing their names: I did the same 'Muller!' 'Brown!' 'Ströbel!' 'Brown!' 'Tschudi!' 'Brown!' 'Röder!' 'Brown!' 'Altmeier!' 'Brown!' 'von Schröder!' 'Brown!' ... An old man – a professor from Tübingen, I think, with heavy glasses and a beard – was talking to Lise. We wrung each other's hands, barking 'Braun!' and 'Brown!' simultaneously. *Snap!* I avoided the girls' glance.

Except for the panorama of the lights of Stuttgart through the plate glass, the house was hideous – prosperous, brand new, shiny,

---

* Sometime earlier I had temporarily abandoned the use of my ordinary Christian name, and, for reasons I've forgotten, adopted my second name, Michael, reverting to normal when this journey was over.

and dispiriting. Pale woods and plastics were juggled together
with stale and pretentious vorticism, and the chairs resembled
satin boxing-gloves and nickel plumbing. Carved dwarfs with red
noses stoppered all the bottles on the oval bar and glass ballerinas
pirouetted on ashtrays of agate that rose from the beige carpets on
chromium stalks. There were paintings – or tinted photographs –
of the Alps at sunset and of naked babies astride Great Danes.
Everything looked better, however, after I'd swallowed two White
Ladies taken from a tray that was carried about by a white-gloved
butler. I helped myself to cigarettes from a seventeenth-century
vellum-bound Dante, with the pages glued together and scooped
hollow, the only book in sight. Down the dinner table, beside
napkins that were half mitres and half Rajput turbans, glittered
a promising arsenal of glasses, and by the time we had worked
our way through them, the scene was delightfully blurred. From
time to time during dinner, I intercepted a puzzled bloodhound
scrutiny from the other end of the table. My host obviously
found me a question mark; possibly a bit of a rotter, and up to
no good; I didn't like him either. I bet he's a terrific Nazi, I
thought. I asked the girls later, and they both exclaimed 'Und
wie!' in vehement unison: 'And how!' I think he found something
fishy, too, about my being on *Du* terms with his unwilling favourites, while he, most properly, was still restricted to *Sie*. (We had
drunk threefold Brüderschaft and embraced in the Cologne style
the night before.) When we were back in the *salon*, the men
armed with cigars like truncheons and brandy rotating in glasses
like transparent footballs, the party began to lose coherence. The
host flogged it along with a jarring laugh even louder than the
non-stop gramophone, between-whiles manoeuvring first Lise and
then Annie into a window-bay whence each extricated herself in
turn like a good-humoured Syrinx. I watched them as I listened to
my namesake Dr Braun, a learned and delightful fogey who was
telling me all about the Suevi and the Alemanni and the Ho-
henstaufens and Eberhardt the Bearded. When the evening broke
up, and Lise and Annie were back in the car, our host stood leaning against the top of the car door, idiotically telling them they
looked like two Graces. I ducked under his arm and slipped in
between them. 'Three now!' Lise said. He looked at me with dis-

favour. 'Ah! And where shall I tell him to drop *you*, junger Mann?'

'At the Graf Zeppelin, please.' I sensed a tremor of admiration on either side: even Lise couldn't have done better.

'Ach so?' His opinion of me went up. 'And how do you like our best hotel?'

'Clean, comfortable and quiet.'

'Tell the manager if you have any complaints. He's a good friend of mine.'

'I will! And thanks very much.'

We had to take care about conversation because of the chauffeur. A few minutes later, he was opening the car with a flourish of his cockaded cap before the door of the hotel and after fake farewells, I strolled about the hall of the Graf Zeppelin for a last puff at the ogre cigar. When the coast was clear I hared through the streets and into the lift and up to the flat. They were waiting with the door open and we burst into a dance.

At half-past nine next morning, we were waving good-bye across a tide of Monday morning traffic. I kept looking upwards and back, flourishing my glittering wand and bumping into busy Stuttgarters until the diminishing torsos frantically signalling from the seventh-storey window were out of sight. I felt as Ulysses must have felt, gazing astern while some island of happy sojourn dropped below the horizon.

I followed the banks of the Neckar, crossed it, and finally left it for good. Suddenly, when it was much too late, I remembered the Kitsch-Museum in Stuttgart; a museum, that is, of German and international bad taste, which the girls had said I mustn't miss. (The décor last night – for this was how the subject had cropped up – could have been incorporated as it stood.) I slept at Göppingen and tried with the help of the dictionary to write three letters in German; to Heidelberg, Bruchsal and Stuttgart. Further on I got a funny joint answer from Lise and Annie; there was a rumpus when Annie's parents got back; not about my actually staying in the flat, which remained a secret to the end. But the bottles we had recklessly drained were the last of a fabulously rare and wonderful vintage that Annie's father had been particularly looking forward to. Heaven only knew what treasured Spätlese from the banks of the Upper Mosel: nectar beyond compare. They had prudently blamed the choice on me. Outrage had finally simmered down to the words: 'Well, your thirsty friend must know a lot about wine.' (Totally untrue.) 'I hope he enjoyed it.' (Yes.) It was years before the real enormity of our inroads dawned on me.

Now the track was running south-south-east across Swabia. Scattered conifers appeared, and woods sometimes overshadowed the road for many furlongs. They were random outposts, separated by leagues of pasture and ploughland, of the great mass, lying dark towards the south-west, of the Black Forest. Beyond it the land rippled away to the Alps.

On straight stretches of road where the scenery changed slowly, singing often came to the rescue; and when songs ran short, poetry. At home, and at my various schools, and among the people who took me in after scholastic croppers, there had always been a lot of reading aloud. (My mother was marvellously gifted in this exacting skill, and imaginative and far-ranging in choice; there had been much singing to the piano as well.) At school some learning by heart was compulsory, though not irksome. But this intake was out-distanced many times, as it always is among people who need poetry, by a private anthology, both of those automatically absorbed and of poems consciously chosen and memorized as though one were stocking up for a desert island or for a stretch of solitary. (I was at the age when one's memory for poetry or for languages – indeed for anything – takes impressions like wax and, up to a point, lasts like marble.)

The range is fairly predictable and all too revealing of the scope, the enthusiasms and the limitations, examined at the eighteenth milestone, of a particular kind of growing up. There was a great deal of Shakespeare, numerous speeches, most of the choruses of *Henry V*, long stretches of *A Midsummer Night's Dream* (drunk in subconsciously and only half understood, by acting Starveling, the shortest part in the play, at the age of six); a number of the Sonnets, many detached fragments; and, generally, a fairly wide familiarity. Several Marlowe speeches followed and stretches of Spenser's *Pro-* and *Epithalamion;* most of Keats's Odes; the usual pieces of Tennyson, Browning and Coleridge; very little Shelley, no Byron. (Amazingly to me today, I scarcely considered him a poet at all.) Nothing from the eighteenth century except Gray's *Elegy* and some of *The Rape of the Lock;* some Blake; *The Burial of Sir John Moore;* bits of *The Scholar Gypsy;* some Scott, fragments of Swinburne, any amount of Rossetti, for whom I had had a long passion, now quite vanished; some Francis Thompson and some Dowson; one sonnet of Wordsworth; bits of Hopkins; and, like all English people with any Irish links, Rolleston's translation of *The Dead of Clonmacnois;* a great deal of Kipling; and some of the verse from *Hassan.* We now move on to Recent Acquisitions: passages from Donne and Herrick and Quarles, one poem of Raleigh, one of Sir Thomas Wyatt, one of Herbert, two of Marvell; a few Border ballads; an abundance of A. E. Housman; some improper stretches of Chaucer (mastered chiefly for popularity purposes at school); a lot of Carroll and Lear. No Chesterton or Belloc, beyond bits of the *Cautionary Tales.* In fact, apart from those mentioned, very little from the present century. No Yeats later than the Ronsard paraphrase and *Innisfree* and *Down by the Salley Gardens;* but this belonged more to singing than reciting; of Pound or Eliot, not a word, either learnt or read; and of younger modern poets now venerable, nothing. If someone had asked me point blank who my favourite contemporary poets were, I would have answered Sacheverell, Edith and Osbert Sitwell, in that order: (*Dr Donne and Gargantua* and *The Hundred and One Harlequins* had appeared in white paper pamphlets while I was at school; I felt I had broken into dazzling new territory). Prose writers would have been Aldous Huxley, Norman Douglas and Evelyn Waugh. This is the end of the short section; but if the road stretched interminably, longer pieces would come to the surface: all *Horatius* and a lot of *Lake Regillus,* hardy survivors from an early craze; *Grantchester;* and the *Rubaiyat of Omar Khayyam* – intact then, now a heap of fragments hard to re-assemble. The standard drops steeply after this: as I pounded along, limericks pinpointed the planet from Siberia to Cape Horn with improper and imaginative acts, and when they came to an end, similar themes would blossom forth in a score of different metres. It is a field where England can take on all challengers.

My bridgehead in French poetry didn't penetrate very far: a few nursery rhymes, one poem of Theodore de Banville, two of Baudelaire, part of one of Verlaine, Yeats's Ronsard sonnet in the original, and another of du Bellay; lastly, more than all the rest put together, large quantities of Villon (this was a very recent discovery, and a passion. I had translated a number of the ballades and rondeaux from the *Grand Testament* into English verse and they had turned out more respectably than any of my other attempts of the same kind). Most of the Latin contribution is as predictable as the rest: passages of Virgil, chiefly, but not entirely, assimilated through writing lines at school: they went faster if one had the text by heart. As nobody seemed to mind who had written them as long as they were hexameters, I used Lucan's *Pharsalia* for a while; they seemed to have just the glibness needed for the task; but I soon reverted to Virgil, rightly convinced that they would last better: my main haunts were the second and sixth books of the *Aeneid*, with sallies into the *Georgics* and the *Eclogues*. The other chief Romans were Catullus and Horace: Catullus – a dozen short poems and stretches of the *Attis* – because the young are prone (at least I was) to identify themselves with him when feeling angry, lonely, misunderstood, besotted, ill-starred or crossed in love. I probably adored Horace for the opposite reason; and taught myself a number of the Odes and translated a few of them into awkward English sapphics and alcaics. Apart from their other charms, they were infallible mood-changers. (One of them – I. ix. *Ad Thaliarchum* – came to my rescue in strange circumstances a few years later. The hazards of war landed me among the crags of occupied Crete with a band of Cretan guerrillas and a captive German general whom we had waylaid and carried off into the mountains three days before. The German garrison of the island were in hot, but luckily temporarily misdirected, chase. It was a time of anxiety and danger; and for our captive, of hardship and distress. During a lull in the pursuit, we woke up among the rocks just as a brilliant dawn was breaking over the crest of Mount Ida. We had been toiling over it, through snow and then rain, for the last two days. Looking across the valley at this flashing mountain-crest, the general murmured to himself:

> Vides ut alta stet nive candidum
> Soracte ...

It was one of the ones I knew! I continued from where he had broken off:

> nec jam sustineant onus
> Silvae laborantes, geluque
> Flumina constiterint acuto,

and so on, through the remaining five stanzas to the end. The general's blue eyes had swivelled away from the mountain-top to mine – and when I'd finished, after a long silence, he said: 'Ach so, Herr Major!' It was very strange. As though, for a long moment, the war had ceased to exist. We had both drunk at the same fountains long before; and things were different between us for the rest of our time together.)

Hotfoot on Horace came Hadrian's lines to his soul – *The Oxford Book of Latin Verse* was about the only prize I carried away from school – and Petronius' ten counter-balancing verses, hinging on the marvellous line: 'sed sic, sic, sine fine feriati'; then some passages of the *Pervigilium Veneris*. After this, with a change of key, come one or two early Latin hymns and canticles; then the *Dies Irae* and the *Stabat Mater*. (Of Latin poets of the two centuries between the classical and the Christian, I scarcely even knew the names; it was a region to be invaded and explored alone, and much later and with great delight.) Last came a smattering of profane Medieval Latin lyrics, many of them from the monastery of Benediktbeuern.* In the brief Greek coda to all this, the sound of barrel-scraping grows louder. It begins with the opening movement of the *Odyssey*, as it does for everyone who has dabbled in the language, followed by bits from the escape of Odysseus from the cave of Polyphemus; unexpectedly, not *Heraclitus*; nothing from the tragic dramatists (too difficult); snatches

---

* As the crow flies, had I but known, it lay only about forty miles S.E. of my point on the Swabian road.

of Aristophanes; a few epitaphs of Simonides, two moon-poems of Sappho; and then silence.

A give-away collection. It covers the thirteen years between five and eighteen, for in the months preceding my departure the swing of late nights and recovery had slowed the intake down to a stand-still. Too much of it comes from the narrow confines of the Oxford Books. It is a mixture of a rather dog-eared romanticism with heroics and rough stuff, with traces of religious mania, temporarily in abeyance, Pre-Raphaelite languor and Wardour Street medievalism; slightly corrected – or, at any rate, altered – by a streak of coarseness and a bias towards low life. A fair picture, in fact, of my intellectual state-of-play: backward-looking, haphazard, unscholarly and, especially in Greek, marked with the blemish of untimely breaking-off. (I've tried to catch up since with mixed results.) But there are one or two beams of hope, and I feel bound to urge in self-defence, that Shakespeare, both in quantity and addiction, overshadowed all the rest of this rolling-stock. A lot has dropped away through disuse; some remains; additions have been appended, but the later quantity is smaller, for the sad reason that the knack of learning by heart grows less. The wax hardens and the stylus scrapes in vain.

Back to the Swabian highroad.

Song is universal in Germany; it causes no dismay; *Shuffle off to Buffalo; Bye, Bye, Blackbird; or Shenandoah; or The Raggle Taggle Gypsies* sung as I moved along, evoked nothing but tolerant smiles. But verse was different. Murmuring on the highway caused raised eyebrows and a look of anxious pity. Passages, uttered with gestures and sometimes quite loud, provoked, if one was caught in the act, stares of alarm. Regulus brushing the delaying populace aside as he headed for the Carthaginian executioner, as though to Lacedaemonian Tarentum or the Venafrian fields, called for a fairly mild flourish; but urging the assault-party at Harfleur to close the wall up with English dead would automatically bring on a heightened pitch of voice and action and double one's embarrassment if caught. When this happened I would try to taper off in a cough or weave the words into a tuneless hum and reduce all gestures to a feint at hair-tidying. But some passages demand an empty road as far as the eye can see before letting fly. The terrible boxing-match, for instance, at the funeral games of Anchises when Entellus sends Dares reeling and spitting blood and teeth across the Sicilian shore – 'ore ejectantem mixtosque in sanguine dentes'! – and then, with his thonged fist, scatters a steer's brains with one blow between the horns – this needs care. As for the sword-thrust at the bridge-head that brings the great lord of Luna crashing among the augurs like an oak-tree on Mount Alvernus – here the shouts, the walking-stick slashes, the staggering gait and the arms upflung should never be indulged if there is anyone within miles, if then. To a strange eye, one is drunk or a lunatic.

So it was today. I was at this very moment of crescendo and climax, when an old woman tottered out of a wood where she had been gathering sticks. Dropping and scattering them, she took to her heels. I would have liked the earth to have swallowed me, or to have been plucked into the clouds.

Herrick would have been safer, Valéry, if I had known him, perfect: 'Calme . . .'

The rain had churned the snow into slush, then blasts from the mountains had frozen it into a pock-marked upheaval of rutted ice. Now, after a short warning drift, the wind was sending flakes along by the million. They blotted out the landscape, turning one side of a traveller's body into a snowdrift, thatching his head with a crust of white and tangling his eyelashes with sticky scales. The track ran along a shelterless hog's back and the wind seemed either to lay a hindering hand on my chest, or, suddenly changing its quarter, to kick me spinning and stumbling along the road. No village had been in sight, even before this onslaught. Scarcely a car passed. I despised lifts and I had a clear policy about them: to avoid them rigorously, that is, until walking became literally in-tolerable; and then, to travel no further than a day's march would cover. (I stuck to this.) But now not a vehicle came; nothing but snowflakes and wind; until at last a dark blur materialized and a clanking something drew alongside and clattered to a halt. It turned out to be a heavy diesel truck with chains on its wheels and a load of girders. The driver opened the door and reached down a helping hand, with the words 'Spring hinein!' When I was

beside him in the steamy cabin he said 'Du bist ein Schneemann!'
– a snowman. So I was. We clanked on. Pointing to the flakes that
clogged the windscreen as fast as the wipers wiped, he said
'Schlimm, niet?' Evil, what? He dug out a bottle of schnapps and
I took a long swig. Traveller's joy! 'Wohin gehst Du?' I told him.
(I think it was somewhere about this point on the journey that I
began to notice the change in this question: 'Where are you
going?' In the north, in Low Germany, everyone had said 'Wohin
laufen Sie' and 'Warum laufen Sie zu Fuss?' – Why are you walking on foot? Recently the verb had been *'gehen'*. For *'laufen'*, in
the south, means to run – probably from the same root as 'lope' in
English. The accent, too, had been altering fast; in Swabia, the
most noticeable change was the substitution of -*le* at the end of a
noun, as a diminutive, instead of -*chen*; *Häusle* and *Hundle*, instead of *Häuschen* and *Hündchen*, for a little house and a small
dog. I felt I was getting ahead now, both linguistically and
geographically, plunging deeper and deeper into the heart of High
Germany ... The driver's *Du* was a sign of inter-working-class
mateyness that I had come across several times. It meant friendly
acceptance and fellow-feeling.)

When he set me down on the icy cobbles of Ulm, I knew I had
reached an important landmark on my journey. For there, in the
lee of the battlements, dark under the tumbling flakes and already
discoloured with silt, flowed the Danube.

It was a momentous encounter. A great bridge spanned it, and
the ice was advancing from either bank to meet and eventually
join amidstream. Inland from the river-wall, the roofs that retreated in confusion were too steep for the snow; the flakes would
collect, bank up, then slide into the lanes with a swish. In the
heart of this warren, Ulm Minster rose, literally saddled, on an
octagon bestriding the west end of the huge nave, with the highest
steeple in the world, and the transparent spire disappeared into
a moulting eiderdown of cloud.

A market day was ending. Snow was being banged from tar-
paulins and basket was slotted into basket. Cataracts of vegetables
rumbled on the bottoms of wagons and the carthorses, many of
them with those beautiful flaxen manes and tails, were being

backed with bad language between the shafts. Scarlet-cheeked women from a score of villages were coifed in head-dresses of starch and black ribbon that must have been terrible snow-traps. They gathered round the braziers and stamped in extraordinary bucket-boots whose like I never saw before or since: elephantine cylinders as wide as the footgear of seventeenth-century postilions, all swaddled inside with felt and stuffed with straw. Dark dialect shouts criss-crossed through the snorts and the neighs. There was a flurry of poultry and the squeal of pigs and cattle were goaded from their half-dismantled pens as the hurdles were stacked. Villagers with flat wide hats and red waistcoats and cart-whips hobnobbed in the colonnades and up and down the shallow steps. There was a raucous and jocular hum of confabulation and smoke among the heavy pillars; and the vaults that these pillars upheld were the floors of medieval halls as big and as massive as tithe barns.

A late medieval atmosphere filled the famous town. The vigorous Teutonic interpretation of the Renaissance burst out in the corbels and the mullions of jutting windows and proliferated round thresholds. At the end of each high civic building a zigzag isosceles rose and dormers and flat gables lifted their gills along enormous roofs that looked as if they were tiled with the scales of pangolins. Shields carved in high relief projected from the walls. Many were charged with the double-headed eagle. This bird was emblematic of the town's status as an Imperial City: it meant that Ulm – unlike the neighbouring towns and provinces, which had been the fiefs of lesser sovereigns – was subject only to the Emperor. It was a Reichstadt.

A flight of steps led to a lower part of the town. Here the storeys beetled and almost touched and in one of the wider lanes was a warren of carpenters and saddlers and smithies and cavernous workshops. Down the middle, visible through a few chopped holes, a river rushed ice-carapaced and snow-quilted under a succession of narrow bridges, to split round an island where a weeping willow expanded to the icicled eaves and then, re-uniting by a watermill so deeply clogged in ice that it looked as if it would never grind again, sped on to hurl itself into the Danube.

This part of the town contained nothing later than the Middle

Ages, or so it appeared. A kind crone outside a harness-maker's saw me peering down a hole in the ice. 'It's full of Forellen!' she said. Trout? 'Ja, Forellen! Voll, voll davon.' How did they manage under that thick shell of ice? Hovering suspended in the dark? Or hurtling along on their Schubertian courses, hidden and headlong? Were they in season? If so, I determined to go a bust and get hold of one for dinner, and a bottle of Franconian wine. Meanwhile, night was falling fast. High up in the snowfall a bell began booming slowly. *Funera plango!* a deep and solemn note. *Fulgura frango!* It might have been tolling for an Emperor's passing, for war, siege, revolt, plague, excommunication, a ban of interdict, or Doomsday: '*Excito lentis! Dissipo ventos! Paco cruentos!*'

As soon as the Minster was open I toiled up the steeple-steps and halted, with heart pounding, above the loft where these bells were hung. Seen through the cusps of a cinquefoil and the flurry of jackdaws and a rook or two that my ascent had dislodged, the foreshortened roofs of the town shrank to a grovelling maze. Ulm is the highest navigable point of the Danube, and lines of barges lay at anchor. I wondered if the ice had crept forward during the night, and where the barges would be hauled to. Water is the one thing that expands when it freezes instead of contracting, and a sudden drop in temperature smashes unwary boats like eggshells. South of the river, the country retreated in a white expanse which buckled into the Swabian Jura. The eastern rim of the Black Forest blurred them; then they rose and merged into the foothills of the Alps and somewhere among them, invisible in a trough with the Rhine flowing into it from the south and out again northwards, Lake Constance lay. Clearly discernible, and rising in peak after peak, the whole upheaval of Switzerland gleamed in the pale sunlight.

It was an amazing vision. Few stretches of Central Europe have been the theatre for so much history. Beyond which watershed lay the pass where Hannibal's elephants had slithered downhill? Only a few miles away, the frontier of the Roman Empire had begun. Deep in those mythical forests that the river reflected for many days' march, the German tribes, Rome's Nemesis, had waited for their hour to strike. The Roman *limes* followed the river's south-

ern bank all the way to the Black Sea. The same valley, function-
ing in reverse, funnelled half the barbarians of Asia into Central
Europe and just below my eyrie, heading upstream, the Huns
entered and left again before swimming their ponies across the
Rhine – or trotting them over the ice – until, foiled by a miracle,
they drew rein a little short of Paris. Charlemagne stalked across
this corner of his empire to destroy the Avars in Pannonia and a
few leagues south-west, the ruins of Hohenstaufen, home of the
family that plunged Emperors and Popes into centuries of vend-
etta, crumbled still. Again and again, armies of mercenaries, lug-
ging siege-engines and bristling with scaling ladders, crawled all
over this map. The Thirty Years War, the worst of them all, was
becoming an obsession with me: a lurid, ruinous, doomed conflict
of beliefs and dynasties, helpless and hopeless, with principles
shifting the whole time and a constant shuffle and re-deal of the
actors. For, apart from the events – the defenestrations and pitched
battles and historic sieges, the slaughter and famine and plague –
astrological portents and the rumour of cannibalism and witch-
craft flitted about the shadows. The polyglot captains of the
ruffian multi-lingual hosts hold our gaze willy-nilly with their
grave eyes and their Velasquez moustaches and populate half the
picture galleries in Europe. Caracoling in full feather against a
background of tents and colliding squadrons, how serenely they
point their batons; or, magnanimously bare-headed and on foot in
a grove of lances, accept surrendered keys, or a sword! Curls flow
and lace or starched collars break over the black armour and the
gold inlay; they glance from their frames with an aloof and high-
souled melancholy which is both haunting and enigmatic: Tilly,
Wallenstein, Mansfeld, Bethlen, Brunswick, Spinola, Maximilian,
Gustavus Adolphus, Bernard of Saxe-Weimar, Piccolomini,
Arnim, Königsmarck, Wrangel, Pappenheim, the Cardinal-Infant
of the Spanish Netherlands, Le Grand Condé. The destroying
banners move about the landscape like flags on a campaign map:
the Emperor's haloed double eagles, the blue-and-white Wittels-
bach lozenges for the Palatinate and Bavaria, the rampant Bohemian lion, the black and gold bars of Saxony, the three Vasa
crowns of Sweden, the black and white check of Brandenburg, the
lions and castles of Castille and Aragon, the blue and gold French

lilies. Ever since then, the jigsaw distribution of Catholics and
Protestants has remained as it was after the Peace of Westphalia.
Each dovetailing enclave depended on the faith of its sovereign,
and occasionally, by a quirk of succession, a prince of the alternative faith would reign as peacefully as the Moslem Nizam over
his Hindu subjects in Hyderabad. If the landscape were really a
map, it would be dotted with those little crossed swords that in-
dicate battles. The village of Blenheim* was only a day's march
along the same shore, and Napoleon defeated the Austrian army
on the bank just beyond the barbican. The cannon sank into the
flooded fields while the limbers and gun-teams and gunners were
carried away by the current. Looking down, I could see a scarlet
banner with the swastika on its white disc fluttering in one of
the lanes, hinting that there was still trouble ahead. Seeing it,
someone skilled in prophecy and the meaning of symbols could
have foretold that three quarters of the old city below would go
up in explosion and flame a few years later; to rise again in a
geometry of skyscraping concrete blocks.

The first sight of the Danube! It was a tremendous vision. In
Europe, only the Volga is longer. If one of the crows that were
fidgeting among the crockets below had flown to my next meeting
place with the river, it would have alighted two hundred miles
east of this steeple. The blast was whistling louder through the
perforated stone of the spire and clouds were advancing fast.

The empty nave, lit only by the marvellous deep-hued gloom of
the glass, was dark by contrast. An organist, rapt with improvis-
ation, was fluting and rumbling in his high lamp-lit nest under a
display of giant pan-pipes. The clustered piers, which looked slender for so huge a place, divided the nave into five aisles and soared
to a network of groins and ribs and liernes that a slight architectural shrug would have flicked into fan-tracery. But it was the
choir-stalls that halted one. A bold oaken outburst of three-dimensional humanism had wrought the finials of the choir-stalls into
the life-size torsos, in dark wood, of the sybils: ladies that is,
dressed in coifs and wimples and slashed sleeves and hatted in

---

* The battle is known as Höchstädt – after the next village – in
Germany and France.

pikehorn head-dresses like the Duchess's in *Alice in Wonderland*. They craned yearning across the chancel towards Plato and Aristotle and an answering academy of pagan philosophers accoutred like burgomasters and led by a burgravial Ptolemy wielding a wooden astrolabe. The vaulted hexagon under the spire was used as a commemorative chapel. The laurel-wreathed and silken colours of Württemberg and Baden regiments from 1914 to 1918 were hanging there in rows: banners bearing black crosses on a white background. The battle-honours inscribed in gold on the fluttering ribands – the Somme, Vimy, Verdun and Passchendaele – were all familiar.

The coloured windows died like fires going out. The clouds had closed over again and the sky presaged snow.

I was haunting cathedrals these days. Only a few hours later I was inside yet another, munching bread and cheese and an onion in one of the transepts. The day's march had been a repetition of yesterday's: I had crossed the Danube bridge; base clouds pursued me with their rotten smoke; the clouds broke and the east wind, once again blurring all in a maelstrom of flakes, had practically brought me to a standstill. Then a benefactor had come to the rescue and deposited me in Augsburg in the late morning. I hadn't expected to reach it till long after dark, if then.

On these Augsburg choir stalls, highly polished free-standing scenes of Biblical bloodshed ran riot. For realism and immediacy they left the carvings of Ulm far behind. On the first, Jael, with hanging sleeves and hatted like a margravine, gripped a coal-hammer and steadied an iron spike among the sleeping Sisera's curls. Judith, likewise dressed in high Plantagenet fashion, held the severed head of Holophernes in one hand while the other buried a sword in the small of his back. Cain's axe was splitting Abel's temple wide open, and David, stooping over the steelclad figure of Goliath, had all but sawn his head off. These wooden duets were only slightly grotesque. Flemings and Burgundians compete with the Germans in wood-carving but they can't catch up with this blunt realism. On tombs and slabs, the figures of high-born laymen – broad- and hard-faced men in full plate armour with their hair clipped in fringes – were outnumbered by the prince-bishops and the mitred landgraves that once ruled in this war-like see. Some were mailclad, some vested in chasubles; and the stone hands joining in prayer were gauntleted or episcopally gloved with gems in a lozenge to mark the points of the stigmata. Tonsured on cushions or bobbed on helms, identical frowns of dominion stamped those rectangular heads, and lances and crosiers were interchangeable at their sides. Under one prelate in heavy ponti-ficals lay an effigy of his skeleton when the worms had finished with him. Further on, from a hanging jaw under the hollow cheek and eye sockets of an aquiline zealot, the death-rattle was nearly audible.

Stark mementoes. But, in compensation, four ravishing scenes from the life of the Virgin hung behind side-altars. 'Hans Hol-bein', the brass plate said; but they were more like Memling in costume and feeling; much earlier in date than the royalties and ambassadors and magnates we all know. They turned out to be by the father and namesake of the best-known Holbein, patriarch of a whole dynasty of Augsburg painters.

I must resist the temptation to enlarge on the fascinating city outside: its abundance of magnificent buildings, the frescoed façade of the Fugger house, the wells canopied with wrought iron. I was pursuing a more general quarry as I munched: no less than the whole feeling and character of pre-baroque German towns. We have been through a number of them; there are more to come. A theory had been forming and clumsy tuning notes have sounded on earlier pages, so I may as well get it off my chest.

The characteristics I have in mind, though of course I didn't know the details, stretch further afield than South Germany: they advance down the Danube, through Austria and into Bohemia, across the mountains of the Tyrol to the edge of Lombardy and through the Swiss Alps and across the Upper Rhine into Alsace; and the real secret about the architecture of these towns is that it is medieval in structure and Renaissance – or the Teutonic in-terpretation of the Renaissance – only in detail. A great wave assembled in Lombardy and Venetia. It mounted, gathered speed, and at last rushed northwards through the passes and down into the plain to break over the German medieval bulk in vast dis-

integrating fans of spray. Curves like the slits in a violin began to
complicate and soften the zigzags of the gables, and, from the
burgeoning crow-steps, florid finials and elaborated obelisks were
soon shooting up. Structurally, the new arcades were medieval
cloisters still, but the detail that proliferated all over them turned
them into elaborately sheltered loggias for a prosperous laity. The
barn-like medieval roofs remained, but, from the arcade to the
eaves, projecting oriels soared in tiers of mullions and armorial
glass as ornately as galleons' poops. They even jutted in spiralling
polygons and cylinders at street corners, abetted in their extravagance by tangles of carved stone and wood. The same ebullient
trend broke loose everywhere . . .

I had been fumbling for a symbol that might hit off this idiosyncrasy and suddenly I found it! In the girls' flat in Stuttgart, turning over a picture book of German history, I stopped at a colour
plate depicting three arresting figures. 'Landsknechts in the time
of the Emperor Maximilian I', was the caption. They were three
blond giants. Challenging moustachios luxuriated over the jut of
their bushy beards. Their floppy hats were worn at killing angles,
and, under the curl of ostrich feathers, the segmented brims spread
as incongruously as the petals of a periwinkle. Two of these men
grasped pikes with elaborate blades, the third carried a musket;
their hands on the hilts of their broadswords tilted up the scabbards behind them. Slashed doublets expanded their shoulders and
quilted sleeves puffed out their arms like Zeppelins; but on top of
all this, their torsos were wrapped slantwise in wide ribbons,
loosely attached to their trunks by a row of bows at an opposite
slant, and bright bands fluttered about their already-voluminous
arms in similar contradictory spirals: scarlet, vermilion, orange,
canary, Prussian blue, grass green, violet and ochre. From buttocks
and cod piece to knee, their legs were subjected to the same contradictory ribbon-treatment, and, with cunning asymmetry, the
bright bands were arranged differently askew on each leg. They
were fluttering criss-cross cages of colour, like maypoles about to
unfurl. The tights below, which ended in wide slash-toed duck-bill
shoes, were striped and parti-coloured. One soldier, with a breastplate over his finery, eschewed all ribbons below the fork. Instead,
his legs were adorned with tiers of fringes as far as mid-calf –

square-ended tapes that sprang out like the umbelliferous rings of
foliage on those marsh plants called mare's tails.

They were swashbuckling, exuberant and preposterous outfits,
yet there was nothing foppish about the wearers: under the flutter
of this blinding haberdashery, they were grim Teutonic soldiers,
and medieval still. All this slashing, which caught on everywhere,
was a Teutonic thing. It began in the late fifteenth century when
miles of plundered silk were sliced up to patch the campaigning
tatters of some lucky mercenaries: they went berserk among the
bales; then, carried away, they started pulling their underlinen
through the gaps and puffing it out. Once launched, the fashion
spread to the courts of the Valois and Tudors and Stuarts and
broke at last into its fullest flower at the field of the Cloth of
Gold.* But the Landsknechts were objects of dread. They swore
and hacked their way through all the religious and dynastic wars
of the Empire; and, while they plied their pikes, buildings were
beginning to go up. When Charles V succeeded Maximilian in
1519, the meridian splendour of the Landsknechts coincided with
a generation of glory that the Holy Roman Empire had not seen
since Charlemagne and would never see again. Through inheritance, conquest, marriage and discovery, Charles's Empire
reached north to the Baltic settlements of the Teutonic knights, to
the old Hanseatic world and the Netherlands; it stretched south to
include the Duchy of Milan and swallowed up the outpost kingdoms of Naples and Sicily; it marched with Turkey on the Middle
Danube and expanded to western Burgundy; then, skipping
France – whose King, however, was the Emperor's prisoner in
Madrid – it leapt the Atlantic from the Pyrenees to the Pacific
shores of Peru.

Once I had got hold of the Landsknecht formula – medieval
solidity adorned with a jungle of inorganic Renaissance detail –
there was no holding me! It came into play wherever I looked: not
only in gables, bell-hampers, well-heads, oriels and arcades – in the

---

* The court-cards in a European pack are a mild version of all this,
and the uniform of the Swiss Pontifical Guard at the Vatican is Michel-
angelo's attempt at standardizing it. There is still a French card game
called Lansquenet.

woodland giants that wrestled in coloured tempera over fifty feet of façade – but in everything. In heraldry, which haunts all German cities, it was omnipresent. The coats of arms that encrust those South German walls were once as simple as upside-down flat-irons with reversed buckets on top: at the touch of the new formula, each shield blossomed into the lower half of a horizontally bisected 'cello, floridly notched for a tilting lance, under a twenty-fold display of latticed and strawberry-leaf-crowned casques, each helmet top-heavy with horns or wings or ostrich or peacocks' feathers and all of them suddenly embowered in mantelling as reckless, convoluted and slashed as spatulate leaves in a whirlwind. The wings of eagles expanded in sprays of separate sable plumes, tails bifurcated in multiple tassels, tongues leapt from beaks and fangs like flames; armour broke out in ribs and fluting and flares and inlaid arabesques. All was lambent. Was it the Landsknecht principle, spreading to typography, that contorted capital letters, twirled the serifs and let loose, round the text of post-Gutenberg blackletter, those reckless, refluent, neverending black flourishes, like ribands kept in motion on the tips of sticks by a conjurer? Typography, bookplates, title pages, headlines, woodcuts, block-engraving ... Dürer, encastled in medieval Nuremberg on his return from Renaissance Venice, spurred it on. The hard outline in German art, the love of complexity ... And Holbein? (Not Cranach. I'd been looking at him that morning in the museum.) Taking their cue – subconsciously, perhaps – from those soldiers, the masons and smiths and joiners must have conspired together; everything that could fork, ramify, coil, flutter, fold back or thread through itself, suddenly sprang to action. Clocks, keys, hinges, door-bands, hilts and trigger-guards ... centrifugal lambency and recoil! The principle is active still.

We have all invented a half-bogus golden age to embower us when we eat and drink away from home. Judging by pubs, this is represented in England by the reign of Elizabeth, with the Regency following close. France's dream dining-land is Rabelais' *Thélème* and the chicken-in-the-pot world of Henry IV; and South Germany's lost paradise covers roughly the same epoch: Landsknecht-time, in fact. Their armies marched and countermarched; but it was not only a time of military and territorial triumph. The stimulating ding-dong of the Reform was at work. The Counter-Reformation was limbering up for a return bout. Luther was fulminating, Erasmus, Reuchlin, Melanchthon and Paracelsus were stooped over their desks; Germany's greatest painters were busy in their studios; books and ideas were on the move. Then, when the Thirty Years War broke out and the deadening years lengthened into decades, all building stopped and artists and writers fell back into eclipse. The Empire was soon sinking into dotage among the cinders. The Landsknechts' high noon was over. The penultimate sparkle of Maria Theresa was only a reprieve, and the perverse and cerebral wonders of Baroque, that flowered among the princes like a springtime in autumn, faded all too soon. (Death came with the Revolution; and the only hope of revival for the Teutonic world lay far away in the north, with the star rising in the Mark of Brandenburg. But the southern Germans and the Austrians never cared for Prussia.) No wonder, then, that the reigns of Maximilian and Charles V should remain the care-free dreamland of the German-speaking world. (Not Valhalla or Asgard at all; these always send them off the rails.) Winecellars, taverns, beer-halls, coffee houses – hundreds of authentic ones were still intact; and the new ones automatically echoed them. So it is not the vomiting crossbowman of an earlier age that haunts such premises, still less the introspective toper after the Thirty Years War. That periwigged figure was morosely waiting for the coloured pastorals to cohere among the gesso tendrils overhead and for the string quartets to begin tuning.

No. It's the bearded guzzler in his harlequin haberdashery, recruited in Swabia, twirling his whiskers and shouting for another bottle. He is the walking epitome and his influence is everywhere: in the tapering coloured globes that form the stems of the wine glasses, in the labels on the green and amber bottles, in the hanging metal signs that creak outside on wrought-iron stanchions; in the unfolding of the carved brackets and the iron involution of banisters, in the folds of the panelling and the calligraphic flourishes of the mural mottoes; in the heavy Bacchic riot of the hewn wooden ivy that inter-twines with the vine shoots and the leaves and the clusters. He is present in the perforation on bench-backs, in the stretchers of the tables, and in the wood and plaster coffering overhead; the tiered tops, the hinges and handles of the stone tankards, the coiling lead that honeycombs the circular window-panes together, the tiles of the stoves looted from the Spanish Netherlands, the very lids of the painted china pipe-bowls – all are his. It is the corroborative detail of dreamland.

Dreamland for me, too, for a while. It was snug among these impedimenta, with sawdust underfoot and hidden in the shag and cheroot smoke that I poured such ideas into my diary. *The Landsknecht touchstone!* (Stale news, I suppose. These discoveries nearly always are.) But it was in the transept of the cathedral that the notion suddenly took shape, detonating over my head and shooting up to triforium-level like a giant exclamation mark in a strip cartoon.

FOUR

Winterreise

NIPPING and eager, the air bites shrewdly and the snow and the wind have obliterated all the details of the journey to Munich. Snow is still falling hard when the scene clears in the late afternoon.

At the Poste Restante counter of the Hauptpost, they handed over a registered envelope crossed with blue chalk; inside, stiff and new, were four pound notes. Just in time! In high spirits I headed for the *Jugendherberge* – one of the very few Youth Hostels that still survived – where the magic word 'student' secured me a bed in a long empty dormitory. I had just placed my rucksack and stick on it in sign of possession when a depressing-looking and pimply newcomer entered and staked a claim on the next bed; infuriatingly: all the others were free. Worse, he sat down, bent on a chat and I was longing to see the town: I had a special goal in view. I made some excuse and dashed down the stairs.

I soon found myself battling down an avenue of enormous width that seemed to stretch to infinity across the draughtiest city in the world. A triumphal arch loomed mistily through the flakes, drew slowly alongside and faded away again behind me while the cold bit to the bone, and when at last a welcoming row of bars appeared, I hurled myself into the first, threw a glass of schnapps through chattering teeth and asked: 'How much further to the Hofbräuhaus?' A pitying laugh broke out in the bar: I had come two miles in the wrong direction: this was a suburb called Schwabing. Swallowing two more schnapps, I retraced my way along the Friedrichstrasse by tram and got off it near a monument where a Bavarian king was riding on a metal horse in front of another colossal and traffic-straddling gateway.

I had expected a different kind of town, more like Nuremberg, perhaps, or Rothenburg. The neo-classical architecture in this boreal and boisterous weather, the giant boulevards, the un-

leavened pomp – everything struck chill to the heart. The proportion of Storm Troopers and S.S. in the streets was unusually
high and still mounting and the Nazi salute flickered about the
pavement like a *tic douloureux*. Outside the Feldherrnhalle, with
its memorial to the sixteen Nazis killed in a 1923 street fight
nearby, two S.S. sentries with fixed bayonets and black helmets
mounted guard like figures of cast-iron and the right arms of all
passers-by shot up as though in reflex to an electric beam. It was
perilous to withhold this homage. One heard tales of uninitiated
strangers being physically set-upon by zealots. Then the
thoroughfares began to shrink. I caught a glimpse down a lane of
Gothic masonry and lancets and buttresses and further on copper
domes hung in convolutions of baroque. A Virgin on a column
presided over a slanting piazza, one side of which was formed by a
tall, Victorian-Gothic building whose great arched undercroft led
to a confusion of lesser streets. In the heart of them stood a massive building; my objective, the Hofbräuhaus. A heavy arched
door was pouring a raucous and lurching party of Brownshirts on
to the trampled snow.

I was back in beer-territory. Half-way up the vaulted stairs a
groaning Brownshirt, propped against the wall on a swastika'd
arm, was unloosing, in a staunchless gush down the steps, the
intake of hours. Love's labour lost. Each new storey radiated great
halls given over to ingestion. In one chamber a table of S.A. men
were grinding out *Lore, Lore, Lore*, scanning the slow beat with
the butts of their mugs, then running the syllables in double time,
like the carriages of an express: '*UND – KOMMT – DER –
FRÜHLingindastal! GRÜSS – MIR – DIE – LORenocheinmal*'.
But it was certain civilian figures seated at meat that drew the
glance and held it.

One must travel east for a hundred and eighty miles from the
Upper Rhine and seventy north from the Alpine watershed to
form an idea of the transformation that beer, in collusion with
almost nonstop eating – meals within meals dovetailing so closely
during the hours of waking that there is hardly an interprandial
moment – can wreak on the human frame. Intestine strife and the
truceless clash of intake and digestion wrecks many German

tempers, twists brows into scowls and breaks out in harsh words and deeds.

The trunks of these feasting burghers were as wide as casks. The spread of their buttocks over the oak benches was not far short of a yard. They branched at the loins into thighs as thick as the torsos of ten-year-olds and arms on the same scale strained like bolsters at the confining serge. Chin and chest formed a single column, and each close-packed nape was creased with its three deceptive smiles. Every bristle had been cropped and shaven from their knobbly scalps. Except when five o'clock veiled them with shadow, surfaces as polished as ostriches' eggs reflected the lamplight. The frizzy hair of their wives was wrenched up from scarlet necks and pinned under slides and then hatted with green Bavarian trilbys and round one pair of elephantine shoulders a little fox stole was clasped. The youngest of this group, resembling a matinée idol under some cruel spell, was the bulkiest. Under tumbling blond curls his china blue eyes protruded from cheeks that might have been blown up with a bicycle pump, and cherry lips laid bare the sort of teeth that make children squeal. There was nothing bleary or stunned about their eyes. The setting may have reduced their size, but it keyed their glances to a sharper focus. Hands like bundles of sausages flew nimbly, packing in forkload on forkload of ham, salami, frankfurter, krenwurst and blutwurst and stone tankards were lifted for long swallows of liquid which sprang out again instantaneously on cheek and brow. They might have been competing with stop-watches, and their voices, only partly gagged by the cheekfuls of good things they were grinding down, grew louder while their unmodulated laughter jarred the air in frequent claps. Pumpernickel and aniseed rolls and bretzels bridged all the slack moments but supplies always came through before a true lull threatened. Huge oval dishes, laden with schweinebraten, potatoes, sauerkraut, red cabbage and dumplings were laid in front of each diner. They were followed by colossal joints of meat – unclassifiable helpings which, when they were picked clean, shone on the scoured chargers like calves' pelvises or the bones of elephants. Waitresses with the build of weight-lifters and all-in wrestlers whirled this provender along and features dripped and glittered like faces at an ogre's banquet. But all too soon the table was an empty bone-yard once more, sound faltered, a look of bereavement clouded those small eyes and there was a brief hint of sorrow in the air. But succour was always at hand; beldames barged to the rescue at full gallop with new clutches of mugs and fresh plate-loads of consumer goods; and the damp Laestrygonian brows unpuckered again in a happy renewal of clamour and intake.

I strayed by mistake into a room full of S.S. officers, Gruppen- and Sturmbannführers, black from their lightning-flash-collars to the forest of tall boots underneath the table. The window embrasure was piled high with their skull-and-crossbones caps. I still hadn't found the part of this Bastille I was seeking, but at last a noise like the rush of a river guided me downstairs again to my journey's end.

The vaults of the great chamber faded into infinity through blue strata of smoke. Hobnails grated, mugs clashed and the combined smell of beer and bodies and old clothes and farmyards sprang at the newcomer. I squeezed in at a table full of peasants, and was soon lifting one of those masskrugs to my lips. It was heavier than a brace of iron dumb-bells, but the blond beer inside was cool and marvellous, a brooding, cylindrical litre of Teutonic myth. This was the fuel that had turned the berserk feeders upstairs into Zeppelins and floated them so far from heart's desire. The gunmetal-coloured cylinders were stamped with a blue HB conjoined under the Bavarian crown, like the foundry-mark on cannon. The tables, in my mind's eye, were becoming batteries where each gunner served a silent and recoil-less piece of ordnance which, trained on himself, pounded away in steady siege. *Mass-gunfire!* Here and there on the tables, with their heads in puddles of beer, isolated bombardiers had been mown down in their emplacements. The vaults reverberated with the thunder of a creeping barrage. There must have been over a thousand pieces engaged! – Big Berthas, Krupp's pale brood, battery on battery crashing at random or in salvoes as hands adjusted the elevation and traverse and then tightened on the stone trigger-guard. Supported by comrades, the walking wounded reeled through the battle smoke and a fresh gunner leaped into each place as it fell empty.

My own gun had fired its last shot, and I wanted to change to a darker-hued explosive. A new *Mass* was soon banged down on the board. In harmony with its colour, it struck a darker note at once, a long Wagnerian chord of black-letter semibreves: *Nacht und Nebel!* Rolling Bavarian acres formed in the inscape of the mind, fanning out in vistas of poles planted pyramidally with the hops gadding over them heavy with poppy-sombre flowers.

The peasants and farmers and the Munich artisans that filled the tables were much nicer than the civic swallowers overhead. Compared to the trim, drilled figures of the few soldiers there, the Storm Troopers looked like brown-paper parcels badly tied with string. There was even a sailor with two black silk streamers falling over his collar from the back of his cap, round the front of which, in gold letters, was written *Unterseeboot*. What was this Hanseatic submariner doing here, so far inland from Kiel and the Baltic? My tablemates were from the country, big, horny-handed men, with a wife or two among them. Some of the older men wore green and grey loden jackets with bone buttons and badgers' brushes or blackcocks' feathers in the back of their hatbands. The bone mouthpieces of long cherrywood pipes were lost in their whiskers and on their glazed china bowls, painted castles and pine-glades and chamois glowed cheerfully while shag-smoke poured through the perforations of their metal lids. Some of them, gnarled and mummified, puffed at cheroots through which straws were threaded to make them draw better. They gave me one and I added a choking tribute to the enveloping cloud. The accent had changed again, and I could only grasp the meaning of the simplest sentences. Many words were docked of their final consonants; 'Bursch' – 'a chap' – for instance, became 'bua'; 'A' was rolled over into 'O', 'Ö' became 'E', and every O and U seemed to have a final A appended, turning it into a disyllable. All this set up a universal moo-ing note, wildly distorted by resonance and echo; for these millions of vowels, prolonged and bent into boomerangs, sailed ricochetting up through the fog to swell the tidal thunder. This echoing and fluid feeling, the bouncing of sounds and syllables and the hogsheads of pungent liquid that sloshed about the tables and blotted the sawdust underfoot, must have been responsible for the name of this enormous hall. It was called the

Schwemme, or horse-pond. The hollowness of those tall mugs aug-
mented the volume of noise like the amphorae which the Greeks
embedded in masonry to add resonance to their chants. My own
note, as the mug emptied, was sliding down to middle C.

Mammoth columns were rooted in the flagstones and the sawdust. Arches flew in broad hoops from capital to capital; crossing
in diagonals, they groined the barrel-vaults that hung dimly above
the smoke. The place should have been lit by pine-torches in stanchions. It was beginning to change, turning now, under my cloud-
ing glance, into the scenery for some terrible Germanic saga,
where snow vanished under the breath of dragons whose red-hot
blood thawed sword-blades like icicles. It was a place for battle-
axes and bloodshed and the last pages of the *Nibelungenlied* when
the capital of Hunland is in flames and everybody in the castle is
hacked to bits. Things grew quickly darker and more fluid; the
echo, the splash, the boom and the roar of fast currents sunk this
beer-hall under the Rhine-bed; it became a cavern full of more
dragons, misshapen guardians of gross treasure; or the fearful
abode, perhaps, where Beowulf, after tearing the Grendel's arm
out of its socket, tracked him over the snow by the bloodstains
and, reaching the mere's edge, dived in to swim many fathoms
down and slay his loathsome water-hag of a mother in darkening
spirals of gore.

Or so it seemed, when the third mug arrived.

Surely I had never seen that oleograph before? Haloed with
stars, the Blessed Virgin was sailing skywards through hoops of
pink cloud and cherubim, and at the bottom, in gold lettering, ran
the words: *Mariä Himmelfahrt.* And those trusses of chair-legs,
the tabby cat in a nest of shavings and the bench fitted with
clamps? Planes, mallets, chisels and braces-and-bits littered
the room. There was a smell of glue, and sawdust lay thick on
the cobwebs in the mid-morning light. A tall man was sand-
papering chair-spokes and a woman was tiptoeing through the
shavings with bread and butter and a coffee pot and, as she
placed them beside the sofa where I lay blanketed, she asked
me with a smile how my Katzenjammer was. Both were utter
strangers.

A *Katzenjammer* is a hangover. I had learnt the word from those girls in Stuttgart.

As I drank the coffee and listened, their features slowly came back to me. At some point, unwillingly emulous of the casualties I had noticed with scorn, I had slumped forward over the Hofbräuhaus table in unwakeable stupor. There had been no vomiting, thank God; nothing worse than total insensibility; and the hefty Samaritan on the bench beside me had simply scooped me up and put me in his handcart, which was full of turned chair legs, and then, wrapping me in my greatcoat against the snow, wheeled it clean across Munich and laid me out mute as a flounder. The calamity must have been brought on by the mixture of the beer with the schnapps I had drunk in Schwabing; I had forgotten to eat anything but an apple since breakfast. Don't worry, the carpenter said: why, in Prague, the beer-halls kept horses that they harnessed to wickerwork coffins on wheels, just to carry the casualties home at the brewery's expense ... What I needed, he said, opening a cupboard, was a 'schluck' of schnapps to put me on my feet. I made a dash for the yard and stuck my head under the pump. Then, combed and outwardly respectable, I thanked my saviours and was soon striding guiltily and at high speed through these outlying streets.

I felt terrible. I had often been drunk, and high spirits had led to rash doings; but never to this hoggish catalepsy.

In the Jugendherberge my rucksack had been tidied away from my unslept-in bed. The caretaker looked in a cupboard in vain and called for the charwoman. No, she said, the only rucksack in the building had departed first thing on the back of their only overnight lodger ... What! Was he a spotty young man? I eked out my inadequate German with a few pointilliste prods. Yes, he had been rather pimply: 'a pickeliger Bua'.

I was aghast. The implications were too much to take in at first. Momentarily, the loss of the diary ousted all other thoughts. Those thousands of lines, the flowery descriptions, the pensées, the philosophic flights, the sketches and verses! All gone. Infected by my distress, the caretaker and the charwoman accompanied me to the police station, where a sympathetic Schupo wrote down all the details, clicking his tongue. '*Schlimm! Schlimm!*' Bad ... So it was;

but there was worse. When he asked for my passport, I reached in the pocket of my jerkin: there was no familiar slotted blue binding there: and I remembered with a new access of despair that I had tucked it down the back of a rucksack pocket for the first time on this journey. The policeman looked grave, and I looked graver still: for inside the passport, for fear of losing it or of spending too much, I had folded the canvas envelope with the four new pounds and this left me with three marks and twenty-five pfennigs in the world, and my lifeline cut for the next four weeks. Apart from this I gathered that wandering about Germany without papers was a serious offence. The policeman telephoned the details to the central police station and said 'We must go to the British Consulate'. We caught a tram and I jolted along beside him. He was formidable in a greatcoat and belted side-arms and a black-lacquered shako and chin-strap. I had visions of being packed home as a distressed British subject, or conducted to the frontier as an undesirable alien and felt as though last night's debauch were stamped on my forehead. I might have been back two years in time, guiltily approaching some dreaded study door.

The clerk at the Consulate knew all about it. The Haupt-polizeiamt had telephoned.

The Consul, seated at a huge desk in a comfortable office under photographs of King George V and Queen Mary, was an austere and scholarly-looking figure in horn-rimmed spectacles. He asked me in a tired voice what all the fuss was about.

Perched on the edge of a leather armchair, I told him, and roughly outlined my Constantinople plan and my idea of writing a book. Then caught up in a fit of volubility, I launched myself on a sort of rambling, prudently censored autobiography. When I finished, he asked me where my father was. In India, I told him. He nodded, and there was a tactful pause. He leant back, with fingertips joined, gazing vaguely at the ceiling, and said: 'Got a photograph?' This rather puzzled me. 'Of my father? I'm afraid not.' He laughed, and said 'No, of you'; and I realized things were taking a turn for the better. The clerk and the policeman led me round the corner to a photomaton shop, which left me with only a few pfennigs. Then I signed the documents waiting in the hall and was summoned back to the Consul's office. He asked me what I proposed to use for money. I hadn't thought yet. I said perhaps I could find odd jobs on farms, walking every other day, till I'd let enough time elapse for some more cash to mount up ... He said 'Well! His Majesty's Government will lend you a fiver. Send it back some time when you're less broke.' After my amazed thanks he asked me how I had come to leave my stuff unguarded in the Jugendherberge; I told him all: the recital evoked another tired smile. When the clerk came in with the passport, the Consul-General signed and blotted it carefully, took some banknotes from a drawer, placed them between the pages and pushed it over to my side of his desk. 'There you are. Try not to lose it this time.' (I've got it in front of me now, faded, torn, dog-eared and travel-stained, crammed with the visas of vanished kingdoms and entry- and exit-stamps in Latin, Greek and Cyrillic characters. The face in the discoloured snap has a dissolute and rather impertinent look. The consular stamp has *gratis* written across it, and the signature is D. *St Clair Gainer*.)

'Do you know anyone in Munich?' Mr Gainer said, getting up. I said I did – that is, not exactly, but I'd got an introduction to a family. 'Get in touch with them,' he said. 'Try and keep out of trouble, and I should avoid beer and schnapps on an empty stomach next time. I'll look out for the book.*

I walked out into the snowy Prannerstrasse like a reprieved malefactor.

Luckily, the letter of introduction had been posted a few days before. But I remembered the name – Baron Rheinhard von Liphart-Ratshoff – so I telephoned, and was asked to stay; and that same evening, in Gräfelfing, a little way out of Munich, I found myself at a lamp-lit table with a family of the utmost charm and

---

* I never saw the rucksack again: I had hoped the diary might have been jettisoned and handed in. Rather oddly the stick, with its twenty-seven plaques, had vanished as well. The loss of the journal still aches now and then like an old wound in bad weather. There was no news either of the 'pickeliger Bua'. I repaid the fiver from Constantinople almost exactly a year later.

kindness. It seemed a miracle that a day so ominously begun could end so happily.

The Lipharts were a White Russian family: more specifically, they were from Esthonia and, like many Baltic landowners, they had taken flight through Sweden and Denmark after the loss of their estates at the end of the war. The castle they lived in – was it called Ratshoff? – became a national museum in Esthonia, and the family settled in Munich. They had none of the austerity that one might associate with descendants of Teutonic knights – in fact, nothing Teutonic at all – and the visual change from solid bulk to these fine-boned Latin-seeming faces was a welcome one. A Greco-esque look stamped this handsome family and they carried off their change of fortune in light-hearted style.

Karl, the eldest son, was a painter, about fifteen years older than me, and as he was short of a sitter for the few days of my stay, I came in handy. We went into Munich every morning and spent peaceful hours of chat in his studio. I listened to anecdotes and scandals and funny stories about Bavaria while the snow piled up on the skylight and the picture dashingly took shape.* When the light began to fail we would wait in a café for Karl's younger brother Arvid, who worked in a bookshop. Here we would hobnob with friends of theirs for an hour or two or have a drink in some-one's house. On a day when there was no painting, I explored as many of the baroque churches and theatres as I could, and spent an entire morning in the Pinakothek. We would catch the train back to Gräfelfing in the evening.

Their parents were captivating survivals of the decades when Paris and the South of France and Rome and Venice were full of northern grandees seeking refuge there from the birch trees and conifers and the frozen lakes of their white and innumerable acres. I could see them, in imagination, lit by the clustering globes of gasoliers on the steps of opera houses and spanking along avenues of lime trees behind carefully matched greys – I could almost catch the twinkle of the scarlet and canary spokes. They would be can-tering among the tombs of the Appian Way or gliding from palace to palace, in wonderful clothes, under a maze of bridges. Much of

---

* It was destroyed by a bomb in the war.

Karl's father's life had been spent in painters' studios and writers' studies, and the house was full of books in half a dozen languages. In my bedroom I was very taken with an old photograph. It showed my host as a young man, dressed to kill and mounted on a beautiful horse in the middle of a pack of foxhounds. Beyond the tophats and the assembled carriages of his guests, the lost castle loomed. The tale of my rucksack, recounted now as a funny story, brought sympathy showering down. What! I'd lost everything? It wasn't too bad, I said, thanks to Mr Gainer's fiver. 'My dear boy, you'll need every penny!' the Baron exclaimed. 'Hang on to it! Karl, Arvid! We must hunt through the attic after dinner.' The attic and various cupboards yielded a splendid rucksack and a jersey, and shirts, socks and pyjamas, a small mountain of things. The whole operation was conducted with speed and laughter, and in ten minutes I was practically fitted out. (I bought the few remaining necessaries next day in Munich for well under a pound.) It was a day of miracles. I was dazed by this immediate and overflowing generosity; but their friendly bohemianism overrode all the reluctance I ought to have felt.

I stayed five days. When leaving-time came, I might have been a son of the house setting forth. The Baron spread maps and pointed out towns and mountains and monasteries and the country houses of friends he would write to, so that I could have a comfortable night now and then, and a bath. 'There we are! Nando Arco at St Martin! And my old friend Botho Coreth at Hochschatten. The Trautmannsdorffs at Pottenbrunn!' (He wrote to them all and it brought a new dimension into the journey.) He and the Baroness were worried about Bulgaria: 'It's full of robbers and comitadjis. You must take care! They're a terrible lot. *And as for the Turks!*' The nature of the hinted menace was obscure.

The evenings were conversation and books. The Baron enlarged on the influence of *Don Juan* on *Evgenye Oniegin* and the decay of German literature and the changes of taste in France: was Paul Bourget read a great deal? Henri de Regnier? Maurice Barrès? I wish I could have answered. Saved from the general loss by its presence in a remote pocket, my only book now was the German translation of *Hamlet*: how true was the German claim that it was as good as the original? 'Not true at all!' the Baron said: 'But it's better than in any *other* foreign language. Just listen!'; and he took down four books and read out Mark Antony's speech in Russian, French, Italian and German. The Russian had a splendid ring, as it always does. The French sounded rather thin and the Italian bombastic and orotund; unfairly but amusingly, he exaggerated the styles as he read. The German, however, had a totally different consistency from any utterance I had heard on this journey: slow, thoughtful, clear and musical, stripped of its harshness and over-emphasis and gush; and in those minutes, as the lamplight caught the reader's white hair and eyebrows and sweeping white moustache and twinkled in the signet ring of the hand that held the volume, I understood for the first time how magnificent a language it could be.

All these kindnesses were crowned with a dazzling consummation. I had said that my books, after the lost diary, were what I missed most. I ought to have known by now that mention of loss had only one result under this roof ... What books? I had named them; when the time came for farewells, the Baron said: 'We can't do much about the others but here's Horace for you.' He put a small duodecimo volume in my hand. It was the Odes and Epodes, beautifully printed on thin paper in Amsterdam in the middle of the seventeenth century, bound in hard green leather with gilt lettering. The leather on the spine had faded but the sides were as bright as grass after rain and the little book opened and shut as compactly as a Chinese casket. There were gold edges to the pages and a faded marker of scarlet silk slanted across the long S's of the text and the charming engraved vignettes: cornucopias, lyres, pan-pipes, chaplets of olive and bay and myrtle. Small mezzotints showed the Forum and the Capitol and imaginary Sabine landscapes; Tibur, Lucretilis, the Bandusian spring, Soracte, Venusia ... I made a feint at disclaiming a treasure so far beyond the status of the rough travels ahead. But I had been forestalled, I saw with relief, by an inscription: 'To our young friend', etc., on the page opposite an emblematic *ex libris* with the name of their machicolated Baltic home. Here and there between the pages a skeleton leaf conjured up those lost woods.

This book became a fetish. I noticed, during the next few days,

that it filled everyone with feelings of wonder akin to my own. On
the second evening – Rosenheim was the first – placed alongside
the resolutely broached new diary on the inn-table of Hohe-
naschau, it immediately made me seem more exalted than the
tramp that I actually was. 'What a beautiful little book!' awed
voices would say. Horny fingers reverently turned the pages. 'Late-
inisch? Well, well . . .' A spurious aura of scholarship and respect-
ability sprang up.

Remembering the advice the mayor of Bruchsal had given me,
the moment I had arrived in this little village, I had sought out the
Bürgermeister. I found him in the Gemeindeamt, where he filled
out a slip of paper. I presented it at the inn: it entitled me to
supper and a mug of beer, a bed for the night and bread and a bowl
of coffee in the morning; all on the parish. It seems amazing to me
now, but so it was, and there was no kind of slur attached to it;
nothing, ever, but a friendly welcome. I wonder how many times I
took advantage of this generous and, apparently, very old custom?
It prevailed all through Germany and Austria, a survival perhaps,
of some ancient charity to wandering students and pilgrims, extended now to all poor travellers.

The Gastwirtschaft was a beetling chalet with cut logs piled to
the eaves. An elaborate balcony ran all the way round it; carved
and fretted woodwork frilled it at every point and a layer of snow
two feet thick, like the cotton-wool packing for a fragile treasure,
muffled the shallow tilt of the enormous wide-eaved roof.

Of the village in the snowy dark outside, nothing has stuck. But
unlike the three overnight halts that follow – Riedering,
Söllhuben and Röttau, that is to say – it is at least marked on
maps.

Each of these little unmarked hamlets seems smaller in retrospect than the other two, and remoter, and more deeply embedded
in hills and snow and dialect. They have left an impression of
women scattering grain in their yards to a rush of poultry, and of
hooded children returning from school with hairy satchels and
muffled ears: homing goblins, slapping along lanes on skis as short
and wide as barrel-staves and propelling themselves with sticks of
unringed hazel. When we passed each other, they would squeak

'*Grüss Gott!*' in a polite shrill chorus. One or two were half gagged by cheekfuls bitten from long slices of black bread and butter.

All was frozen. There was a particular delight in treading across the hard puddles. The grey discs and pods of ice creaked under hobnails and clogs with a mysterious sigh of captive air: then they split into stars and whitened as the spiders-web fissures expanded. Outside the villages the telegraph wire was a single cable of flakes interrupted by birds alighting and I would follow the path below and break through the new and sparkling crust to sink in powdery depths. I travelled on footpaths and over stiles and across fields and along country roads that ran through dark woods and out again into the white ploughland and pasture. The valleys were dotted with villages that huddled round the shingle roofs of churches, and all the belfries tapered and then swelled again into black ribbed cupolas. These onion-domes had a fleetingly Russian look. Otherwise, especially when the bare hardwoods were replaced by conifers, the décor belonged to Grimms' Fairy Tales. 'Once upon a time, on the edge of a dark forest, there lived an old woodman, with a single beautiful daughter', it was that sort of a region. Cottages that looked as innocent as cuckoo-clocks turned into witches' ginger-bread after dark. Deep and crusted loads of snow weighed the conifer-branches to the ground. When I touched them with the tip of my new walking stick, up they sprang in sparkling explosions. Crows, rooks and magpies were the only birds about and the arrows of their footprints were sometimes crossed by the deeper slots of hares' pads. Now and again I came on a hare, seated alone in a field and looking enormous; hindered by the snow it would lope awkwardly away to cover, for the snow slowed everything up, especially when the rails and the posts beside the path were buried. The only people I saw outside the villages were woodcutters. They were indicated, long before they appeared, by the wide twin grooves of their sledges, with cart-horses' crescent-shaped tracks stamped deep between. Then they would come into view on a clearing or the edge of a distant spinney and the sound of axes and the rasp of two-handed saws would reach my ears a second after my eye had caught the vertical fall or the horizontal slide of the blades. If, by the time I reached them, a tall tree was about to come down, I found it impossible to move on. The sledge-horses, with icicled fetlocks and muzzles deep in their nosebags, were rugged up in sacking and I stamped to keep warm as I watched. Armed with beetles, rustic bruisers at work in a ring of chips and sawdust and trodden snow banged the wedges home. They were rough and friendly men, and one of them, on the pretext of a strange presence and with a collusive wink, was sure to pull out a bottle of schnapps. Swigs, followed by gasps of fiery bliss, sent prongs of vapour into the frosty air. I took a turn with the saw once or twice, clumsily till I got the hang of it, unable to tear myself away till at last the tree came crashing down. Once, arriving on the scene just as the loading of the dismembered tree was complete, I got a lift on the sledge, and swished along behind two of those colossal chestnuts with flaxen manes and tails and ornate jingling collars. The trip ended with more schnapps in a Gastwirtschaft, and a departure sped by dialect farewells. It shot through my mind that if I were up against it further on, I might do worse than hitch on to one of these forest teams, as one of the woodmen half jocularly suggested, and hack away for my keep.

Otherwise, except for birds, most of these white landscapes were empty, and I would crunch along adding the track of my hobnails to their criss-cross of little tridents. Fired by the Baron's example, I tried to get by heart, from Schlegel and Tieck's pocket translation, the passages of *Hamlet, Prinz von Dänemark* which I knew in English. 'Whether 'tis better in the mind to suffer . . .' came rumbling out over the snow in its new guise:

> Ob's edler im Gemüt, die Pfeil' und Schleudern
> Des wütenden Geschicks erdulden, oder,
> Sich waffnend gegen eine See von Plagen,
> Durch Widerstand sie enden

until I got to 'It is a fear of something after death/that undiscovered country from whose bourne/no traveller returns':

> Nur dass die Furcht vor etwas nach dem Tod –
> Das unentdeckte Land, von des Bezirk
> Kein Wandrer wiederkehrt

Again, anyone bumping into me unawares, like the crone on the Ulm road, would have taken me for drunk; in a literary sense they would have been right.

Every mile or so wooden calvaries, hewn and painted with rustic velleities of baroque, stood askew beside the path. Streaming wounds mangled the gaunt figures and exposure had warped or split them along the grain. Haloes of tarnished brass put out spikes behind the heads; the brows were clumsily hooped already with plaits of real thorns and sheltered by pointed snow-laden chevrons. They might have been the lineal replacements, changed every few generations, of the first Christian emblems which St Boniface, hot-foot from Devonshire, had set up in Germany. He converted the country a hundred years after St Augustine had arrived in Kent; and not much more than two centuries after Hengist and Horsa had landed in Britain while their German kinsmen were bursting into Gaul and into these trans-Danubian woods. This saint from Devonshire was not the only Englishman to help drive the old gods out: monks from south-east England, the West Country and the Shires were soon seated on all the earliest bishops' thrones of Germany.

Vague speculation thrives in weather like this. The world is muffled in white, motor-roads and telegraph-poles vanish, a few castles appear in the middle distance; everything slips back hundreds of years. The details of the landscape – the leafless trees, the sheds, the church towers, the birds and the animals, the sledges and the woodmen, the sliced ricks and the occasional cowmen driving a floundering herd from barn to barn – all these stand out dark in isolation against the snow, distinct and momentous. Objects expand or shrink and the change makes the scenery resemble early woodcuts of winter husbandry. Sometimes the landscape moves it further back in time. Pictures from illuminated manuscripts take shape; they become the scenes which old breviaries and Books of Hours enclosed in the O of *Orate, fratres*. The snow falls; it is Carolingian weather ... Set on the way by my Villon craze, I had discovered and devoured Helen Waddell's *Mediaeval Latin Lyrics* and the *Wandering Scholars* the year before and had seized on the Archpoet and the *Carmina Burana*; and I wasn't slow, in the present circumstances, to identify myself

with one of those itinerant medieval clerks. In an inn or a cowshed, when I scratched away the ice-ferns in the morning and the
winter scene widened, the illusion was complete:

> Nec lympha caret alveus,
>   nec prata virent herbida,
> sol nostra fugit aureus
>   confinia;
> est inde dies niveus,
>   nox frigida.

It was the world all round me! 'De ramis cadunt folia . . .' they had
fallen long ago. 'Modo frigescit quidquid est . . .' icicles, barring
the scene out of doors, dripped from the eaves in confirmation.

There was something meditative and consoling about this dim
season, except towards evening, when the sun – invisible through
the clouds, reduced to a silvery blur or expanded to an orange
globe like a winter cherry – began to set. Then rooks fell silent; the
pink after-glow faded on faraway peaks; the light dwindled over
the grey fields; and life ebbed with a shudder like a soul leaving
the body. All was suddenly quiet and ghostly and I longed for the
first glimpse of the lamp-light streaming through the windows of
my destined village. I lost my way now and then through mis-
understanding instructions at a farm or a cottage; sometimes dialect or lack of teeth or the wind had garbled them. Heading in the
twilight for one of those three uncharted villages, I had a moment
of panic. I was long past the last signpost: it had pointed to
Pfaffenbichl and Marwang – I remember these two names because
the first was ridiculous and the second rather sinister. All at once
it was dark and the snow was coming down fast. I was feeling my
way by a wooden rail when I lost touch and fell stumbling in a
drift and floundered in circles but couldn't find the rail. I must
have strayed into a field. Luckily I found a ruined barn and fum-
bled my way to the door. I lit a match and cleared the snow and
the ancient cow-pats and owls' pellets out of a corner and, pulling
on every stitch of extra clothing from my rucksack, resigned
myself to the thought of sheltering there till daybreak. The sun
had only just set.

I usually had an apple and a hunk of bread and a flask, but not

this time. There was no light to read by or dry wood for a fire, the
cold was getting worse and the wind was driving snow through a
score of gaps. I huddled in a ball with my arms round my knees,
stirring every few minutes to stamp and flap my arms. Too low for
wolves, I thought melodramatically; or was it? After a while I
stopped the singing with which I was trying to pass the inter-
minable hours. There was nothing for it but to sit clenched and
shivering in this prehistoric burial posture and listen to my teeth
rattling. Every now and then I seemed to fall into a sort of catalepsy. But suddenly – was it midnight, or one in the morning? or
later perhaps? – the wind fell and I heard voices, quite near, and
jumped up and ran out shouting. There was silence, then someone
called back. I could make out two faint blurs. They were villagers
returning home. What was I doing there, on such a night? I told
them. 'Der arme Bua!' They were all sympathy. But it was only
half-past eight and the village was a mere two or three hundred
metres away, just round the end of the hill ... And within five
minutes, there were the roofs and the belfry and the lighted doorway. The carpet of lamplight unrolled across the snow and the
flakes floating past the windows were turning to sequins. Inside
the inn the lamplit and steaming rustics round the table, veiled in
the smoke of their lidded pipes, were maundering away with
slurred vowels over their mugs. It was no good trying to explain.

'Hans.'
'What?'
'Can you see me?'
'No.'
'Well, the dumplings are enough.'
The inn-keeper's wife, who was from Munich, was illustrating
the difficulties of the dialect by an imaginary conversation be-
tween two Bavarian peasants. They are seated on either side of a
table, helping themselves from a huge dish of *Knödel*, and it is
only when the plate of one of them is piled high enough with
dumplings to hide him from view that he stops. In ordinary
German, this dialogue would run: 'Hans!' 'Was?' 'Siehst Du
mich?' 'Nein.' 'Also, die Knödel sind genug.' But in the speech of
Lower Bavaria, as closely as I can remember, it turns into: 'Schani!'

'Woas?' 'Siahst Du ma?' 'Na.' 'Nacha, siang die Kniadel knua.'
Such sounds were mooing and rumbling in the background all
through this Bavarian trudge.

   The inns in these remote and winter-bound thorpes were warm
and snug. There was usually a picture of Hitler and a compulsory
poster or two, but they were outnumbered by pious symbols and
more venerable mementoes. Perhaps because I was a foreigner,
politics seldom entered the conversations I had to share in; rather
surprisingly, considering the closeness of those villages to the
fountain-head of the Party. (It was different in towns.) Inn-talk,
when it concerned the regional oddities of Bavaria, was rife with
semi-humorous bias. Even then, many decades after Bismarck's
incorporation of the Bavarian Kingdom into the German Empire,
Prussia was the chief target. A frequent butt of these stories was a
hypothetical Prussian visitor to the province. Disciplined, blink-
ered, pig-headed and sharp-spoken, with thin vowels and stripped
consonants – every 'sch' turning into 's' and every hard 'g' into 'y'
– this ridiculous figure was an unfailing prey for the easy-going
but shrewd Bavarians. Affection for the former ruling family still
lingered. The hoary origins and the thousand years' sway of the
Wittelsbachs were remembered with pride and their past follies
forgiven. So august and gifted and beautiful a dynasty had every
right, these old people inferred, to be a bit cracked now and then.
The unassuming demeanour of Prince Ruprecht, the actual Pretender – who was also the last Stuart Pretender to the British
throne – was frequently extolled; he was a distinguished doctor in
Munich, and much loved. All this breathed homesickness for a
past now doubly removed and thickly overlaid by recent history. I
liked them for these old loyalties. Not everyone is fond of Bavarians: their fame is mixed, both inside Germany and out and one
hears damning tales of aggressive ruthlessness. They seemed a
rougher race than the civilized Rhinelanders or the diligent and
homely Swabians. They were, perhaps, more raw in aspect and
more uncompromising in manner; and – trivial detail! – an impression remains, perhaps a mistaken one, of darker hair. But there
was nothing sinister about the farm people and foresters and
woodcutters I spent these evenings with. They have left a memory
of whiskers and wrinkles and deep eye sockets, of slurred speech

and friendly warmth and hospitable kindness. Carved wood
teemed in every detail of their dwellings, for from the Norwegian
fiords to Nepal, above certain contour-lines, the upshot of long
winters, early nightfall, soft wood and sharp knives is the same. It
soars to a feverish zenith in Switzerland, where each winter begets
teeming millions of cuckoo clocks, chamois, dwarfs and brown
bears.

On one of these evenings, an accordion player set everyone
yodelling. I can't bear it now, but I listened in rapture then. In the
last of these villages I found myself rolling about on the floor in a
friendly wrestling match with a village boy of about my own age.
It ended in an inextricable clinch and a draw, from which we rose
covered in sweat and sawdust, limping through acclaim towards
the reviving beer mugs.

In thanks for shelter in farms, or for sojourns that the parish
had imposed, I sketched the farmers and inn-keepers and their
wives and presented them with the results and through politeness
or lack of sophistication, they looked pleased. I will go into the
merits of this output later. At one point, it plays an important
part in this story.

It was different in towns.

In all those chance conversations in coffee-houses and beer-halls
and wine-cellars I was a most inadequate foil. Just how inadequate, I must try to convey, even if it slows things up for a
couple of pages.

'A *dangerous mixture of sophistication and recklessness* . . .'
those words in my housemaster's report would have been nearer
the mark if 'sophistication' had been replaced by 'precocity plus
backwardness'. At all events, the mixture had produced nothing
faintly resembling a grasp of politics and I'm forced to confess that,
apart from a few predictable and almost subconscious prejudices,
politically speaking, I didn't care a damn. It was still possible for
people to know each other fairly well without the dimmest idea of
their opinions; and, at the King's School, Canterbury, discussion
raged on every theme but this.

It goes without saying that in a small, tradition-haunted public
school of such improbable antiquity – founded a few decades after

Justinian closed the pagan academy at Athens – the atmosphere
was likely to be conservative, and it was; but it was conservatism
of an inexplicit kind, unaggressive because it was unchallenged –
at least, at the age of sixteen and a half it was, which is when I
vanished from the scene; but deep in the bloodstream nevertheless.
There were rumours of sporadic heterodoxy higher up but they
were few, and not fierce, and no firebrands like the two-man jac-
querie of Esmond Romilly and Philip Toynbee had ever broken in
to scatter manifestos and drive away with a carload of straw
boaters. Communism, in such surroundings, still suggested the
beards, the fur hats and the steaming bombs of old-fashioned cartoons; it was a concept almost too exotic for conjecture. The few
boys with Socialist leanings were thought to be harmless, but a bit
odd; and, where they might have seemed dashing a couple of years
later, they were then thought rather dim. Socialism sounded grey
and without charm and Labour M.P.s conjured up visions of steel-
rimmed spectacles, homespun cloth, cocoa and seed-cake and long
killjoy faces bent on dismantling – what? Here an odd medley of
targets would be bandied across fifth-form studies: What indeed?
Why, the Empire, for a start! The Fleet! The Army! Established
religion – 'except Methodist chapels'; Gibraltar, the Lords, judges'
wigs, kilts, bearskins, public schools ('No, steady on!'), Latin and
Greek, Oxford and Cambridge – 'the Boat race too, most likely';
'county cricket for a cert' – steeplechasing, shooting, fox-hunting,
flat-racing, the Derby, betting, country-life, farming – ('I bet
they'd plough up everything for swedes and beetroots if they got
the chance!') What about London? Why, the Palladium and the
Aldwych would be turned into lecture halls or bloody temperance
canteens. (The preceding notions were imported, rather than
formed on the spot. They were fragments left over from outbursts
and lamentations at home. The level may have been higher; but I
think this reconstruction is about right.) Talk would languish and
a pensive gloom descend. Then someone might say: 'It's a pity
something can't be done about those poor chaps on the dole'; and
the gloom would deepen; then: 'It's rotten luck on all those
miners.' Awkward silence would prolong itself while these liberal
thoughts fluttered overhead. Then someone might tactfully put
Rhapsody in Blue or *Ain't Misbehavin'* on the gramophone and

steer the talk into happier channels: musical comedies, domestic scandal, Tallulah Bankhead, slow bowling or the fast passages in Juvenal.

My early days in London saw little advance on this; rather the reverse. The fellow crammers' pups from other establishments that I knocked about with at first were mostly a year older than me, or more; and their early departure from school had been prompted by backwardness rather than iniquity. They were wide-eyed, pink-cheeked and innocent boys with tidy hair; cornets and ensigns in the larva phase, cramming painfully for their exams and bent on an early mastery of the customs of their future regiments. They shunned flannel bags for whole suits and choked happily behind ties that were silk autobiographies knotted in high starched collars. Lock had helmeted them in hard hats till after Goodwood. Brigg, or Swaine & Adeney, sworded them with umbrellas that no cloud-burst would ever unfurl, and – ah! how enviably! – Lobb, Peel and Maxwell, on their fathers' accounts, had shod them in boned and gleaming shoes. With brows knit, they concentrated on not carrying parcels in London, on puffing at Turkish or Egyptian cigarettes rather than stinkers – even if they didn't want to smoke at all – and on eschewing the arcane blacklist of verbal usage that regimental traditions condemned. There was earnest talk, but it revolved round breeches-makers, gunsmiths and spurriers and hairdressers and their lotions, and the rival claims, in the evening, of carnations and gardenias. Arlen-ish anxieties! They were absurd and rather delightful. I was dazzled by all this juvenile dandyism; it seemed the height of worldly maturity and I did my best to keep up. With expert advice on pattern and cut I pondered eclectically in shops as hushed as cave-palaces at the bottom of the sea, and bills mounted up. In the fullness of time, there was a Simla–London row about them, with bewilderment more than anger at the Simla end; how could I be quite so silly? Some of the bills weren't paid till years after these travels ended. Decorous d'Orsay-esque canters under the plane trees with these new friends, especially when Hyde Park was still covered with dew, seemed a perfect beginning to the day, and in winter I sped across country on borrowed steeds. They were very nice to me, because I was the youngest and because genuine rashness, linked with a

kind of clownish exhibitionism, whose secret I had learnt long ago
and sedulously cultivated, always won a dubious popularity. I
was even forgiven, after diving into a lake at a ball, for only
remembering when climbing out covered in slime and duckweed
that my tails were borrowed.

It was about then that the first doubts about soldiering in peace-
time began. Mermaid voices – the world of Literature and the Arts
– were secretly beckoning. My friends, however much they might
grumble about shortness of ready cash, would have enough later
to enliven soldiering with all the country pursuits they loved and
plenty over for painting London red, and in a more elaborate and
seemly style than our uncomplex weekly binges allowed. These
would begin among the brass and the baize-curtained settles and
the print-covered walls of Stone's Chop-House in Panton Street – a
Leach illustration for Surtees, destroyed in the Blitz – and twice
they ended in Vine Street: ('Did you have a nice time last night,
Richard?' 'Perfect, Aunt Kitty. Just what I like: a vomit and a
brush with the Police.') Also, if they tired of the Army, they could
leave it. But what about living on one's pay, as I would have to? It
might have worked had I felt utterly and exclusively vowed to a
military life. But suddenly it seemed that the whole idea had taken
shape *faute de mieux*; and, quite clearly, I was as ill-endowed for
thrift in the face of temptation as I was for discipline. How would
I manage, year after year, with no war in sight, never getting
abroad, perhaps? As it happened, only one of this small set was
destined for the infantry; armed at all points with arcane foot-
guard vetoes, he was the one who was strictest, in a voice which
had scarcely broken yet, about usage and attire; but dynastic loy-
alty had vowed the others, practically from birth, to paternal cavalry regiments and every so often, they were cast down by the
thought that, Hussars and Lancers though they would be, the
cavalry was being motorized fast. Wheels, armour-plating, nuts,
bolts and caterpillar-tracks were closing in and soon, outside the
Household Cavalry and the two first regiments of heavy Dragoons, there would not be a whinny within earshot except from
their own loose-boxes. But all their longings remained true to boot
and saddle, and these feelings were catching. I was infected with
their equestrian yearnings and moments of hope would spring:

Why not India? Plenty of horses there. And with the extra allowances, why not?

After this, at regular intervals, unloosed by my voices-in-the-next-room relationship to India, fostered by long gazing at faded photographs, and almost wholly unrelated to reality, unavowable dreams intoxicatingly and fleetingly took shape. Sashed, and in chain-mail epaulettes with a striped puggaree twisted round a conical Multani cap and its fringed tail flying loose with the speed of the charge, I would be pointing along a canyon with a sabre while a squadron of irregular horse, their pennanted lances lowered, thundered behind; the bullets of ten-rupee jezails, meanwhile, consistently missing, whistled past our ears. In another scene in this secret *camera obscura* I was seconded like Strickland Sahib, thanks to an effortless mastery of a dozen native tongues and their dialects, for special duties: unrecognizable under my rags I would disappear for months into the lanes and the bazaars of seething frontier cities. The scenery of the next slide was set beyond the Himalayas: how many weeks from Yarkand to Urumchi? There, sheltered from the blizzards of the Pamirs under the black and snow-laden tent-flap, narrow-eyed over the hookah and indistinguishable from the shaggy chieftains cross-legged all round me, I played out the last chukkah of the Great Game ... Invariably, as they dissolved, these deadly secret scenes made room for a final lantern-slide which was more convincing than all the rest and in much sharper focus. Squad-drill barked in the offing, recruits formed fours with a ragged triple crash, a bugler blew 'Defaulters', and for miles around, Hampshire drizzle soaked into the gorse and pines and streamed over Aldershot windows. The adjutant meanwhile, pointing wearily at the mess-bills and cheques on his desk, said: 'You realize this can't go on? The Colonel will see you now. He's waiting for you.'

Once I dropped the idea of soldiering, the mermaid voices which had all the time been softly, and then less softly, calling me away from those friendly cornets of horse, now held me in thrall. The world of Literature and Art ... I didn't find it. But through new friends and via the Cavendish Hotel, I think, I felt I had stepped through a looking-glass to wander in a bracing and brand new region. In this breezy, post-Stracheyan climate, it was cheerfully and explicitly held that all English life, thought and art were irredeemably provincial and a crashing bore and the sack from school, to my surprise, was hailed as a highly creditable feat; failure to join the Army was better still: 'The Army! I should hope *not* indeed. The very idea!' I tried to explain that it had not been for ideological reasons and that I thought the King's commission a heavy honour; but, jovially overridden, I remained traitorously silent next time. An exotic radiance played over this new world. Bright with fireworks and shot with sulphuric sparks, it was an extension into real life of half a dozen books I had just read. The left-wing opinions that I occasionally heard were uttered in such a way that they seemed a part merely, and a minor part, of a more general emancipation. This was composed of eclectic passwords and symbols – a fluent awareness of modern painting, for instance, or a familiarity with new trends in music; neither more important nor less than acquaintance with nightlife in Paris and Berlin and a smattering of the languages spoken there. The atmosphere was far removed from cocoa and Methodism; principle never interfered with fastidious hedonism – expensive clothes and elaborate ties – and the only proletarian leanings I could discern probably sprang more from a physiological need for tough company than from dogma. How brilliantly the author of 'Where Engels Fear to Tread'* depicts the protagonist of this particular aspect of Thirties' London! He soars from the page like a genie out of a bottle, and the symbols he leaves on evaporation are not hammers or sickles but a scattering of jewels and the tail feather of a lyre-bird. No wonder that the 'Left Wing' and 'Communism' seemed little more than light siege-pieces aimed at the stuffiness of the old. This was the target, and shocks the tactics along the Ritz-Café Royal-Gargoyle front and a great salient of country houses. Of course I knew that these flashes were the frivolous symptoms of an enormous political movement. But I had no inkling of the immeasurable influence that it was about to exert on people of my age and not a hint of the unquestioning ardour and the disillusioned palinodes that lay in wait for most of my later friends.

---

* In *The Condemned Playground* by Cyril Connolly.

I never heard communism seriously propounded or argued; perhaps I was too deeply preoccupied with my own dissipations; and,
as it turned out in the end, it was a way of thought that I was
denied or spared by a geographical fluke. From the end of these
travels till the War, I lived, with a year's interruption, in Eastern
Europe, among friends whom I must call old-fashioned liberals.
They hated Nazi Germany; but it was impossible to look eastwards for inspiration and hope, as their western equivalents –
peering from afar, and with the nightmare of only one kind of
totalitarianism to vex them – felt able to do. For Russia began
only a few fields away, the other side of a river; and there, as all
her neighbours knew, great wrong was being done and terrible
danger lay. All their fears came true. Living among them made
me share those fears and they made stony ground for certain
kinds of grain.

This is a long rigmarole, but it does show how ill-prepared I was
for any form of political argument. In this respect, I might have
been sleep-walking.

Those Bavarian inn conversations reflected opinions which ran
from the total conviction of party-members to the total opposition
of their opponents and victims; with the difference that the first
were loud and voluble while the second remained either silent or
non-committal until they were alone with a single interlocutor.
Being English was relevant to all this, for though the Germans'
attitude to England varied, it was never indifferent. A few, like the
near-albino in Heidelberg, showed loathing. The War inevitably
cropped up: they resented that we had been on the winning side,
but didn't seem to blame us – always with the proviso that Germany would never have lost if she hadn't been stabbed in the
back; and they admired England, in a certain measure for reasons
that were seldom heard in respectable English circles any more.
For past conquests, that is, and the extent of the colonies, and the
still apparently undiminished power of the Empire. When, with
education and practice the colonies could rule themselves, I would
urge at this point, they would be given their independence. Not at
once, of course; it would take time ... (This was the theory we
had all been brought up on.) Looks of admiration, partly rueful

and partly ironical, at what they considered the size of the lie and the extent of its hypocrisy, were the invariable response.

In these exchanges I was held up by ignorance and by anxiety to hide it; and my limited German, though it was often a stumbling block, sometimes helped to mask its true depths. How I longed to be better equipped! When they asked, and they always did, what the English thought of National Socialism, I would stick repetitively to three main objections: the burning of the books, of which lurid photographs had filled the newspapers; the concentration camps which had been set up a few months before; and the persecution of the Jews. This procedure was irritating, I could see, but not wholly ineffective. Anyway, the reactions and arguments are too familiar for repetition.

In all of these conversations there was one opening I particularly dreaded: I was English? Yes. A student? Yes. At Oxford, no? No. At this point I knew what we were in for.

The summer before, the Oxford Union had voted that 'under no circumstances would they fight for King and Country'. The stir it had made in England was nothing, I gathered, to the sensation in Germany. I didn't know much about it. In my explanation – for I was always pressed for one – I depicted the whole thing as merely another act of defiance against the older generation. The very phrasing of the motion – 'Fight for King and Country' – was an obsolete cliché from an old recruiting poster: no one, not even the fiercest patriot, would use it now to describe a deeply-felt sentiment. My interlocutors asked: 'Why not?' 'Für König und Vaterland' sounded different in German ears: it was a bugle-call that had lost none of its resonance. What exactly did I mean? The motion was probably 'pour épater les bourgeois', I floundered. Here someone speaking a little French would try to help. 'Um die Bürger zu erstaunen? Ach, so!' A pause would follow. 'A kind of joke, really,' I went on. 'Ein Scherz?' they would ask. 'Ein Spass? Ein Witz?' I was surrounded by glaring eyeballs and teeth. Someone would shrug and let out a staccato laugh like three notches on a watchman's rattle. I could detect a kindling glint of scornful pity and triumph in the surrounding eyes which declared quite plainly their certainty that, were I right, England was too far gone in degeneracy and frivolity to present a problem. But the distress I could detect on the face of a silent opponent of the régime was still harder to bear: it hinted that the will or the capacity to save civilization was lacking where it might have been hoped for. Veterans of the War showed a sort of unpartisan sorrow at this falling-off. It sprang from the ambiguous love-hate for England that many Germans felt. They recalled the trenches and the stubborn fighting qualities of 'die Tommies'; then they compared them to the pacifist voters in the Union, and shook their heads. There was a sorrowing, Horatian note in this. Not from such sires, these veterans seemed to say, were sprung the youths who dyed the sea red with Punic blood and struck down Pyrrhus and mighty Antiochus and grim Hannibal.

These undergraduates had landed their wandering compatriots in a fix. I cursed their vote; and it wasn't even true, as events were to prove. But I was stung still more by the tacit and unjust implication that it was prompted by lack of spirit. I urged that there had always been an anti-militarist strain among the English in peacetime. But when the blast of war blew in their ears, they imitated the action of the tiger, stiffened the sinews, summoned up the blood, and disguised fair nature with hard-favoured rage, etc. It didn't cut much ice.

Appalling things had happened since Hitler had come into power ten months earlier; but the range of horror was not yet fully unfolded. In the country the prevailing mood was a bewildered acquiescence. Occasionally it rose to fanaticism. Often when nobody was in earshot, it found utterance in pessimism, distrust and foreboding, and sometimes in shame and fear but only in private. The rumours of the concentration camps were still no louder than a murmur; but they hinted at countless unavowable tragedies.

In one of those lost Rhineland towns, I can't remember which, I had a glimpse of how quick the change-over had been for many Germans. In a workmen's bar late at night I made friends with several factory hands in overalls who had come off a late shift. They were about my age, and one of them, an amusing, clownish character, said: why didn't I doss down on his brother's camp bed at his place? When we climbed the ladder to his attic, the room turned out to be a shrine of Hitleriana. The walls were covered with flags, photographs, posters, slogans and emblems. His S.A. uniform hung neatly ironed on a hanger. He explained these cult objects with fetishist zest, saving up till the last the centrepiece of his collection. It was an automatic pistol, a Luger parabellum, I think, carefully oiled and wrapped in mackintosh, accompanied by a pile of green cardboard boxes packed with bullets. He stripped and reassembled the pistol, loaded the magazine and smacked it home and ejected it again, put on a belt and crossbrace with a holster, whipped the gun in and out like a cowboy, tossed it in the air and caught it, spun it round by the trigger-guard and danced about with one eye shut, going through the motions of aiming and firing with loud clicks of the tongue ... When I said that it must be rather claustrophobic with all that stuff on the walls, he laughed and sat down on his bed, and said: '*Mensch!* You should have seen it last year! You would have laughed! Then it was all red flags, stars, hammers and sickles, pictures of Lenin and Stalin and Workers of the World, Unite! I used to punch the heads of anyone singing the *Horst Wessel Lied!* It was all the *Red Flag* and the *International* then! I wasn't only a Sozi, but a Kommi, ein echter Bolschewik!' He gave a clenched fist salute. 'You should have seen me! Street fights! We used to beat the hell out of the Nazis, and they beat the hell out of us. We laughed ourselves silly – *Man hat sich totgelacht.* Then suddenly, when Hitler came into power, I understood it was all nonsense and lies. I realized Adolf was the man for me. All of a sudden!' He snapped his fingers in the air. 'And here I am!' What about all his old pals, I asked. 'They changed too! – all those chaps in the bar. Every single one! They're all in the S.A. now.' Had a lot of people done the same, then? A *lot?* His eyes opened wide. 'Millions! I tell you, I was astonished how easily they all changed sides!' He shook his head dubiously for a moment. Then a wide, untroubled smile divided his face, as he spilled the bullets like rosary beads through the fingers of one hand into the palm of the other. 'Sakra Haxen noch amal! We've scarcely got any Sozis or Kommis left to pitch into!' He laughed merrily. What did his parents think about it all? I had met them on the way up – rather a nice, seedy-looking old couple listening to the wireless by the kitchen stove. He shrugged and looked depressed. '*Mensch!* They don't understand anything. My father's old-fashioned: only thinks about the Kaiser and Bismarck and old Hindenburg – and now he's dead, too – anyway, he helped the Führer to get where he is! And my mother, she knows nothing about politics. All she cares about is going to church. She's old-fashioned too.'

On the road running east from my last Bavarian halt in Traunstein the sudden clear weather showed how close I was getting to the Alps. The clouds had vanished and the great range soared out of the plain as abruptly as a wall rises from a field. The snow-covered masses climbed and gleamed, slashed with blue shadows; dark loops of fir and the peaks of the Kitzbühl Alps and the East Tyrol overlapped in the sky above a deep mesh of shadowy valleys. A signpost pointed south and along a valley at the end of which Bad Reichenhall lay. On the ledge above, Berchtesgaden was perched, only known, as yet, for its abbey and its castle and its view over the wide Bavarian lowlands.

But I steered east and reached the banks of the Salzach late in the afternoon. A red, white and black pole barred the road. Inside the customs-house hung the last picture of the Führer. Uniform sleeves were ringed by the last swastika armbands and in a few minutes, beside a barrier striped red and white, an Austrian official was stamping my passport: 24 *January 1934.*

By nightfall I was gazing at the statues and wandering down the baroque colonnades of Salzburg in search of a café. The windows, when I found one, looked out on a fountain adorned by stampeding horses and stalactitic with icicles.

FIVE

The Danube: Seasons and Castles

ONLY glimpses of Salzburg remain: bell-towers, bridges, piazzas, fountains, a dome or two and an impression of cloisters which might all have been flown here by djinns and reassembled as an Italian Renaissance city the wrong side of the Alps.

But I didn't tarry, and for a depressing reason. The evocative smell of hot ski-wax drifted through many of the windows and swarms of people, little older than me and all bound for the mountains, were clumping the streets with skis over their shoulders. They filled the arcades and the cafés and shouted joyfully to each other as though they were already swooping about the high slopes; worse still, some were English. I loved ski-ing and all this made me feel lonely and out of things. So, early next morning, turning my back on the Salzkammergut and the lakes and the beckoning peaks of Styria and the Tyrol, I slipped away; and soon I was plodding north-west and ever further from temptation through the woods of Upper Austria. I slept in a barn near the village of Eigendorf – too small a hamlet for any map – and the next two nights in Frankenburg and Ried. One of them, spent in a loft where all the racks were filled with apples, was sweet-smelling almost to swooning point. Little has stuck from early Austrian days except the charm of these minor mountains.

St Martin, one of Baron Liphart's castles, the earliest of those houses of friends to whom he had written on my behalf, is my first real landmark. To avoid arriving out of the blue, I telephoned before setting out, and learnt that the owner was in Vienna; but he had asked his agent to look after me if I turned up. Graf Arco-Valley, a great favourite of many English people, called 'Nando' (but not by me as we never met*) had been at Oxford or Cambridge a couple of generations earlier. The schloss was shut up, the

---

* Alas! Too late now. He died in the 1960s.

friendly agent told me. But we wandered through its twilit rooms and walked about under the trees in the park. Finally he gave me a feast in the cheerful and pretty inn, urging me to tuck in with the assiduity of a jolly uncle taking a nephew out from school. There were a couple of musicians, a zither-player and a violinist, and everybody sang. He told me at breakfast he had telephoned to the next schloss marked down on the Liphart itin- erary: I would be welcome any time, they had said. (Things were beginning to look up! I would have given anything to know what my kind sponsor in Munich had written. It was a change to have favourable reports circulating.) As a result, after a second cow- shed sojourn near Riedau, I found myself in the corner tower of another castle two evenings later, wallowing in a bath of ancient shape, enclouded by the scent of the cones and the pine-logs that roared like caged lions in the huge copper stove.

The word 'schloss' means any degree of variation between a fortified castle and a baroque palace. This one was a fair sized manor-house. I had felt shy as I ploughed through the snow of the long avenue late that afternoon; quite baselessly. To go by the solicitude of the trio at the stove-side in the drawing-room – the old Count and his wife and their daughter-in-law – I might, once again, have been a schoolboy asked out for a treat, or, better still, a polar explorer on the brink of expiring. 'You must be *famished* after all that walking!' the younger Gräfin said, as a huge tea appeared: she was a beautiful dark-haired Hungarian and she spoke excellent English. 'Yes,' said the elder, with an anxious smile. 'We've been told to feed you up!' Her Husband radiated silent benevolence as yet another silver dish appeared. I spread a third hot croissant with butter and honey and inwardly blessed my benefactor in Munich.

The Count was old and frail. He resembled, a little, Max Beer- bohm in later life, with a touch of Franz Joseph minus the white sidewhiskers. (Next day he wrote a chit to some private gallery in Linz on the back of a visiting card. After his name was printed: K.u.K. *Kämmerer u. Rittmeister i.R.** 'Imperial and Royal

* Ruhestand.

Chamberlain', that is, 'and retired Captain of Horse'. All through Central Europe the initials 'K.u.K.' – *Kaiserlich und Königlich* – were the alliterative epitome of the old Dual Monarchy. Only candidates with sixteen or thirty-two quarterings, I learnt later, were eligible for the symbolic gold key that court chamberlains wore on the back of their full-dress uniforms. But now the Empire and the Kingdom had been dismembered and their thrones were empty; no doors opened to the gold keys, the heralds were dispersed, the regiments disbanded and the horses dead long ago. The engraved words croaked loud of spent glories. Rare then, each of those symbols by now must be one with the translucent red button, the unicorn-embroidered robe and the ruby and jade clasp of a mandarin of the first class at the count of Manchus: '*Finis rerum*, and an end of names and dignities and whatsoever is terrene . . .') I admire his attire, the soft buckskin knee-breeches and gleaming brogues and a grey and green loden jacket with horn buttons and green lapels. These were accompanied out-of-doors by the green felt hat with its curling blackcock's tail-feather which I had seen among a score of walking sticks in the hall. It was in Salzburg that I had first admired these Austrian country clothes. They were similar in kind, but less splendid in detail, to the livery of the footmen who kept bringing in those silver dishes. There was a feeling of Lincoln green about them, woodland elegance that the Count carried off with the ease of a courtier and a cuirassier.

I made myself as tidy as I could after my bath. At dinner the Count, drawing on a well-stored but failing memory, recalled ancient journeys he had made as a young A.D.C., attached to an Archduke who was a passionate shot. Out of affability to me, I think, his reminiscences were all connected with the British Isles. 'Grandes battues' in County Meath were recalled, and almost antediluvian pheasant-stands at Chatsworth and late-Victorian grouse-drives at Dunrobin; house parties of untold magnificence. ' – Und die Herzogin von Sutherland!' he sighed: 'eine Göttin!' A goddess! Ancient balls were conjured up and dinners at Marlborough House; there were discreet hints of half-forgotten scandals; and I saw, in my mind's eye, hansoms bound for assignations, bowling up St James's and turning into a gaslit

Jermyn Street. When the name of a vanished grandee escaped his memory, his wife would prompt him. His mind wandered back and away to the estates of a cousin in Bohemia – 'The Czechs have taken them away now,' he said with another sigh – and a wild boar shoot which had been held there in honour of Edward VII when he was still Prince of Wales: 'Er war scharmant!' I was fascinated by all this. As I listened, the white gloved hand of the Lincoln green footman poured out coffee and placed little silver vermeil-lined goblets beside the Count's cup and mine. Then he filled them with what I thought was schnapps. I'd learnt what to do with that in recent weeks – *or so I thought* – and I was picking it up to tilt it into the coffee when the Count broke off his narrative with a quavering cry as though an arrow from some hidden archer had transfixed him: 'NEIN! NEIN!' he faltered. A pleading, ringed and almost transparent hand was stretched out and the stress of the moment drove him into English: 'No! No! Nononono – !'

I didn't know what had happened. Nor did the others. There was a moment of perplexity. Then, following the Count's troubled glance, all our eyes alighted simultaneously on the little poised silver goblet in my hand. Then both the Countesses, looking from the torment on the Count's face to the astonishment on mine, dissolved in saving laughter, which, as I put the goblet back on the table, spread to me and finally cleared the distress from the Count's features too, and replaced it with a worried smile. His anxiety had been for *my* sake, he said apologetically. The liquid wasn't schnapps at all, but incomparable nectar – the last of a bottle of a liqueur distilled from Tokay grapes and an elixir of fabulous rarity and age. When we had recovered I felt glad that this marvellous drink had been rescued, above all for the Count's sake – it was too late a stage in life for any more shocks – and ashamed of my pot-house ways; but they were too kind-hearted for the feeling to last long.

The Count retired early, kissing first the hands and then the cheeks of his wife and daughter-in-law. When he said good night to me, his hand felt as light as a leaf. With his free hand he gave my forearm a friendly pat and faded away down a lamp-lit grove of antlers. Then the elder Gräfin, who had put on spectacles and spread her needlework on her lap, said, 'Now come and tell us all about your travels.' So I did my best.

At this dead time of the year, when agriculture had come to a halt, most of the dwellers in these castles were dispersed until harvest or shooting or school holidays should muster them again. When I think of these havens, later castles at other seasons intrude their memories and the resulting confusion of unlabelled lantern-slides composes a kind of archetypal schloss, of which each separate building becomes a variation.

An archetypal schloss ... At once, in my mind's eye, an angular relic of the Dark Ages confronts the wind on top of a crag. More slowly, a second vision begins to cohere. Staircases entwine. Allegorical ceilings unfold. Conch-blowing tritons, at the heart of radiating vistas of clipped hornbeam, shoot plumes of water at the sky. Both visions are true. But finally, a third category emerges: a fair-sized country house, that is, which combines the castle-principle with a touch of the monastery and the farm. It is usually beautiful and always pleasing and sometimes age or venerability demand sterner epithets. A rustic baroque, even if it is only a later superimposition on a much older core, is the presiding style. There are shingle roofs, massive walls whitewashed or mottled with lichen and rectangular and cylindrical towers capped with pyramids or cones or with wasp-waisted cupolas of red or grey tiles. Cavernous gateways breach the arcades of thick and flattened arches. There is a chapel and stables and a coachhouse full of obsolete carriages; barns and waggons and sledges and byres and a smithy; then fields and hayricks and woods. Indoors, a pattern of flagstones rings underfoot, or the lighter resonance of polished wood. The spans of elliptical and snow-white cross-vaults spring low in the corners of the rooms and between them flared embrasures taper to tall double windows that are tight shut and ice-flowered in winter, with bolsters between them to foil draughts. In summer the tilt of the slatted shutters guides the glance downwards to leaf-shadows on cobblestones and a battered fountain or a sundial. The pockmarked statues are curdled with lichen. Scythes swish through deep hayfields. There is an interlock of orchards and slanting meadows; and beyond them, cattle and woods and a

herd of deer that lift all their antlers simultaneously at the sound
of a footfall.

As I shut my eyes and explore, looking-glasses throw back the
faded reflections: the corroborative detail assembles fast. In
portraits,* the solemn seventeenth-century magnates in lace
collars and black breastplates are out-numbered by descendants in
Addisonian periwigs and powder. Later, by slender figures romantically moustached, and dressed in white uniforms that conjure up
pictures of Sarah Bernhardt in *l'Aiglon*. Lancers' torsoes taper into
their sashes like bobbins. Red and white ribbons cross their breasts
and sometimes the Golden Fleece sprouts from those high star-
crusted collars. Hands rest on the hilt of a sabre looped with a
double-headed-eagle sabretache.† Others nurse a plumed shako, a
dragoon's helmet or an uhlan's czapka with a square top like a
mortar-board and tufted with a tall aigrette. In later pictures, pale
blue replaces these snowy regimentals, in melancholy homage to
the progress in firearms and marksmanship since the battle of
Königgrätz. The passion for the chase breaks out over the walls
and stags' antlers spread their points among the panoplies. There
are elks' horns from the frontiers of Poland and Lithuania, bears
from the Carpathians, the tushes of wild boars twisting up like
moustaches, chamois from the Tyrol and bustards, capercailzies
and blackcock; along every available inch of the passages, the twin
prongs of roe deer, calligraphically inscribed with a faded date and
the venue, multiply forever. A respectable assembly of books fills
the library. There is a missal or two in the hall, the *Wiener Sal-
onblatt* and *Vogue* lie anachronistically about the drawing-room
and perhaps a poetical grandson or great-niece has left a pocket-
volume of *Hyperion* or the *Duino Elegies* on a window-sill. Minia-
tures and silhouettes constellate the spaces between the portraits
and the looking-glass. Heraldic details abound: crowns or

---

* For all their charm, few of these portraits, except in castles of
great splendour, are at all well painted.

† By a minor freak of history, the only uniforms where these vanished insignia survive are those of a regiment of the British Army:
Franz Josef was honorary colonel-in-chief of the Queen's Dragoon
Guards. They commemorate him still with the Habsburg double-eagle
cap badge and the Radetzky March.

circlets with nine, seven or five pearls celebrate the owner's rank and stamp his possessions as plentifully as brands on a ranch. On a handy shelf the small gilt volumes of the *Almanach de Gotha*, a different colour for each degree, fall open automatically, like the Baronetage in the hands of Sir Walter Elliot of Kellynch Hall, at the castellan's own family. Biedermeier tables are crowded with photographs. Scores of summers have faded the green, the royal blue, the canary and the claret-coloured velvet of their frames. Between his embossed crown and a signature turned yellow with age, Franz Joseph presides like an *agathos daimon*. The Empress, goddess-like among a photographer's cardboard turrets, gazes into the distance with her hand on the head of an enormous deer-hound. Sewn into her habit, she clears prodigious fences; or with a swan-like turn of her throat, she looks over her bare shoulder under piled-up tiers of thick plaits or cascading coils that are sprinkled with diamond stars.

The libraries of all these castles contained Meyer's *Kon-versations-lexikon*. As soon as I decently could, I would beg to be let loose among its many volumes, with the plea that questions had cropped up on the road that it was a torment to leave un-solved. This often caused surprise, always pleasure: at the least, it solved the problem of entertainment, and sometimes it stirred a kindred curiosity, leading to searches in the library through dense columns of Gothic type. *Meyer* was sometimes backed up by the *Larousse XXème Siècle* or the *Encyclopaedia Britannica*; once, miraculously, in Transylvania, and once, later on, in Moldavia, all three were present. Atlases, maps and picture books were loaded into one's arms at bedtime.

Shaded paraffin lamps, I think, not electricity, light up a few of these rooms after dark. I'm sure candles lit the music when I turned over for someone at the piano – I can see the glitter of their flames in the removed rings at the end of the keyboard as clearly as I can hear the lieder of Schubert and Strauss and Hugo Wolf, and *Der Erlkönig* at last. Music played a leading part in all these households. The sound of practising winds along passages, sheet music and bound scores scatter the furniture. The variously shaped instrument cases gathering dust in the attics bear witness to palmier days when the family and its staff and its guests would

assemble for symphonies. Now and then, the pipes of an organ
cluster in the hall, and a gilt harp gleams in a corner of the library
with all its strings intact.

After I had said good night and made my way book-laden along
an antlered corridor and up a stone spiral to my room, it was hard
to believe I had been sleeping in a byre the night before. There is
much to recommend moving straight from straw to a four-poster,
and then back again. Cocooned in smooth linen and lulled by the
smell of logs and beeswax and lavender, I nevertheless stayed
awake for hours, revelling in all these delights and contrasting
them with joy to the now-familiar charms of cow-sheds and hay-
lofts and barns. The feeling would still be there when I woke up
next morning and looked down from the window.

The last sunrise of January was sliding across a lawn, catching
the statues of Vertumnus and Pales and finally Pomona at the far
end and stretching their thin and powdery shadows on the untouched snow. Rooky woods feathered the sky-line and there was
a feeling in the air that the Danube was not far.

Castles were seldom out of sight. Clustering on the edge of
country towns, recumbent with sleepy baroque grace on wooded
ledges or beetling above the tree tops, they loomed from afar. One
is aware of their presence all the time, and when the traveller steps
over the border of a new sphere, he feels like Puss-in-Boots when
the peasants tell him that the distant chateau and the pastures
and the mills and the barns belong to the Marquis of Carabas. A
new name impinges. For a stretch it is Coreth or Harrach or Traun
or Ledebur or Trautmannsdorff or Seilern; then it dies away and
gives place to another. Perhaps I struck lucky; for when, on the
road or during halts at an inn, the theme of the local castle-dwellers cropped up, as they invariably did, there were no Cobbett-like
diatribes. The villagers would speak of the local castellan and his
family in the possessive tones they might have used for a font or a
roodscreen of great antiquity in the parish church. Feelings were
often warmer than this; and when bad luck, gambling, extravagance or even total imbecility had sent a local dynasty into decline, this eclipse of a familiar landmark was bewailed as yet
another symptom of dissolution.

This hovering Ichabod feeling was everywhere epitomized by old photographs of Franz Josef, battered and faded but cherished; rather strangely, perhaps. His reign had been a succession of private tragedies and public though peripheral erosion. Every few decades some irredentist-loosened fragment of the Empire was detached or – occasionally and worse still – rashly annexed. But these regions were far away at the Empire's fringes, their inhabitants were foreign, they spoke different languages, and life at the heart of the Empire was still serene and cheerful enough to muffle these shocks and omens. After all, most of that huge assembly of countries, slowly and peacefully acquired through centuries of brilliant dynastic marriages – 'Bella gerunt alii; tu, felix Austria, nubes!' – was still intact; and until 1919 – when the centrifugal break-up spared only the Austrian heartlands – a buoyant douceur de vivre had pervaded the whole of life. Or so it appeared to them now, and many seemed to look back to those times with the longing of the Virgilian farmers and shepherds in Latium when they remembered the kind reign of Saturn.

At Eferding, where I stayed the night, the baroque palace that filled one side of the central square belonged to a descendant of Rüdiger von Starhemberg, the great defender of Vienna in its second siege by the Turks. The name was once more on everyone's lips, owing to the present Prince Starhemberg's role as commander of the Heimwehr: a Home Guard or militia, I was told, ready to foil any attempted seizure of power by either of the political extremes. I had seen columns of this corps on country roads, dressed in grey uniforms and semi-military ski-caps, shouldering raw-hide knapsacks with the brindled and piebald marking turned outwards. Rather mild they had seemed, to eyes and ears attuned to the fiercer tempo and the stamping and barking the other side of the German border; but they did not escape the accusation of fascism by one half of their opponents. After Dr Dollfuss, Starhemberg's picture was the one most often seen in public places: which – again compared to Germany – was not much. They showed a tall, handsome young man with a high-bridged nose and a rather weak chin.

*

The scene was beginning to change. My path followed a frozen woodland stream into a region where rushes and waterweed and marsh vegetation and brambles and shrubs were as densely entangled as a primeval forest. Opening on expanses of feathered ice, it was like a mangrove swamp in the Arctic circle. Encased in ice and snow, every twig sparkled. Frost had turned the rushes into palisades of brittle rods and the thickets were loaded with icicles and frozen rainbow-shooting drops. Of birds, I could only see the usual crows and rooks and magpies, but the snow was arrowed with forked prints. It must have teemed with water-fowl at a different time of year and with fish too. Nets were looped stiffly in the branches and a flat-bottomed boat, three quarters sunk, was frozen in for the winter. It was a white, hushed region under a spell of catalepsy.

The hush was broken by a succession of claps from a lagoon. A heron was slowly hoisting itself off the ice; then a spiral of slower wingbeats lifted it to the top of a Lombardy poplar that was dark with a multitude of dishevelled nests. Its mate, looking enormous as it paced a white pool, cumbrously followed it; and a minute later, I could see their beaks projecting side by side. They were the only ones there, wintering it out in the nearly-empty heronry. The other nests would fill up towards the close of the tadpole season.

It was a marvellous place; an unusual place; I couldn't quite make it out – half mere, half frozen jungle. It finished at a bank where a row of poplars was interspersed with aspen and birch and willow among blackberry-thickets and hazel. On the other side of this barrier the sky suddenly widened and a great volume of water was flowing dark and fast. In midstream, cloudy with the hemispherical ghosts of weeping-willows, an island divided the rush of the current. There was an answering line of ice on the other bank, then reeds and woods and a fluctuation of timbered mountain.

This second meeting with the Danube had taken me unawares; I had reached it half a day sooner than I thought! As it streamed through those wooded and snowbound ranges the river made an overpowering impression of urgency and force.

My map, when I dug it out, said that the mountains opposite were part of the Bohemian Forest. They had followed the north

bank ever since the river had entered Austria a mile or two east of
Passau, about thirty miles upstream.

'In cold weather like this,' said the innkeeper of a Gastwirtschaft further down, 'I recommend Himbeergeist.' I obeyed
and it was a lightning conversion. Spirit of raspberries, or their
ghost – this crystalline distillation, twinkling and ice-cold in its
misty goblet, looked as though it were homeopathically in league
with the weather. Sipped or swallowed, it went shuddering
through its new home and branched out in patterns – or so it
seemed after a second glass – like the ice-ferns that covered the
window panes, but radiating warmth and happiness instead of
cold, and carrying a ghostly message of comfort to the uttermost
fimbria. Fierce winters give birth to their antidotes: Kümmel,
Vodka, Aquavit, Danziger Goldwasser. Oh for a thimble full of
the cold north! Fiery-frosty potions, sequin-flashers, rife with
spangles to spark fuses in the bloodstream, revive fainting limbs,
and send travellers rocketing on through snow and ice. White fire,
red cheek, heat me and speed me. This discovery cast a glow over
the approach of Linz. A few miles on, round a loop of river, the
city appeared. It was a vision of domes and belfries gathered under
a stern fortress and linked by bridges to a smaller town at the foot
of a mountain on the other bank.

When I got to the fine sweeping piazza in the middle of the
city I chose a promising-looking coffee house, kicked off the snow,
went in and ordered two boiled eggs. *Eier im Glas!* It was my latest
passion. The delight of tapping the eggs all over with a bone
spoon before removing the fragmented shell and sliding the fragile
contents into a tumbler intact, then a slice of butter . . . travellers'
joys. I had chosen more luckily than I knew; for as well as staying
me with eggs, the young proprietor and his wife put me up for
two nights in their flat over the shop. Better still, next day being
Sunday, they lent me some boots and took me ski-ing. The whole
of Linz was picnicking on the Pöstlingsberg – the mountain that
rose from the opposite bank – and then swirling down its icy and
rutted slopes. Starting without any practice, I was soon battered
black and blue, but the sorrows of Salzburg were exorcized.

I hobbled round Linz by twilight. Pargeted façades rose up,
painted chocolate, green, purple, cream and blue. They were
adorned with medallions in high relief and the stone and plaster
scroll-work gave them a feeling of motion and flow. Casemented
half-hexagons jutted from the first storeys, and windowed three-
quarter-cylinders blunted the corners, both of them soaring to the
line of the eaves where they shelved into wasp-waists and re-
expanded spherically to the same circumference, forming buoyant cupolas and globes; and domes and pinnacles and obelisks
joined these decorative onions along the city's skyline. At ground-
level, spiral commemorative columns rose twirling from the flagstones of the piazzas and hoisted radiating, monstrance-like,
counter-Reformation bursts of gold spikes in mid-air. Except for
the fierce keep on the rock, the entire town was built for pleasure
and splendour. Beauty, space and amenity lay all about. In the
evening Hans and Frieda, my hosts, took me to a party in an inn
and next morning I set off down the Danube.

But not immediately. On their suggestion, I took a tram a few
miles off my track and then a bus, to the Abbey of St Florian. The
great baroque convent of Augustinian Canons stood among low
hills, and the branches of the thousands of apple trees all round it
were crusted with lichen and bright with rime. The buildings, the
treasures and the marvellous library, all – excepting the pictures –
have merged in a universal and coruscating oblivion. Just before
leaving, I stood for a moment in front of the twin belfries with a
friendly Canon. Following his pointing forefinger, we gazed along
a succession of freak gaps in the mountains. As the crow flies, this
trough runs south-west for over a hundred and sixty miles, clean
across Upper Austria to the northern marches of the Tyrol and
Upper Bavaria to a point where the peak of the Zugspitze just
discernibly floats, half-ghostly and half-gleaming.

When I turned my back on these ranges, the pictures indoors
still crowded my mind. They unloosed vague broodings on how
large a part geography and hazard play in one's knowledge and
one's ignorance of painting.

It had struck me in Holland that an average non-expert, gallery-sauntering inhabitant of the British Isles would know the names, and a little of the work, of scores of Dutch, Flemish and Italian painters and of twenty Frenchmen at the very least. Equally certainly, of half a dozen Spaniards: all thanks to geography, religion, the Grand Tour and the vagaries of fashion. But his total – mine, that is – for the entire German-speaking world is three: Holbein; Dürer; and, palely loitering, Cranach. Holbein, because he seems almost English, and Dürer because he is the sort of genius one can't help knowing about, an original and universal phenomenon, well up on the slope leading to the Da Vinci class. Recent visits to a few German galleries, especially in Munich, had now given more substance to Cranach and added Altdorfer and Grünewald to this list.

Though these painters are unlike each other, they do have some important things in common. They all come from southern Germany. They were all born in the last forty years of the fifteenth century. All of them were active in the early decades of the sixteenth, first under the Emperor Maximilian – 'the Last of the Knights', a belated survivor of the Middle Ages – and then under his half-Spanish, High Renaissance grandson and successor, Charles V. The whole of German painting seems to crowd into this sixty years' span: a sudden abundance, with nothing but medieval workshops to herald it and no real follow-up. It was Germany's moment, brought about by the Renaissance in Italy and by the spread of humanist studies at home and stimulated and tormented by the rise of Protestantism. Luther's active life fits the time-span almost to a second; and all five painters finished on the Protestant side. (Grünewald, the oldest, was deeply troubled and finally reduced to inaction. Holbein, the youngest, took things in his stride. It is hard to think of them as contemporaries but their lives overlapped for forty years.) Two main channels of approach and flight linked south Germany with the outside world. The more natural one followed the Rhine to Flanders and led straight to the studios of Brussels and Bruges and Ghent and Antwerp. The other crossed the Alps through the Brenner Pass and followed the Adige to Verona, where an easy path unwound to Mantua, Padua and Venice. Fewer took the second way but it was the more decisive in the end. It was a fruitful polarity and German painting was spinning, as it were, on a Van der Weyden–Mantegna axis.

As I walked along the Danube, I was traversing, without knowing it, an important minor sub-division of art history. 'The
Danube School', an arbitrary term which is often enclosed in in-
verted commas, covers exactly the period we have been talking
about and it embraces the Danube basin from Regensburg to
Vienna, taking in Bohemia to the north as far as Prague, and to
the south the slopes of the Alps from the Tyrol to Lower Austria.
Dürer and Holbein, although they are from the near-Danubian
towns of Nuremberg and Augsburg, are not included: the one is
too universal, the other, perhaps, too sophisticated or a decade or so
too late. Grünewald, geographically, is a fraction too far west and
they probably need him for an equally arbitrary Rhenish School.
Otherwise, he would fit in admirably. This leaves Cranach and
Altdorfer: Danubian stars of the first magnitude among a swarm
of lesser-known regional masters.

On the evidence I encountered then, I hated Cranach more with
each new picture. Those pale-haired, equivocal minxes, posturing
in muslin against the dark, were eerie and uncongenial enough;
but, in juxtaposition with the schadenfreude of his martyrdoms,
they become deeply sinister; and this thought flowed on directly
to the stark detail of the minor masters of the Danube School and
perhaps, if one followed it through, to the whole disturbing theme
of realism in Germany.

Some of these Danube School paintings are wonderful. Others
are either moving or touching or likeable and, to a stranger like
me, they had an immediate appeal which had no connection with
their technical Renaissance advances, about which I knew
nothing. Indeed, the aspect that took my fancy was precisely the
medieval and the Teutonic spirit that completely changed the Renaissance atmosphere of these pictures: the emerald green of the
sward, that is, the sap green of the woods, the dark conifer forests
and bosky spurs of Jurassic limestone; the backgrounds full of
snowy spikes – distant glimpses, without a doubt, of the Gross-
glockner, the Reifhorn, the Zugspitze and the Wildspitze. This is
the scenery through which the flight into Egypt, the journey of
the Magi and the footpaths to Cana and Bethany uncoil! A barn
with leaky thatch shelters the Nativity in an Alpine glade. It is

among fir-cones and edelweiss and gentians that the Transfigurations, Temptations, Crucifixions and Resurrections take place. The actors in a picture by Wolf Huber are Swabian peasant girls, bewildered gaffers with tangled beards, goodies with dumpling cheeks, crab-apple crones, marvelling ploughboys and puzzled woodmen – a cast of Danube rustics in fact, reinforced, in the wings, by a whole bumpkin throng. The scenes they present have enormous charm. They are not naïve pictures, very far from it; but the balance between rusticity and sophistication is such that to contemplate one of them is to sit on a log under a northern welkin while the incidents of scripture are wonderingly and urgently whispered in one's ear. They affect one like folk-tales in thick Swabian or in Tyrolese or Bavarian or Upper Austrian dialect. Everything rustic and simple in these pictures is wonderfully real; a convincing earthiness reigns side by side with a most melting piety. But, unless the woods and the undergrowth are goblin country, there is little hint of a spiritual or supernatural feeling in these happenings – except in a different and an adverse sense. For example, in some of these canvasses and panels the laws of gravity seem to exert an unnaturally powerful pull. The angels, unlike their soaring congeners in Italy or Flanders, are poor flyers and ill-equipped for staying up long. The severe Bürgermeister's features of the Holy Child have the ferocity, sometimes, of a snake-strangling infant Hercules. He looks heavier than most mortal babies. Once these symptoms have been observed, everything else begins to go wrong, and in a way that is rather hard to define. Complexions become pasty and suet-like, eyes narrow to knowing and spiteful slits and sparks of madness kindle. The middles of faces are simultaneously flaccid and clenched, as though a bad diet had prematurely rotted away every tooth in their heads, and often, for no clear reason, features start sliding out of shape. Noses fall askew, eyes grow bleary and mouths hang open like those of snowmen or village idiots. There is something enigmatic and unexplained about this spreading collapse. It has no bearing on the holiness or the villainy of the character affected and, clearly, nothing to do with technical capacity. It is as though a toxin of instability and dissolution had crept into the painter's brain.

But, when the theme shifts from pastoral scenes to martyrdoms, their intentions become baffling beyond all conjecture. These pictures are the opposite of their equivalent Byzantine scenes. There the executioner and his victim wear an identical expression of benign aloofness, and the headsman, as an artisan of beatitude flourishing a sword-shaped key to salvation, has an equal claim on our approval. Italians may not attempt this detachment in their martyrdoms, but feelings for sacredness and dignity in the painter's mood engage both the striker and the struck in a ceremonial choreography of grandeur that keeps horror at a distance.

Not here. Meaty, unshaven louts with breastplates crooked, hanging shirt-tails and codpieces half-undone have just reeled out of the Hofbräuhaus, as it were, reeking of beer and sauerkraut and bent on beating someone insensible. A victim is found and they fall on him. Leering and winking with bared teeth and lolling tongues, they are soon sweating with exertion. These ostlers, butchers, barrel-makers, and apprentices, and Landsknechts in moulting frippery are expert limb-twisters, lamers, stoners, floggers, unsocketers and beheaders to a man, deft with their bright tools and rejoicing at their task. The painters' windows must have looked out on scaffolds where the wheel, the block and the gallows drew frequent crowds. Certain details, which are more rare in other painters, recur with great regularity here. Four burly tormentors, with their crossed staves bending under their weight, force an enormous crown of thorns on their victim's head and a fifth batters it home with a three-legged stool. When another prepares him for scourging, he places a boot for purchase in the small of the victim's back and hauls on the bound wrists till his veins project. The heavy birch-rods need both hands to wield them and broken twigs and smashed scourges soon litter the floor. At first the victim's body looks flea-bitten. It is spotted later on, like an ocelot's, with hundreds of embedded thorns. At last, after a score of indignities, the moribund carcass is nailed in place and hoisted aloft between two pot-bellied felons whose legs are snapped askew like bleeding sticks. The last touch of squalor is the cross itself. Ragged-ended and roughly barked lengths of fir and silver-birch have been so clumsily botched together that they bend under the weight of the victim as though about to collapse, and the special law of gravity, tearing the nail-holes wider, dislocates the fingers and expands them like a spider's legs. Wounds fester, bones break through the flesh and the grey lips, wrinkling concentrically round a tooth-set hole, gape in a cringing spasm of pain. The body, mangled, dishonoured and lynched, twists in *rigor mortis*. It hangs, as Huysmans says in his description of Grünewald's altar-piece in Colmar, 'comme un bandit, comme un chien'. The wounds turn blue, there is a hint of gangrene and putrefaction in the air.

Yet somehow, and most contradictorily, Grünewald escapes the category I have in mind. The thorn-speckled carcass on the cross is part of an old formula; the horror is extreme; but, thanks to the harrowing poignancy of the attendant mourners and some exempting streak of genius, it is a feeling of drama and tragedy that has the last word,* removing it – for me, that is – to the atmosphere and mood of 'Woofully araid', the extraordinary poem on the Passion by his exact English contemporary, Skelton.†

Critics and apologists blame these cruel scenes on the infectious savagery of the Peasants' War of 1523. This shattering sequel to the religious conflict left few southern Germans untouched. Even if some of these pictures were painted earlier – and the Isenheim altarpiece, for one, antedates it by a decade – the cruel temper of the times may well have influenced contemporary painting. But,

---

* There are, too, mystical and medical causes, abstruse but valid, for the erupting and purulent Isenheim details. They were expressly stipulated by the Antonite monks in their directions to the painter. The altarpiece was destined for their Isenheim hospital which was dedicated to the cure of diseases of the skin and the blood, plague, epilepsy and ergotism, and the details are depicted for a strange reason. Contemplation of these painted symbols by the patients comprised the initial stage of their healing. It was a religious act in which the promise of miraculous healing was held to reside.

† The refrain, with the spelling modernised, is:

> Woefully arrayed,
> My blood, man,
> For thee ran,
> It may not be nayed;
> My body blue and wan,
> Woefully arrayed.

even if it did, the results are unusual and ambiguous: the horrors of the Thirty Years and Peninsula Wars affected Callot and Goya in a way that leaves no doubt about their attitude to those wars or the purpose of their work. What, then, are these? Grim heirlooms from the Dark Ages, unenlightened by the Renaissance but animated by its techniques, bursting out under savage stimuli? Perhaps. But religious painting is, *ipso facto*, didactic. What do these pictures enjoin? It is impossible to say. At Byzantium, an impartial grace exalted both the virtuous and the wicked and joined their hands in abstraction. Here, an opposite agency is at work. Good and evil, kneaded from the same yeastless dough, are united in squalor until both become equally base; and in this equality in abjection, horror chases pity away. Dignity and tragedy take wing together, and one gazes in perplexity. Are saints being martyred or felons slowly dispatched? On whose side is the painter? No answer comes.

Perhaps the mood was inescapable. There are certainly traces of it, much reduced, in a few of Altdorfer's pictures. But he outshines his fellow-Danubians like a lyre-bird among carrion-crows. He was from Regensburg. I hadn't been there yet – I missed it when I turned south at Ulm – but I have seen it since, and it explains much. Here, at the northernmost point of the river, a hundred and thirty miles upstream from the Abbey of St Florian, the ancient stronghold of Ratisbon spans the Danube with a bridge that rivals all the great bridges of the Middle Ages. Those battlements and steeples, wrapped in myth, dominate one of the most complete and convincing medieval cities of the world. Anyone who has wandered in these streets can understand why the holy pastorals which his colleagues turned into dialect folk-tales, shift, under his hand, into the mood and the scenery of legends. The episodes of scripture – which are nowhere more splendidly manifest than in his great altarpiece at St Florian's – are suddenly clothed in the magic and the glamour of fairy stories; fairy stories, moreover, where the Mantua–Antwerp axis, uncoiling brilliant strands into the fabric, has been most potently spinning. Under the gothic interlock of cold whites and greys that canopy hallowed scenes in Flanders, the Biblical characters, clad in robes of lilac and mulberry and lemon and the shrill sulphur hue Mantegna loved, evolve and posture with convincing Renaissance splendour. Pontius Pilate – velvet-clad, mantled in dark sapphire, tasselled and collared like an Elector and turbaned like a Caliph – twists his sprinkled hands betwen ewer and salver under a magnificent baldaquin of scumbled gold. Through the lancets and the cinquefoils and beyond the diamond panes, the fluted rocks ascend and the woods and cliffs and cloud-banks of Gethsemane frame a luminous and incandescent sunset that presages Patinir. Though the centurions are knights in dark armour, no mortal smith ever wrought those helmet-wings and metal flourishes and knee-flutes and elbow-fans, even on the anvils of Augsburg and Milan in Maximilian's reign. It is the fabulous harness that flashed later on every pre-Raphaelite Grail-seeker and greaved and gauntleted the paladins in the Coloured Fairy Books. Shifting from Divinity to sacred fable, the same ambience of magic isolates lonely knights among millions of leaves and confronts St Eustace and the stag with its antlered crucifix in a forest of hazards and spells.

He is very various. Tufted with spurge and dockweed, a tumble-down cowshed flickers strangely across the meadows with the grisaille highlights of the Nativity. Transparent Babylonian palaces pile capricious tiers of arcaded galleries among shoals of cloud. Palaces, moreover, which are elaborated with the almost-completely mastered secrets of perspective which Dürer had brought back from Bologna and Venice. Intoxicating times! It must have been as though Dürer, from the tallest tower in Nuremberg, had floated an invisible geometry over Franconia: a geometry which webbed the air with dotted lines, gridded mountainous duchies, soared across Swabia and Austria and Saxony in chessboard vistas and carelessly loosed off volleys of parallels towards the sovereign bishoprics of the Rhine.*

I didn't know it then but some of his country-pictures – wilder-

---

* But his perspective was still short of solution! The ends of all those volleys pepper the target area with near-misses, instead of converging on a single bull's eye, as, half a century before, Brunelleschi had discovered and Alberti had written that they should. The northward journey of ideas was beset with delays.

nesses with no scriptural episode, nothing human, not even a
tumbling Icarus to justify their existence – are the first pure landscape paintings in Europe. I only understood on a journey years
later how faithfully his landscape echoes the actual Danube. It
was his amazing *Alexanderschlacht* – Alexander's victory over
Darius at Issus – that pointed the way: I was looking upstream
from Dürnstein (on that later journey) with my mind full of the
great picture I had been recently gazing at, when an apocalyptic
flash revealed that the painted stretch of water in the picture was
no Asian river, not even the Granicus. It was the valley of the
Danube in the throes of one of its hundreds of battles. It must
have been. But, on this first visit, how could I have realized it? The
battle in the painted canyon is fought out under a lurid October
sunset and the rival armies, like windswept cornfields bristling
with lances and poppied with banners, collide in an autumnal
light. Whereas the battlefield on my first encounter was dulled
with snow, with all contours muffled and fanfares hushed.

The link between journeys and painting, especially this sort of
journey, is very close. There was plenty to think about as I made
my way through the snow-bound monastic orchards; and it occurred to me, in the silent fields that followed, and for the hun-
dredth time since my landing in Holland, that so far one painter
had presided over every stage of this *Winterreise*. When no buildings were in sight, I was back in the Dark Ages. But the moment a
farmhouse or a village impinged, I was in the world of Peter Brueghel. The white flakes falling beside the Waal – or the Rhine or
the Neckar or the Danube – and the zigzag gables and the muffled
roofs, were all his. The icicles, too, and the trampled snow, the logs
piled on the sledges and the peasants stooped double under loads of
faggots. When children with woollen hoods and satchels burst out
of a village school with a sudden scamper of miniature clogs, I
knew in advance that in a moment they would be flapping their
arms and blowing on mittened fingers and clearing a space to beat
a top in, or galloping down a lane to slide on the nearest brook,
with everyone – children, grown-ups, cattle and dogs – moving
about in the wake of their own cloudy breath. When the wintry
light crept dimly from slits close to the horizon or an orange sun

was setting through the branches of a frozen osier-bed, the identity was complete.

I headed north-east, treading downhill through the snow, and each step sank deeper. Rooks crowded the trees and the fields below were white and grey parallelograms bordered by many willows. Streams crossed them under lids of ice to join a slatey loop of the river; and the hushed and muffled scenery was the background of Brueghel's *Hunters in the Snow*. Only the hunters themselves were missing, with their spears and their curly-tailed dogs.

I crossed the river to the lights of Mauthausen by a massive and ancient bridge. A tall fifteenth-century castle thrust out into the river and, under its walls, Hans and Frieda were on the quay, true to the vaguest of rendezvous; and I realized, as we waved to each other from afar, that another cheerful evening lay ahead.

A foothill path next day. The river Enns, which I had crossed by twilight, came winding out of its valley and into the Danube, where it turned downstream to plait a long pale green strand of clear mountain water into the dun-coloured flux. I fetched up at Perg, which lies a few miles from the northern shore. The river, flooding the frozen fields, had been wandering in a tangle of deviant and rejoining streams; at Ardagger, the mountains closed in again. Each time this happened, solemnity invaded.

I slept in the village of Grein that night, just upstream from a wooded and many-legended island. Old perils haunt these defiles. The name itself is thought to be onomatopoeia for the cry of a sailor drowning in one of the whirlpools, for the rapids and reefs of this stretch of the Danube smashed up shipping for centuries. Sailors who fell overboard were allowed to drown: they were looked upon as propitiatory offerings to some Celtic or Teutonic god still surviving in secret from both pre-Roman and pre-Christian times. The Romans, before confronting this menacing reach, threw coins into the stream to placate the river-god Danubius; and later travellers took the sacrament before making the passage. Maria Theresa's engineers made the journey safer, but the hidden spikes were never completely destroyed till the 1890s. Until then everything hung on the pilot's skill and to some degree it still does; the creases and ruffles turning into sudden cartwheel-twirls amidstream bear witness to the commotion below. To outwit these hazards, vessels were lashed together like catamarans and steadied by hawsers from the shore. Those travelling upstream were towed by teams of horses and oxen – twenty, thirty and sometimes fifty strong – and escorted by troops of pikemen, to keep robbers at bay. The battlements of Werfenstein, whose castellans lived by wrecking and by plunder, beetle greedily over the rapids: but Barbarossa's army, heading for the Third Crusade, was too numerous to tackle. The castle-dwellers gazed through the arrow-slits and gnawed their knuckles with frustration as the Crusaders trudged downstream.

The Danube, particularly in this deep gorge, seemed far wilder than the Rhine and much lonelier. How scarce was the river traffic by comparison! Perhaps the fear of ice-jams kept boats at anchor. I could walk for hours without hearing a siren. At rare intervals a string of barges, usually from one of the Balkan Kingdoms, would toil upstream with a cargo of wheat. After delivering their freight and loading up with planks or paving stones, they would glide downstream again with the current. These cargoes were quarried and felled from the banks. Huge horseshoe-cavities were blasted out of the cliffs, and the mountains, from the water's edge to their summits, were a never-ending stand of timber. Deep in snow, the nearly perpendicular rides sundered the forests in long white stripes that were scattered with thousands of felled tree-trunks like the contents of spilled match-boxes. Smaller trunks were cut and stacked in clearings and I could hear the sound of the felling and the voices of the woodmen long before I saw them. From the riverside, every mile or so, rose the zing of a circular saw and the echo of planks falling where cloudy ghosts covered in sawdust were dismembering sledge-load after sledge-load of forest giants.

The only other men in these woods were foresters: loden-clad figures in clouted boots who live among deer and squirrels and badgers and polecats. One of them, every now and then, with a gun in the crook of his arm and ice on his whiskers and his eyebrows and a pipe with a lidded china bowl, would materialize

among the trees like a vision of Jack Frost. Sometimes we would
keep each other company for a mile or two while Brueghel dogs
trotted alertly ahead. There was plenty of game in these mountains; the cloven slots I noticed in the snow were the prints of
roedeer, as I had thought, and once or twice I caught brief glimpses
of them, standing at gaze for a moment, then bounding for cover
with a scattering of snow from the low branches. But Styria and
the Tyrol, the gamekeepers all agreed, those were the places! I
learnt that when a young hunter stalks and lays low his first stag,
his Jäger marks the occasion with a sort of woodland blooding
that sounds so hoarily ancient and redolent of feudal forest law –
or the defiance of it – that the little ceremony has stuck in my
mind ever since. The Jäger breaks off a branch and strikes the
novice three times across the shoulders, quite hard, saying as he
does so, a line for each swish:

> Eins für den Herrn,
> Eins für den Knecht,
> Eins für das alte Weidmannsrecht!*

Massed shadows, tilting down from the sierras, filled the bottom
of the canyon. Here the Danube followed a winding corridor
which expanded without warning to giant circular ballrooms and
closed again just as abruptly; and for leagues on end this widening
and shrinking ravine was empty of all but a cottage and a barn or
two and a scattering of castles and lonely towers and hermitages,
all crumbling to fragments. They broke through the forest mass,
disintegrating on vertiginous spikes of rock high overhead. As
I climbed the hill-path, the ruins fell level and then dropped
below and the mountains opposite changed from a wall of
branches into a maze of moraines and clefts and buttresses with a
ripple of meadows and solitary hamlets along their crests, all of
them invisible till now and basking in the sunlight which was
denied the lower world. Increasing height laid bare new reaches of
the river like an ever-lengthening chain of lakes, and for those rare
stretches where the valley ran east and west, the sunrise and the
sunset lay reflected and still and an illusion lifted each lake a step

---

* 'One for the lord, one for the serf, one for the ancient woodman's
right.'

higher than its predecessor until they formed gleaming staircases climbing in either direction; and at last the intervening headlands lost touch with the other shore and the watery stairs, now far below, cohered in a single liquid serpent.

At first, only a saw or an axe or the bang of a gun broke the silence of these forests. Soon other sounds would impinge: snow sliding from a branch, a loose rock starting a small avalanche, an occasional barge sending its siren ricochetting from cliff to cliff. Hidden streams, hardly noticed at first, were seldom out of ear-shot; but the waterfalls, though they were visible for miles, seemed inaudible until I was on them. I could see them cataracting from ledge to ledge, dividing and joining again, vanishing under the trees and dropping in long parabolas to the river; and all in silence, with seemingly as little motion as white horsetails sway-ing in the faintest of breezes. Then my path would round a spur of rock and a murmur which had been growing slowly was all at once loud as thunder. From a ledge stalactitic with icicles tons of pale liquid jadeite crashed among the rocks, and the spray of its impact loaded the branches with fans of frozen drops. A trough of boulders and a tunnel of ice and frozen bracken rushed it to the cliff's edge and there, in a cloud of mist, flung it clear of the clustering stalactites and the tree-tops and sent it booming into the abyss and out of sight. Then the ensuing furlongs would hush the roar and slow the headlong pace to the ruffle of a far-away horsetail again.

The millions of pine needles that cross-hatched the sunbeams sprinkled the paths with an entrancing broken light. An icy zest crackled among the branches, and I paced through these sparkling woods like a Huron. But there were moments in the early morning when the dense conifers and the diaphanous skeletons of the hard-woods were as insubstantial as plumage, and the early mists, hov-ering in the valleys, floated the transparent peaks on air and enclosed the rock-pinnacles in diminishing smoke-rings of vapour. At these moments the landscape below seemed to have moved far from Central Europe, further even than Red Indian forests; all the way to China. The painter's red-inkstone cypher, trailing its lightly brushed-in kite's tail of ideograms, should have stamped the pallor of the sky.

Footpaths corkscrewed down-hill from these uplands; down, down until the trees thinned and the sunlight died away. Meadows would appear, then a barn, then an orchard and a churchyard and threads of smoke ascending from the chimney pots of a riverside hamlet; and I was back among the shadows.

> Et jam summa procul villarum culmina fumant
> Majoresque cadunt altis de montibus umbrae.

There was always a Golden Hart or a White Rose for bread and cheese among the huddle of roofs, or for a coffee and Himbeergeist. Often, half in a bay of the mountains and half on a headland, a small and nearly amphibian Schloss mouldered in the failing light among the geese and the elder-bushes and the apple trees. Dank walls rose between towers that were topped with cones of mounting shingle. Weeds throve in every cranny. Moss mottled the walls rose between towers that were topped with cones of moult-masonry which the rusting iron clamps tried to hold together, and buttresses of brick shored up the perilously leaning walls. The mountains, delaying sunrise and hastening dusk, must have halved again the short winter days. Those buildings looked too forlorn for habitation. But, in the tiny, creeper-smothered windows, a faint light would show at dusk. Who lived in those stone-flagged rooms where the sun never came? Immured in those six-foot-thick walls, overgrown outside with the conquering ivy and within by genealogical trees all moulting with mildew? My thoughts flew at once to solitary figures . . . a widowed descendant of a lady-in-waiting at the court of Charlemagne, alone with the Sacred Heart and her beads, or a family of wax-pale barons, recklessly inbred; bachelors with walrus moustaches, bent double with rheumatism, shuddering from room to room and coughing among their lurchers, while their cleft palates called to each other down corridors that were all but pitch dark.

After supper and filling in my diary in the front room of the inn in Persenbeug – I think I must have been staying there on the charitable-burgomaster principle – I started to sketch the inn-keeper's daughter Maria while she busied herself over a basket of darning. I was talking to her about my visit to St Florian: either it

had been the wrong time for sightseers or a day when the Abbey
was officially shut. The janitor was adamant. I told him it was my
only chance – I had come all the way across Europe to see the
Abbey; and at last, when I must have sounded on the brink of
tears, he had begun to melt. He had handed me over to the
friendly Canon in the end, who showed me all. Maria laughed. So
did a man at the next table who lowered the *Neue Freie Presse*,
and looked over his spectacles. He was a tall and scholarly-looking
figure with a long amusing face and large blue eyes. He was
dressed in leather breeches and a loden-jacket, and a big dark dog
with Brueghel tendencies called Dick lay quietly beside his chair.
'You did the right thing,' he said. 'In Germany you would only
have got in by shouting.' Maria and two watermen, the only other
people in the Gastzimmer, laughed and agreed.

The Danube inspires those who live on its banks with an infectious passion. My companions knew everything about the river.
They rejoiced in the fact that, after the Volga, which was almost
too far away to count, it was the largest river in Europe; and the
man in loden added that it was the only one that flowed from
west to east. The watermen were full of lurid descriptions of the
hazards of the Strudengau and their tales were amply borne out
by the others. The man in loden, I discovered, spoke perfect English, but except in the frequent case of a word I didn't understand,
he stuck to German out of politeness to the others. The Danube,
he said, played a role in the *Nibelungenlied* that was just as important as that of the Rhine. I hadn't read it yet but I admitted I
had never connected the story with any river but the latter. 'Nor
has anyone!' he said. 'That's because of Dr Wagner! Magnificent
sounds, but very little to do with the actual legend.' Which part of
the Danube? '*Exactly here!* All the way downstream, right into
Hungary.'

We looked out of the window. The flood was rushing by under
the stars. It was the widest river in Europe, he went on, and the
richest by far in interesting life. Over seventy different kinds of
fish swim in it. It had its own species of salmon and two distinct
kinds of pike-perch – stuffed specimens of a few of them were hung
round the walls in glass cases. The river was a link between the
fish of Western Europe and those that populated the Dniestr, the

Dniepr, the Don and the Volga. 'The Danube has always been an invasion route,' he said. 'Even above Vienna, you get fish that never venture west of the Black Sea otherwise. At least, extremely seldom. True sturgeon stay in the Delta – alas! – but we get plenty of their relations up here.' One of them, the sterlet, was quite common in Vienna. It was delicious, he said. Sometimes they ventured as far upstream as Regensburg and Ulm. The biggest of them, another sturgeon-cousin called the Hausen, or *Acipenser Huso*, was a giant that sometimes attained the length of twenty-five feet, and, in very rare cases, thirty; and it could weigh as much as two thousand pounds. 'But it's a harmless creature,' he went on. 'It only eats small stuff. All the sturgeon family are short-sighted, like me. They just fumble their way along the bottom with their feelers, grazing on water plants.' He shut his eyes and then, with a comic expression of bewilderment, extended his fingers among the wine glasses with an exploratory flutter. 'It's true home is the Black Sea and the Caspian and the Sea of Azov. But the real terror of the Danube is the *Wels*!' Maria and the watermen nodded their heads in sad assent, as though a Kraken or the Grendel had been mentioned. The *Silurus glanis* or Giant Catfish! Though it was smaller than the Hausen, it was the largest purely European fish and it sometimes measured thirteen feet.

'People say they eat babies if they fall in the water,' Maria said, dropping a half-darned sock into her lap.

'Geese, too,' one of the watermen said.

'Ducks,' the other added.

'Lambs.'

'Dogs.'

'Dick had better look out!' Maria appended.

My polymath neighbour's reassuring pats on the shaggy scalp at his side were rewarded by a languorous gaze and a few tail-thumps, while his master told me that a swallowed poodle had been cut out of a catfish a year or two before.

'They are terrible creatures,' he said, 'terrible and extraordinary.'

I asked him what they looked like and he repeated the question ruminatively to himself. 'Beastly!' he said at last. 'You see, they

THE DANUBE: SEASONS AND CASTLES   159

have no scales, they are quite smooth. Dull-coloured and slimey. But the face! That's the thing! It has great blunt features and hateful little staring eyes.' As he spoke, he lowered his brows in a scowl and somehow contrived to make the large frank eyes behind the lenses contract and protrude simultaneously in a glare of venomous rage – 'and its mouth!' he went on, 'its mouth is the worst of all! It's underslung and fitted with rows of terrifying little teeth.' He widened his mouth to a slit that sank balefully at both ends and thrust out his lower jaw in a hideous Habsburg jut. 'And it has long, long whiskers,' he said, spreading his finger-tips across both his cheeks, 'sweeping out on either side.' He fanned them airily away and over his shoulders like the long barbels of the giant catfish streaming in the current. *It looks like this!* he said, slowly rising from his chair and, as he did so, he thrust the dreadful mask towards us across the wine glasses. It was as if the great fish had swum in silently through the door. Maria said *'Herr Jesus!'* with a nervous laugh, and the dog jumped up and barked excitedly. Then his features resumed their normal cast, and he sat back again smiling at our amazement.

I had chanced on a gold mine! 'Inquire Within About Everything': flora, fauna, history, literature, music, archaeology – it was a richer source than any castle library. His English, mastered from governesses with his brothers, was wide in range, flawless in its idiom and polished by many sojourns in England. He was full of stories about the inhabitants of Danubian castles, of which he was one, as I had more or less gathered from the others' style in addressing him: his lair was a battered Schloss near Eferding, and it was the empty heronry I had noticed there which had first excited him when he was a boy about the fauna of the river. He had a delightful Bohemian, scholar-gipsy touch.

He was on his way back from an antiquarian visit to Ybbs, the little town immediately across the river. His goal there had been the carved tomb of Hans, Knight of Ybbs: 'A figure,' he said, 'of knock-out elegance!' He showed me a snapshot the parish priest had given him. (It was so striking that I crossed the river to see it next day. The Knight, standing in high relief in a rectangle which is deeply incised with gothic lettering, was carved in 1358. Falling in battle in the same decade as Crécy and Poitiers, he was an exact contemporary of du Guesclin and the Black Prince: at the very pinnacle, that is, of the age of chivalry. He is in full plate armour and the fingers of his right gauntlet curl round the shaft of a lance from which a pennant flutters. Those of the other, under an elbow bent at an angle which shifts the breastplated torso to one side from a wasp waist, are spread on the cross-hilt of a two-handed sword, to which a notched shield is strapped. His pointed steel cap is ridged like an almond and chain mail covers cheek, chin and throat like a nun's wimple; similar to that arrangement, with starched linen in lieu of metal, which gives a knight-like look to the nuns in some Orders. A huge oak-leaf-crested and slit-eyed tilting helm balances on one of his plated shoulders. The sinuous flow of the carving gives a lively, poetical and debonair stance to the Knight which is probably unique in such effigies.)

At the mention of the Ritter von Ybbs, I asked him the exact meaning of *von*. He explained how a 'Ritter von' and an 'Edler von' – Knight, or Nobleman, 'of' somewhere – were originally feudal landowners holding a fief, and usually an eponymous one, in knight's fee. Later it simply became the lowest rank in the scale of titles. Its fiendish aura in England, due to the military bent of Prussian junkers, is absent in Austria where a milder, squire-ish feeling hovers about the prefix. This was the cue for an excursus on Central European aristocracy, conducted with great brio and the detachment of a zoologist. I had got the hang of it on broad lines; but what about those figures who had intrigued me in Germany: landgraves, margraves, rhinegraves and wildgraves? Who was the Margravine of Bayreuth and Anspach? The answers led him to a lightning disquisition on the Holy Roman Empire and how the tremendous title had pervaded and haunted Europe from Charlemagne to the Napoleonic Wars. The roles of the Electors – the princes and prelates who chose the Emperors until the Crown became an unofficial Habsburg heirloom, when they ratified it still – were at last made clear. Between his election and accession, I learnt, a prospective Emperor was styled King of the Romans. 'Why!' he said, 'there was an English one, King John's son, Richard of Cornwall! And his sister Isabella married the Emperor Frederick II, the *stupor mundi*! But Richard never succeeded, poor fellow – as you know' – a tacit, all-purpose nod seemed the best response here – 'he died of grief when his son Henry of Almain was murdered by Guy de Montfort at Viterbo. Dante writes about it . . .' By this time I had stopped being surprised at anything. He explained the mediatization of lesser sovereign states when the Empire was dissolved; and from here, at a dizzy pace, he branched into the history of the Teutonic Knights, the Polish szlachta and their elective kings, the Moldowallachian hospodars and the great boyars of Rumania. He paid brief tribute to the prolific loins of Rurik and the princely progeny they scattered across the Russias, and the Grand Princes of Kiev and Novgorod, the Khans of Krim Tartary and the Kagans of the Mongol Hordes. If nothing had interrupted, we would have reached the Great Wall of China and flown across the sea to the Samurai world.* But something re-called us nearer home: to the ancient, almost Brahminic Austrian rules of eligibility and the stifling Spanish ceremony of the Court which had survived from the times of Charles V. He was critical of the failures of the nobility at crucial moments, but he was attached to it nevertheless. The proliferation of central European titles came under mild fire. 'It's much better in England, where all but one reverts to Mister in the end. Look at me and my brothers! All handle and no jug.' Would he have liked titles to be done away with?† 'No, no!' he said, rather contradictorily. 'They should be preserved at all costs – the world is getting quite dull enough. And they are not *really* multiplying – history and eco-logy are against them. Think of the Oryx! Think of the Auckland Island Merganser! The Great Auk! The Dodo!' His face was div-ided by a grin: 'You ought to see some of my aunts and uncles.' But a moment later his brow was clouded by concern. 'Everything is going to vanish! They talk of building power-dams across the Danube and I tremble whenever I think of it! They'll make the wildest river in Europe as tame as a municipal waterworks. All those fish from the East – they would never come back! Never,

---

* I loved all this. I was soon suspiciously expert in all the relevant socio-historical lore, to which others might give a grosser name. But I would have been genuinely taken aback if anyone had taxed me with snobbery.

† They had been, officially, but nobody paid the slightest attention

never, never!' He looked so depressed that I changed the subject by asking him about the Germanic tribes who had once lived here – the Marcomanni and the Quadi – I couldn't get their odd names out of my head. 'What?' He cheered up at once. Those long-haired Wotan-worshippers, who peered for centuries between the tree-boles, while the legionaries drilled and formed tortoise on the other bank? His eyes kindled, and I drank in more about the Völkerwanderungen in a quarter of an hour than I could have gleaned in a week with the most massive historical atlases.

The others had stolen away to bed hours before. The third bottle of Langenlois was empty and we stood up too. He paused in front of a glass case in which a bright-eyed and enormous stuffed trout was swimming urgently through a tangle of tin water-weed. 'It's a pity you didn't go on over the hills from St Florian,' he said. 'You would have got to the little town of Steyr, and the Enns valley' – this was the green tributary I had watched curling out of the hills opposite Mauthausen – 'It's only half a dozen miles. Schubert wrote the Trout quintet there. He was on a walking tour, like you.'

He whistled the tune as we strolled along the snow-covered quay, with Dick bounding ahead and sliding comically out of control on the concealed ice. The steeple of Ybbs stood clear above the roofs and the tree-tops the other side. Above the roofs of our own shore, almost inevitably, a large baroque castle soared into the starlight. 'You see the third window on the left?' the polymath asked. 'It's the room where Karl, our last Emperor was born.' After a pause, he went on whistling the tune of The Trout. 'I always think of streams running down to the Danube,' he said, 'whenever I hear it.'

SIX

The Danube: Approach to a Kaiserstadt

NEXT morning, after we had rowed across to Ybbs and back, conversation in the sunny front room of the inn flowed on till luncheon. The sun was well down the sky when I set out, and by nightfall I found myself in a mildly spurious kind of hunters' tavern in a valley only five miles further on. There was an open stove and the walls were laden wth guns, hunting knives, horns, animal traps, badgers, moorhens, weasels, pheasant and deer. Everything was made of wood, leather or horn and the chandelier was an interlock of antlers. There were even some genuine foresters among the people out for the evening from Krems. A tireless accordionist accompanied the singing and through the thickening haze of wine, even the soppiest songs sounded charming. 'Sag beim Abschied leise "Servus" ', 'Adieu, mein kleiner Gardeoffizier', and 'In einer kleinen Konditorei'. Songs from the *White Horse Inn* followed, and regimental marches of the most unmilitary kind, like the *Deutschmeistermarsch* ('Wir sind rom K.u.K. Infanterieregiment'), the Kaiserjäger and Radetzky Marches and the *Erzherzog-Johann-Lied*. Musically speaking, London never plucks at the heart-strings. But Paris, from Villon to Maurice Chevalier and Josephine Baker, never stops, nor does Naples, nor, above all, does Vienna: 'Good night Vienna'; 'Ich möcht mal wieder in Grinzing sein'; 'Wien, Wien, nur du allein!' – they followed each other staunchlessly and the eyes of the singers grew mistier and mistier with homesickness. Then we moved on to the rival dreamland of Styria and the Tyrol: peaks, valleys, forests, streams, cowbells, shepherds' flutes, chamois and eagles: 'Zillertal, du bist mein Freud'!', 'Fern vom Tirolerland', 'Hoch vom Dachstein an' ... Everything became blurred and golden. The one I liked most was the *Andreas-Hofer-Lied*, a moving lament for the great mountain leader of the Tyrolese against Napoleon's armies, executed in Mantua and mourned ever since. I found myself, with two new friends, still singing it in the small hours as we descended the valley. We passed the luminous vision of a watermill fossilized in ice and snow. When we reached the river, we rowed across to a circular bastion and a tall belfry glimmering among the trees on the other bank. As we climbed the steps into the starry town of Pöchlarn, a window opened and told us to stop making such a noise.

We were invading one of the most important Danubian landmarks of the *Nibelungenlied!* The polymath had said it was the only place in the whole saga where no slaughter had broken out. The Margrave Rüdiger entertained the Nibelungen-Burgundians in this very castle, feasting them in coloured tents pitched all over the meadows. They were celebrating a betrothal with dancing and songs to the viol. Then the great army rode away to Hungary and their doom. 'And none of them,' the poet says, 'ever got back alive to Pöchlarn.'

The mountains had once more loosened their hold on the river and the little towns succeeded each other at shorter intervals. Those across the water slid into view quietly posing above their reflections with a two-dimensional and stage-like solemnity. The gabled coloured façades, entwined with ironwork and symmetrically leaved with shutters, joined in a line of scenery that ran the length of each quay. A few arches pierced this back-drop. Russet or sulphurous cupolas were lifted above the roofs. Higher still there was always a castle and stream-beds descended the darkly timbered valleys. But the quays and the nets and anchors along the water's brink might have belonged to small maritime ports.

Strictly speaking, the Bohemian Forest had come to an end some way upstream. The old Kingdom of Bohemia, which had belonged to the Empire for the last three centuries, vanished when it became part of Czechoslovakia in 1919. It had always been landlocked by surrounding states. How could the famous stage-direction – 'The Coast of Bohemia' – have ever slipped from Shakespeare's pen? When he introduced it in *The Winter's Tale*, Bohemia wasn't a half-mythical country, like 'Illyria' in *Twelfth Night*. Its whereabouts and its character were as well known as Navarre in *Love's Labour's Lost*, or Scotland in *Macbeth*. In fact, as an important Protestant stronghold, it was particularly famous at the time. The Elector Palatine – the Protestant champion of Europe – was married to Princess Elizabeth, and three years after Shakespeare's death he was elected to the throne of Bohemia. (The Winter Queen again! Shakespeare must have known her well and, according to some, the bridal masque in *The Tempest* was written for their betrothal.) How could Shakespeare have thought that her Kingdom was on the sea?

As I marched downstream, inspiration struck. 'Coast' must originally have meant 'side' or 'edge', not necessarily connected with 'sea' at all! Perhaps this very path was the Coast of Bohemia – at any rate, the Coast of the Forest: near enough!*

Let us run quickly through the relevant part of the story. The King of Sicily is unjustly convinced that Perdita, his infant daughter, is the bastard offspring of his Queen Hermione by his former friend and guest, the King of Bohemia. Antigonus, a faithful old courtier determined to save Perdita from her father's anger, flees from the court with the baby under his cloak, and takes ship for Bohemia. By what route? Shakespeare doesn't say. He would scarcely have gone *via* the Black Sea. I saw him sailing from Palermo, landing at Trieste, travelling overland, then embarking in Vienna in a vessel sailing upstream. The ship, running into a terrible storm, probably among the Grein whirlpools, founders. Antigonus, the old courtier, scrambles ashore – perhaps just under the castle of Werfenstein! – and then, amid thunder and lightning, he just has time to perch the swaddled Perdita in a safe place when the second of Shakespeare's most famous stage directions – 'Exit pursued by bear' – comes into force. (Bears have died out in the Austrian mountains, but there were plenty then.) While the beast in question devours Antigonus in the wings, enter an old shepherd. He sees Perdita and carries the little bundle home, and, finally brings her up as his daughter. Sixteen years later comes the marvellous sheep-shearing feast, with its promise of recognition and a happy ending and its magical speeches. It was probably celebrated in one of those upland farms . . .

---

* True Bohemia – the modern Czech frontier – began twenty-five miles further north.

I hastened along the banks to get to Vienna a day earlier: 'Sir: Perhaps I can shed a little new light on a matter which has puzzled generations of scholars.' The mock-modest fuse that would touch off the bombshell began forming and re-forming . . .

Who first misquoted and launched the phrase 'the Coast of Bohemia'? The correct stage-direction, as I discovered on my first morning in Vienna, runs: 'Bohemia: A desert country near the Sea'.

It was total collapse.

At night the stars flashed in a cloudless void. Nothing but an early, brief mist dimmed the pale skies in the morning and the snow on the peaks was coloured at both ends of each day by almost too poignant a flush. I felt that I had been let loose among a prodigality of marvels, and the thought was made more exhilarating still by the illusion of privacy. This landscape might have been an enormous and unending park, scattered with woods and temples and pavilions, for often the only footprints in the snow were mine.

Through the last water-meadow, before the mountains resumed their grip, I was approaching one of those landmarks. High on a limestone bluff, beneath two baroque towers and a taller central dome, tiers of uncountable windows streamed away into the sky. It was Melk at last, a long conventual palace cruising above the roofs and the trees, a quinquereme among abbeys.

No janitor was about. A young Benedictine, finding me loitering in the gatehouse, took me in tow, and as we crossed the first great courtyard, I knew I was in luck. He spoke beautiful French; he was learned and amusing and the ideal cicerone for all that lay ahead.

Afterwards, it was in confused musical terms that the stages of our progress strung themselves together in my memory. This is how they resound there still. Overtures and preludes followed each other as courtyard opened on courtyard. Ascending staircases unfolded as vaingloriously as pavanes. Cloisters developed with the complexity of double, triple and quadruple fugues. The suites of state apartments concatenated with the variety, the mood and the décor of symphonic movements. Among the receding infinity of

gold bindings in the library, the polished reflections, the galleries
and the terrestrial and celestial globes gleaming in the radiance of
their flared embrasures, music, again, seemed to intervene. A
magnificent and measured polyphony crept in one's ears. It was
accompanied by woodwind at first, then, at shortening intervals,
by violins and violas and 'cellos and then double basses while a
sudden scroll-work of flutes unfurled in mid-air; to be joined at last
by a muted fanfare from the ceiling, until everything vibrated
with a controlled and pervading splendour. Beyond it, in the
church, a dome crowned the void. Light spread in the painted
hollows and joined the indirect glow from the ovals and the lu-
nettes and the windows of the rotunda. Galleries and scalloped
baldachinos and tiered cornices rose to meet it; and the soft light,
falling on the fluted pilasters and circles of gold spokes, and on the
obelisks wreathed with their sculpted clouds, suffused the honeycomb side-chapels and then united in a still and universal radiance.
Music might just have fallen silent; unless it were about to begin.
In the imagination, instruments assembled – unseen cymbals just
ajar that would collide with a resonance no more strident than a
whisper; drums an inch below their padded sticks with palms
ready to muffle them; oboes slanting, their reeds mute for a
moment more; brass and woodwind waiting; fingers stretched motionless across the wires of a harp and fifty invisible bows poised
in the air above fifty invisible sets of strings.

For me the famous buildings were a peak in a mountain range
of discovery which had begun at Bruchsal and continued long
afterwards. Again and again during these weeks I was to find
myself wandering through great concavities illuminated by
reflections from the snow. Sunlight flared in lintels and broken
pediments, and streamed in over snowy sills so close to the ceilings
that they gave a last lift to the *trompe l'oeil* Ascensions and
Transfigurations and Assumptions as they poured across them
and quickened the white and cream wreaths of stucco holding
them aloft: garlands doubly etherealized by the reverberated radiance of the snowflakes, and composed of all that reed and palm-
leaf and tendril and scallop and conch and the spines of the murex
can inspire.

In this high baroque style, halted at a point on the frontier of rococo where the extravagant magic of later decades is all implicit, how easily the same aesthetic mood glides from church to palace, from palace to ballroom, from ballroom to monastery and back into church again! Paradox reconciles all contradictions. Clouds drift, cherubim are on the wing, and swarms of putti, baptized in flight from the Greek Anthology, break loose over the tombs. They try on mitres and cardinals' hats and stumble under the weight of curtains and crosiers while stone Apostles and Doctors of the Church, who are really encyclopedists in fancy dress, gaze down indulgently. Female saints display the instruments of their martyrdom as light-heartedly as dice-boxes and fans. They are sovereign's favourites, landgravines dressed as naiads; and the androgynous saint-impersonating courtiers who ogle the ornate ceilings so meltingly from their plinths might all be acting in a charade. Sacred and profane change clothes and penitents turn into dominoes with the ambiguity of a masqued ball.

In the half-century following Melk, rococo flowers into miraculously imaginative and convincing stage scenery. A brilliant array of skills, which touches everything from the pillars of the colonnade to the twirl of a latch, links the most brittle and transient-seeming details to the most magnificent and enduring spoils of the forests and quarries. A versatile genius sends volley after volley of fantastic afterthoughts through the great Vitruvian and Palladian structures. Concave and convex uncoil and pursue each other across the pilasters in ferny arabesques, liquid notions ripple, waterfalls running silver and blue drop to lintels and hang frozen there in curtains of artificial icicles. Ideas go feathering up in mock fountains and float away though the colonnades in processions of cumulus and cirrus. Light is distributed operatically and skies open in a new change of gravity that has lifted wingless saints and evangelists on journeys of aspiration towards three-dimensional sunbursts and left them levitated there, floating among cornices and spandrels and acanthus leaves and architectural ribands crinkled still with pleats from lying long folded in bandboxes. Scripture pastorals are painted on the walls of the stately interiors. Temples and cylindrical shrines invade the landscape of the Bible. Chinese pagodas, African palms, Nile pyramids and then a Mexican volcano and the conifers and wigwams of Red Indians spring up in Arcady. Walls of mirror reflect these scenes. They bristle with sconces, sinuous gold and silver boundaries of twining branches and the heaped-up symbols of harvest and hunting and warfare mask the joins and the great sheets of glass answer each other across wide floors and reciprocate their reflections to infinity. The faded quicksilver, diffusing a submarine dusk, momentarily touches the invention and the delight of this looking-glass world with a hint of unplanned sadness.

But one is always looking up where those buoyant scenes in grisaille or pastel or polychrome, unfolding elliptically in asymmetric but balancing girdles of snowy cornice, enclose room after room with their resplendent lids. Scriptural throngs tread the air among the banks of vapour and the toppling perspectives of the balustrades. Allegories of the seasons and chinoiserie eclogues are on the move. Aurora chases the Queen of the Night across the sky and Watteau-esque trios, tuning their lutes and their violins, drift by on clouds among ruins and obelisks and loosened sheaves. A sun declining on a lagoon in Venice touches the rims of those clouds and veils the singing faces and the plucked strings in a tenuous melancholy; irony and pity float in the atmosphere and across the spectator's mind, for there is little time left and a closing note sounds in all these rococo festivals.

Ceremonious and jocund, Melk is high noon. Meridian glory surounded us as a clock in the town struck twelve. The midday light showered on the woods and a yellow loop of the Danube and a water-meadow full of skaters, all foreshortened as they wheeled and skimmed beneath the flashing line of windows. We were standing at the centre of a wide floor and peering – under a last ceiling-episode of pillars and flung cloud where the figures rotated beneath a still loftier dayspring of revelation – at a scene like a ballroom gallop getting out of hand. Draperies whirled spiralling up biblical shanks and resilient pink insteps trod the sky. We might have been gazing up through a glass dance-floor and my companion, touching me on the elbow, led me away a couple of paces and the scene reeled for a second with the insecurity of Jericho, as *trompe l'oeil* ceilings will when a shift of focus inflicts the

beholder with a fleeting spasm of vertigo. He laughed, and said:
'On se sent un peu gris, vous ne trouvez pas?'

A bit tipsy . . . It was quite true. We had been talking about the
rococo interplay of spiritual and temporal, and for a few instants,
at these last words, my companion was transformed as well: habit,
scapular, cowl and tonsure had all vanished and a powdered queue
uncoiled down his brocaded back from a bow of watered silk. He
was a Mozartian courtier. His light-hearted voice continued its
discourse as he stood with his left hand poised on his sword knot.
With explanatory sweeps of a clouded cane in his right, he un-
ravelled the stratagems of the ceiling-painter; and when, to
balance the backward tilt of his torso, he advanced a leg in a
Piranesi stance, I could all but hear a red heel tap on the chessboard floor.

One of the Abbey's bells began tolling on a more insistent note
and, with an apology from my mentor, who was safely back in his
native century, we hastened our step. In a few minutes I was
several fields away, high above the Danube with the dome and the
cupolas already dropping out of sight below a clump of trees.
Twin gold crosses followed them and the cross on the dome last of
all. Nothing remained in those hills to give the Abbey's presence
away. The vanished pinnacles might have been the pigeon-loft of a
farm.

Un peu gris. It was too mild a term.

The footpath along the southern bank was leading me into the
heart of the Wachau, a region of the Danube as famous as those
stretches of the Rhine I had travelled at Christmas or the Loire in
Touraine. Melk was the threshold of this unspeakably beautiful
valley. As we have seen by now, castles beyond counting had been
looming along the river. They were perched on dizzier spurs here,
more dramatic in decay and more mysteriously cobwebbed with
fable. The towered headlands dropped sheer, the liquid arcs
flowed round them in semicircles. From ruins further from the
shore the land sloped more gently, and vineyards and orchards descended in layers to the tree-reflecting banks. The river streamed
past wooded islands and when I gazed either way, the seeming

water-staircase climbed into the distance. Its associations with the *Nibelungenlied* are close, but a later mythology haunts it. If any landscape is the meeting place of chivalrous romance and fairy tales, it is this. The stream winds into distances where Camelot or Avalon might lie, the woods suggest mythical fauna, the songs of Minnesingers and the sound of horns just out of earshot.

I sat under a birch tree to sketch Schloss Schönbühel. Gleaming as though it were carved ivory, it sprang out of a pivot of rock which the river almost surrounded and ended in a single and immensely tall white tower crowned with a red onion cupola. 'It's the castle of the Counts Seilern,' a passing postman said. Smoke curled from a slim chimney: luncheon must have been on the way. I imagined the counts seated expectantly down a long table, hungry but polite, with their hands neatly crossed between their knives and forks.

A falcon, beating its wings above an unwary heron half-way up this northern bend, would command the same view of the river as mine. I had climbed to the ruins of Aggstein – unnecessarily steeply, as I had strayed from the marked pathway – and halted among the battlements of the keep to get my breath back. This gap-toothed hold of the Künringers teems with horrible tales; but I had scrambled up here for a different reason. The polymath's talk, two nights before, had made me long to look down on this particular reach.

There is nothing more absorbing than maps of tribal wanderings. How vaguely and slowly nations float about! Lonely as clouds, overlapping and changing places, they waltz and reverse round each other at a pace so slow as to be almost stationary or work their expanding way across the map as imperceptibly as damp or mildew. What a relief it is when some outside event, with an actual date attached to it, jerks the whole sluggishly creeping osmotic complex into action!

I mentioned earlier that we – or rather, the polymath – had talked about the Marcomanni and the Quadi, who had lived north of the river hereabouts. The habitat of the Marcomanni lay a little further west; the Quadi dwelt exactly where we were sitting. 'Yes,' he had said, 'things were more or less static for a while . . .'

He illustrated this with a pencil-stub on the back of the *Neue Freie Presse*. A long sweep represented the Danube; a row of buns indicated the races that had settled along the banks; then he filled in the outlines of eastern Europe. '... and suddenly, at last,' he said, 'something happens!' An enormous arrow entered the picture on the right, and bore down on the riverside buns, 'The Huns arrive! Everything starts changing place at full speed!' His pencil leaped feverishly into action. The buns put forth their own arrows of migration and began coiling sinuously about the paper till Mitteleuropa and the Balkans were alive with demons' tails. 'Chaos! The Visigoths take shelter south of the lower Danube, and defeat the Emperor Valens at Adrianople, *here!*' – he twisted the lead on the paper – 'in 476. Then – in only a couple of decades' – a great loop of pencil swept round the tip of the Adriatic and descended a swiftly-outlined Italy '—we get Alaric! Rome is captured! The Empire splits in two—' the pace of his delivery reminded me of a sports commentator '—and the West totters on for half a century or so. But the Visigoths are heading westwards,' an arrow curved to the left and looped into France, which rapidly took shape, followed by the Iberian peninsula. 'Go West, young Goth!' he murmured as his pencil threw off Visigothic kingdoms across France and Spain at a dizzy speed. 'There we are!' he said; then, as an afterthought, he absentmindedly pencilled in an oval across northern Portugal and Galicia, and I asked him what it was. 'The Suevi, same as the Swabians, more or less: part of the whole movement. But *now*,' he went on, '*here go the Vandals!*' A few vague lines from what looked like Slovakia and Hungary joined together and then swept west in a broad bar that mounted the Danube and advanced into Germany. 'Over the Rhine in 406: then clean across Gaul – ' here the speed of his pencil tore a ragged furrow across the paper ' – through the Pyrenees three years later – here they come! – then down into Andalusia – hence the name – and *hop!* –' the pencil skipped the imaginary straits of Gibraltar and began rippling eastwards again ' – along the north African coast to' – he improvised the coast as he went, then stopped with a large black blob – '*Carthage!* And all in thirty-three years from start to finish!' His pencil was busy again, so I asked him the meaning of all the dotted lines he had started sending out from Carthage into

the Mediterranean. 'Those are Genseric's fleets, making a nuisance
of themselves. Here he goes, sacking Rome in 455! There was lots
of sea activity just about then.' Swooping to the top of the sheet,
he drew a coast, a river's mouth and a peninsula: 'That's the Elbe,
there's Jutland.' Then, right away in the left hand corner, an acute
angle appeared, and above it, a curve like an ample rump; Kent
and East Anglia, I was told. In a moment, from the Elbe's mouth,
showers of dots were curving down on them. ' – and there go your
ancestors, the first Angles and Saxons, pouring into Britain only a
couple of years before Genseric sacked Rome.' Close to the Saxon
shore, he inserted two tadpole figures among the invading dots:
what were they? 'Hengist and Horsa,' he said, and refilled the
glasses.

This was the way to be taught history! It was just about now
that a second bottle of Langenlois appeared. His survey had only
taken about five minutes; but we had left the Marcomanni and the
Quadi far behind ... The polymath laughed. 'I forgot about them
in the excitement! There's no problem about the Marcomanni,' he
said. 'They crossed the river and became the Bayuvars – and the
Bayuvars are the Bavarians – I've got a Markoman grandmother.
But the Quadi! There are plenty of mentions of them in Roman
history. Then, all of a sudden – none! They vanished just about the
time of the Vandals' drive westward ...' They probably went
along with them too, he explained, as part of the slipstream ... 'A
whole nation shimmering upstream like elvers – not that there are
any eels in the Danube,' he interrupted himself parenthetically,
on a different note. 'Not native ones, unfortunately: only visitors
– suddenly, the forests are empty. But, as nature hates a vacuum,
not for long. A new swarm takes their place. Enter the Rugii, all
the way from southern Sweden!' There was no room on the *Neue
Freie Presse*, so he shifted a glass and drew the tip of Scandinavia
on the scrubbed table top. 'This is the Baltic Sea, and here they
come.' A diagram like the descent of a jellyfish illustrated their
itinerary. 'By the middle of the fifth century they were settled all
along the left bank of the Middle Danube – if "settled" is the word –
they were all such fidgets.' I'd never heard of the Rugii. 'But I
expect you've heard of Odoaker? He was a Rugian.' The name,
pronounced in the German way, did suggest something. There

were hints of historical twilight in the syllables, something momentous and gloomy . . . but what? Inklings began to flicker.

Hence my ascent to this ruin. For it was Odoacer, the first barbarian king after the eclipse of the last Roman Emperor. ('Romulus Augustulus!' the polymath had said. 'What a name! Poor chap, he was very good-looking, it seems, and only sixteen.')

Behind the little town of Aggsbach Markt on the other bank, the woods which had once teemed with Rugians rippled away in a fleece of tree-tops. Odoacer came from a point on the north bank only ten miles downstream. He dressed in skins, but he may have been a chieftain's, even a king's son. He enlisted as a legionary, and by the age of forty-two he was at the head of the winning immigrant clique in control of the Empire's ruins, and finally King. After the preceding imperial phantoms, his fourteen years' reign seemed – humiliatingly to the Romans – an improvement. It was not a sudden night at all, but an afterglow, rather, of a faintly lighter hue and lit with glimmers of good government and even of justice. When Theodoric replaced him (by slicing him in half with his broadsword from the collar-bone to the loins at a banquet in Ravenna) it was still not absolutely the end of Roman civilization. Not quite; for the great Ostrogoth was the patron of Cassiodorus and of Boëthius, 'the last of the Romans whom Cato or Tully could have acknowledged for their countryman'. But he slew them both and then died of remorse; and the Dark Ages had come, with nothing but candles and plainsong left to lighten the shadows. 'Back to the start,' as the polymath had put it, 'and lose ten centuries.'

Grim thoughts for a cloudless morning.

In Mitter Arnsdorf I stayed under the friendly roof of Frau Oberpostkommandeurs-Witwe Hübner – the widow, that is, of Chief-Postmaster Hübner – and sat talking late.

She was between sixty and seventy, rather plump and jolly, with a high-buttoned collar and grey hair arranged like a cottage loaf. The photograph of her husband showed an upright figure in a many-buttoned uniform, sword, shako, pince-nez and whiskers that were twisted into two martial rings. She was glad of someone to talk to, she told me. Usually her only companion in the evenings was her parrot Toni, a beautiful and accomplished macaw that whistled and answered questions pertly in Viennese dialect, and sang fragments of popular songs in a quavering and beery voice. He could even manage the first two lines of *Prinz Eugon, der edle Ritter*, in celebration of Marlborough's ally, the conqueror of Belgrade.

But his mistress was a born monologuist. Ensconced in mahogany and plush, I learnt all about her parents, her marriage and her husband, who had been, she said, a thorough gentleman and always beautifully turned out – 'ein Herr durch und durch! Und immer tip-top angezogen.' One son had been killed on the Galician Front, one was a postmaster in Klagenfurt, another, the giver of the parrot, was settled in Brazil, one daughter had married a civil engineer in Vienna, and another – here she heaved a sigh – was married to a Czech who was very high up in a carpet-manufacturing firm in Brno – 'but a very decent kind of man,' she hastened to add: 'sehr anständig.' I soon knew all about their children, and their illnesses and bereavements and joys. This staunchless monologue treated of everyday, even humdrum matters but the resilience and the style of the telling saved it from any trace of dullness. It needed neither prompting nor response, nothing beyond an occasional nod, a few deprecating clicks of the tongue , or an assenting smile. Once, when she asked rhetorically, and with extended hands: 'So what was I to do?' I tried to answer, a little confusedly, as I had lost the thread. But my words were drowned in swelling tones: 'There was only one thing to do! I gave that umbrella away next morning to the first stranger I could find! I couldn't keep it in the house, not after what had happened. And it would have been a pity to burn it ...' Arguments were confronted and demolished, condemnations and warnings uttered with the lifting of an admonitory forefinger. Comic and absurd experiences, as she recalled them, seemed to take possession of her: at first, with the unsuccessful stifling of a giggle, then leaning back with laughter until finally she rocked forward with her hands raised and then slapped on her knees in the throes of total hilarity while her tears flowed freely. She would pull herself together, dabbing at her cheeks and straightening her dress and her hair with deprecating self-reproof. A few minutes later,

tragedy began to build up; there would be a catch in her voice:
'... and next morning all seven goslings were dead, laid out in a
row. All seven! They were the only things that poor old man still
cared about!' She choked back sobs at the memory until sniffs and
renewed dabs with her handkerchief and the self-administered con-
solations of philosophy came to the rescue and launched her on a
fresh sequence. At the first of these climaxes the parrot interrupted a pregnant pause with a series of quacks and clicks and the
start of a comic song. She got up, saying crossly, 'Schweig, du
blöder Trottel!',* threw a green cloth over the cage and silenced
the bird; then picked up the thread in her former sad key. But in
five minutes the parrot began to mutter 'Der arme Toni!' – (Poor
Toni) – and, relenting, she would unveil him again. It happened
several times. Her soliloquy flowed on as voluminously as the
Danube under her window, and the most remarkable aspect of it
was the speaker's complete and almost hypnotic control of her
listener. Following her raptly, I found myself, with complete sin-
cerity, merrily laughing, then puckering my brows in com-
miseration, and a few minutes later, melting in sympathetic
sorrow, and never quite sure why. I was putty in her hands.

Sleep was creeping on. Gradually Frau Hübner's face, the
parrot's cage, the lamp, the stuffed furniture and the thousand
buttons on the upholstery began to lose their outlines and merge.
The rise and fall of her rhetoric and Toni's heckling would be
blotted out for seconds, or even minutes. At last she saw I was
nodding, and broke off with a repentant cry of self-accusation. I
was sorry, as I could have gone on listening for ever.

When I crossed the bridge at Mautern and saw the low country
opening eastward, I knew that a big change was coming. I hated
the thought of leaving this valley. After something to eat beside
the barbican of Krems I doubled back, halting for a coffee in Stein
by the statue of St John Nepomuk, whose monument dominates
the little town. He had been appearing frequently along the road.
This Bohemian saint, the champion of the inviolacy of the confessional, became a great favourite of the Jesuits. They have set

---

* 'Shut up, you silly fool!'

him up with so twirling a posture and such a spin of cassock and stole that the surrounding air might be rifled. The vineyards on the hill above filled a thousand buckets at vintage time, someone told me. The cliffs are warrened with cask-lined caves.

In a mile or two, safely back in the wide and winding canyon, I got to Dürnstein. It was a little town of vintners and fishermen. Tilting uphill from the water's edge, it was shored with buttresses, pierced by arches, riddled with cellars and plumed with trees. Where the ice and the current allowed it, the Danube reflected the violin curves of the church and an Augustinian priory and a seven-teenth-century schloss. It was another Starhemberg castle, half of it jutting into the river, half embedded in the fabric of the town.

From the west barbican a long crenellated wall ran steeply up the mountainside to the tip of a crag that overhung both the town and river. Obeying the polymath – in this, as in all things – I was soon clambering about the wreckage of the stronghold that covered this low mountain top. Lancets pierced the remains of the battlemented walls, there were pointed arches and a donjon; but, except for the clustering stumps of the vaulting, all trace of a roof had gone and firs and hazel-saplings grew thick in the crumbling cincture. This wreckage was the fortress where Richard Coeur de Lion had been imprisoned.

I had forgotten how this – the result of a quarrel on the Third Crusade – had come about and when I had listened to it, over the inn-stove a few nights before, it had seemed extremely odd. It is briefly this. At the end of the siege of Acre the victorious sov-ereigns marched into the town and hoisted their banners. Richard, seeing the flag of Leopold, Duke of Austria, fluttering, as he thought, presumptuously close to his own, flew into a rage and had it hauled down and thrown into the moat. Mortally insulted, Leopold left Palestine, abandoned the Crusade and returned to Austria. Next year, Richard was summoned to England by the misgovernment of Prince John. He broke off his victorious cam-paign against Saladin and, to dodge his Christian enemies (who were understandably numerous), set off in disguise. Reaching Corfu, he embarked in a pirate ship which was tossed off her course by the autumn storms and wrecked at the head of the Adriatic. From here his only way lay overland through hostile states; worst of all, through the Duchy of his enemy. In a tavern near Vienna, his disguise was penetrated by some of Leopold's men and he was taken prisoner – betrayed, some say, by his commanding looks; according to others, by the careless splendour of his gloves – and donjoned incognito on this crag. How he was rescued by Blondel, his minstrel and fellow-troubadour – who is said to have discovered him by singing outside every likely prison until his friend's voice answered with the second verse – has always sounded too good to be true. But on the spot, it is impossible to doubt it.*

Wandering along the river's bank just before sunset, I felt I would like to settle and write here for ages. Meditating, admonishing and blessing, a team of sainted and weather-fretted Abbots

---

* Leopold handed Richard over to his suzerain, Henry VI Hohenstaufen, the son of Barbarossa and the father of the *Stupor Mundi*. Leopold himself belonged to the house of Babenberg. (It was still nearly a hundred years before the Habsburgs, who were great lords in Swabia, began their centuries of rule over both Austria and the Empire.) The enormous ransom demanded for King Richard was never entirely paid.

There is a strange and perplexing coda to all this. Four knights of Richard's father had murdered St Thomas à Becket two decades earlier. One was Hugo de Morville, and when the crowd from the nave had tried to come to the rescue, he had kept them at bay with his sword while Tracy, Brito and Fitzurse struck down the Archbishop in the north-west transept. We know the sequel; the flight to Saltwood, to Scotland, then the outcast solitude of the four murderers in Morville's Yorkshire castle; penance, rehabilitation, possibly pilgrimage to the Holy Land. According to a tradition, Morville died there in 1202 or 1204 and was buried in the porch (now indoors) of the Templar's Hostel at Jerusalem, which became the Mosque of El Aksa.

But the poet Ulrich von Zatzikhoven says that when Leopold transferred the King to the Emperor's custody in 1193, Richard's place was taken by a hostage. This was a knight called Hugo de Morville, who lent the poet a volume containing the Legend of Lancelot in Anglo-Norman verse, from which he translated the famous *Lanzelet*, who thus followed Sir Percival and Tristan and Yseult into German mythology. Some authorities think the two Morvilles are the same. I hope they are right.

postured with operatic benignity along the Canons' balustrade. Their haloes were dripping with icicles; snow had filled the clefts of their mitres and furred the curls of their pastoral staves. I could hear the sigh of the river just below. When I leant over the balustrade, it rose to a roar. Under the bare chestnut branches, the current was rushing by, flurrying the reflections which the lights on the other bank dropped into the flood. Beyond King Richard's castle the forested uplands of the north bank suddenly broke off. A precipice dropped sheer and at its foot, meadows and orchards followed the river upstream in a three-mile-long question-mark. Halfway, dissolving in the blue of the dusk, an island hovered over its own flawed image.

The cliff possesses an acoustic foible which I have never met anywhere else. I remembered it, standing in the same place, and hearing it again, three decades later. A tug, with a string of barges and a flag that was unidentifiable in the failing light, was creeping upstream against the press of the current. When its siren sounded, after a delay of three seconds the long-drawn out boom was joined by an echo from the cliff which was exactly an octave higher, forming a chord; and when the lower note ended, the higher outlived it solo for another three seconds and died away.

Crossing the river by the little ferry from Dürnstein, I struck southward. By early afternoon I was approaching an enormous white building that I had espied the day before from the ruins of Dürnstein. It was the Benedictine Abbey of Göttweig, a stately rectangle lifted high above the hills and forests, with a cupola at each corner. Having enlarged so freely on the wonders of Melk, I daren't say much about Göttweig: only that it is a resplendent and worthy rival to its great sister abbey at the other end of the Wachau.

Snow-clouds were assembling as I took the uphill path. I overtook a boy of my own age, a bookish shoemaker called Paul, who had taught himself English. He was a great friend of the monks, I learnt, but I think he would have liked to have taken monastic vows himself if family responsibilities had not stood in the way. The most famous part of the Abbey is the Grand Staircase, a wide, shallow and magnificent flight where elaborate lanterns alternate with immense monumental urns at each right-angle turn of the broad marble balustrade. Paul told me that Napoleon is believed to have ridden his horse up these stairs: he passed this way, crossing the river near Krems, in the late autumn of 1805, between the victories of Ulm and Austerlitz.

He led me along an upper cloister to see an Irish monk of immense age and great charm. His words are all lost, but I can still hear his soft West of Ireland voice. Except for his long Edgar Wallace cigarette holder, our host could have sat for a picture of St Jerome. I envied his airy and comfortable cell, his desk laden with books, and his view over the mountains and the river. The Danube was a distant gleam now, winding far away through hills where the dusk and clouds were assembling.

It was snowing hard when we started down after dark. I spent the night under Paul's roof, in the little village of Maidling im Tal, a mile or two down the valley. We had a cheerful and noisy feast with his brothers and sisters in a room next to the shop.

Next day it was snowing even harder. The magic Danubian weather was over. Paul suggested halting there till it improved but I was committed to a plan made two days before, and I reluctantly set off.

It was the eleventh of February, the morning of my nineteenth birthday. As I still had festive notions about anniversaries, I had planned to spend the end of it under a friendly roof. Not that Paul's wasn't; but, before setting out from Dürnstein, I had telephoned to some more friends of Baron Liphart who lived an easy half day's walk from Güttweig. The line had been bad and the faint voice of the Gräfin at the other end sounded a bit surprised. But she managed to convey across the chaotic wires that they longed for news of their old friend in Munich. I was expected about tea-time.

It snowed and blew all the way. The Schloss, when it took shape at last through the whirling flakes, really was a castle. It was a huge sixteenth-century pile with a moat and battlements surrounded by a wide white park. Its dark towers would have awed Childe Roland; they called for a blast of the slughorn. I battled my way there and found a man shovelling out a path that filled up again as fast as he dug, and asked him, at the top of my voice, where the front door was – it was snowing too hard to see much in the falling dark. Which Count did I want, he bawled back: what Christian name? It sounded as if there were two or more brothers about: mine was Graf Joseph; he led me into a courtyard. I was caked and clogged and thatched like a snowman, and when I got into the hall a grey-green butler helped me to beat and brush it off, hospitality seconded by Graf Joseph, who had come down the stairs.

He must have been just old enough to have flown a 'plane at the end of the war – its propeller stood in the hall – but he looked younger, and his wife was younger still, with a gentle and thoughtful look, and a touch of shyness, I thought. (She belonged to that interesting Greek community of Trieste which had been settled there for centuries, and formerly ran the shipping and trade of the Adriatic. The city had only ceased to be part of Austria-Hungary in 1918; and, though they retained their Greek language and Orthodox faith and a patriotic concern with Greek matters, they were much intermarried with Austrians and Hungarians.) They both talked excellent English, and after the ferocious weather out of doors, it seemed a miracle to be sitting on the edge of an armchair in this haven of soft lamp- and firelight, lapping up whisky and soda from a heavy cut-glass tumbler. Two handsome and slender dogs were intertwined in slumber on a white bearskin rug; and one of the painted figures on the wall, I noticed at once, was in total harmony with my recent historico-snobbish craze. It was an ancestor, famous in the Thirty Years War, and at the Treaty of Westphalia, with an ugly, intelligent and humorous face, shoulder length hair, Vandyke moustache and beard, and the chain of the Fleece round his shoulders. He was all in black, in the Spanish fashion which had become general after the Habsburg marriage with Joan the Mad.

This was all very well. But, from the friendly but puzzled faces of my hosts, I understood that, apart from my all-but-inaudible telephone conversation, they had no notion of any impending visit. No letter had reached them from Munich. My telephone call had conveyed an impression, I think, of some Englishman motoring to Vienna proposing himself for tea or a drink. Instead of this

urbane imaginary absentee, they were confronted by an affable
tramp with a knapsack and hobnailed boots. When we had been
talking about our Munich friends for half an hour, a moment of
silence prolonged itself for a few seconds; and, during the gap
made by this angel's overflight, a swarm of anxieties and doubts
and uncharacteristic scruples rushed into my mind. I felt suddenly
convinced that they longed to be alone. Perhaps they had just
heard bad news; other visitors might be expected at any moment;
or they might simply be bored stiff: why not? Anyway, I was
convinced that a stranger's presence might be a curse past bearing,
and this loss of nerve gave way to a touch of insanity: *perhaps
they thought I was a burglar?* I heard myself clumping to my feet
and inventing, in a strangled voice, an excuse for departure. I had
to catch a train that night, I said, in order to meet a friend arriving
in Vienna by train next day. The unconvincing lameness and
confusion of this invention called up looks of surprise, then bewilderment and finally concern as though they had a mild lunatic
on their hands. At which station was I meeting my friend? Des-
perately, and at a venture, I said, the Western one ... luckily, a
Westbahnhof *did* exist. When was I meeting this friend? 'Oh – at
noon.' 'Then *that's* all right,' they said. 'You can't possibly go on
tonight in weather like this! We'll get you to the station in plenty
of time for your rendezvous in Vienna.' I think it must have been
obvious that the entire rigmarole was nonsense, but none of us
could say so. They may have guessed that it had been prompted
by diffidence. My fears had been chimerical; but I was committed
to my mythical programme. In spite of all this, dinner and the
evening were easy and delightful. When I outlined my future
journey, they were full of suggestions, my hostess made me take
down the names and addresses of kinsmen and friends on the way
who might help, especially in Hungary, and she promised to write
to them. (She did. It made a great difference later on.) I didn't let
on about my birthday; what *could* I have been expecting?

The Gräfin, opening her letters over breakfast, gave a joyful cry
and waved one over her head. It was the Baron's, re-forwarded
several times! She read it out, and, on the strength of its splendid
tenor, I thought of telling the truth about my Vienna improvis-
ation but I didn't quite dare.

The day was dark and threatening. Why didn't I stay on a bit? How I would have liked to! But I was entangled in a fiction that no one believed and there was no way out. We were talking in the library, snugly surrounded by books, when the man in green announced that the car was waiting. No good saying, now, that I would rather walk to the station: I would have missed my unwanted train and been late for my phantom rendezvous ... But when we said good-bye, they looked truly worried, as though I were not quite safe on my own.

I sailed away, half-cocooned in a fur rug, in the back of an enormous car that swished its way, under an ever-darkening sky, to a little country station on the St Pölten–Vienna line. A few warning flakes were falling when we arrived and the chauffeur jumped out, carrying my rucksack and stick. He wanted to help at the ticket office, put me into a corner seat and see me off.

Here was a new panic. Even had I wanted to go by train, I hadn't enough money for the ticket. All this brought on a recrudescence of last night's folly: someone had told me – *who, and where?* – that one tipped chauffeurs in Central Europe. Taking my stick and shouldering the rucksack, I found four coins in my pocket, and pressed them on the chauffeur with mumbled thanks. He was a white-haired, friendly and cheerful old man, a former coachman, I think. He had been telling me, over his shoulder on the way, how he too had loved wandering about as a young man. He looked surprised and distressed at this sudden unwanted largesse – he didn't in the least expect me to try to keep up with the Liechtensteins – and he said, with real feeling, 'O nein, junger Herr!' and almost made as though to give the wretched coins back. Leaving him with his coronetted cap in his hand, scratching his head with a puzzled and unhappy look, I dashed in confusion into the station for cover and oblivion and watched him get slowly back in the car and drive off. The station master, who had exchanged friendly greetings too, headed for the office to sell me a ticket. Instead, I gave him an ambiguous wave, slunk out again and strode fast along the Vienna road, Looking back in a minute or two, I saw him standing on the platform, staring bemusedly at my dwindling figure. I wished I were dead.

*

There was another serious cause for anxiety. The coins that had made up that ridiculous tip had been the last. Not a *groschen* remained. With luck, four pounds would be waiting in Vienna, but till then I would have to trust to farms and cowsheds.

The day matched the general distress. Low mountains rose on either side of a gloomy road. The snowflakes became scarce and sticky and finally stopped altogether. A fierce gust ran along the valley and clashed the laden branches, shaking down cascades of snow. All at once the clouds, which had been growing steadily darker, burst open. The snow, pitted like smallpox for a second, turned to slush and the whole sky was dissolving in water and sound.

I got into a barn just in time and despondently surveyed the grim scene from a heap of straw. After an hour of wild thunder and lightning the storm dwindled to a stubborn downpour and a few intermittent rumbles. The sky was dark as twilight. I pressed on when the rain slackened, and sat through the next deluge in an almost pitch-dark church. On a lonely stretch of road the driver of a lorry, creeping along slowly for fear of skidding, pulled up and shouted to me to climb in behind.

Snug under lashed tarpaulin in a nest among piled planks, a scarlet-cheeked girl with a kerchief tied under her chin was sitting with a basket of eggs by her side and her arms clasped round her knees. I huddled beside her, and the drops hammered down on the re-fastened waterproof. She shook hands politely, asked me my name and told me hers was Trudi. Then she said, grinning with enjoyment: 'Hübsches Wetter, nicht?' and laughed: 'Nice weather, eh?' She gave me a slice of cake sprinkled with caraway seeds out of her basket and I was half-way through it when a loud quack came from the other side. A huge bird was sitting in a second basket held there by a zigzag of strings: 'Er ist schön, nicht wahr?' She was taking this handsome drake to her grandmother who lived with five unhusbanded ducks in Vienna. Her parents had a farm the other side of St Pölten, she told me; she was fifteen, the eldest of six: how old was I? Nineteen yesterday. She shook my hand again solemnly and wished me 'herzliche Glückwünsche zum Geburtstag'. Where did I come from, with that funny accent? When I told her, she clicked her tongue. What a long way from home.

The rain had sunk to a steady drizzle and the truck crawled on through the slush while we huddled together and sang. It was impossible to make out much in the dark, but Trudi said we must be in the Wienerwald by now; Strauss's Vienna Woods. But there were no lights on the horizon where Vienna should have begun to show. When the lorry pulled up, we could hear voices, and then a torch was flashed on us by a helmeted soldier with a slung rifle and fixed bayonet and we saw that we were in a built-up street, and already inside Vienna. But torches were the only lights on the pavements and the gleam of candles behind window-panes. A breakdown, apparently.

When the truck put us down, the people in front said they didn't know what was going on. There had been some disorders in Linz. I took the egg basket, and Trudi the drake, and she put her free arm companionably through mine. The drake, which had been asleep most of the journey, was wide awake now and quacking frequently. The atmosphere in the street was inexpressibly dismal. There was a sound of more thunder, or something like it. After a mile or so, barbed wire barriers closed the way and a couple of helmeted soldiers, again with their bayoneted rifles slung, peered into the baskets. One of them started handling the eggs rather clumsily and Trudi told him, with considerable firmness, to mind what he was doing. He let us through, and when we asked him what was up, he answered: the hell of a mess.

What *was* going on? A general strike, as well as a breakdown? The noise we had taken for thunder boomed again, followed by a scattering of sharper reports. Trudi, with a wide, hopeful grin and sparkling eyes, said 'Perhaps it's War!' – not out of blood-thirstiness, but anything for a change. 'It must be the Nazis again! They're always shooting at people, throwing bombs, starting fires! *Pfui Teufel!*' She had to go to the north of the city, and I was heading for the centre. At the point where our ways parted, she asked for my handkerchief and handed it back with a dozen eggs knotted inside: 'There!' she said. 'A birthday present for you! Don't bump them about.' She hitched the basket in the crook of one arm and the drake, with a quack or two, over the other. She turned round after a few steps to shout cheerful post-valedictory wishes for good luck.

The sooty and rain-pocked snow, banked along the pavements, showed in pale lines. Once or twice the beam of a searchlight moved beyond the roofs. The distant rumbling, interspersed with the crackle of small arms and a few continuous bursts, was unmistakably gunfire now. At another road block, I asked a policeman if there were a Jugendherberge in Vienna where I might sleep for the night. He conferred with a colleague: the Heilsarmee, they said, was the only place. I didn't understand the word – something Army? – and I got in a muddle about their directions. One of them came along with me for a furlong or two. He knew Vienna as little as I did; he had only arrived from the country that afternoon; but he knocked at lighted windows and asked the way. When I asked him whether it were a Nazi putsch, he said no, not this time: in fact, just the opposite. It was trouble between the Army and the Heimwehr on one side and demonstrating Social Democrats on the other. He didn't know any details. No papers had appeared. Trouble had started early that morning in Linz and then spread. There was martial law, and an outbreak of strikes, hence the darkness and general chaos. I said it didn't seem fair to use weapons against unarmed political demonstrators. At the word 'unarmed' he stopped and looked at me in surprise, and repeated the word: 'unbewaffnet?' He gave a grim laugh and said 'You don't seem to know much about things here, young man. They've got thousands of weapons that they've been keeping hidden for years. Rifles, machine-guns, bombs, everything! All over the country. It's an armed battle over there in the Nineteenth District!'

That was all he knew about it. It was not till later that it was possible to get a very slightly clearer idea of events. Afterwards, the dead on both sides were reckoned in hundreds by the government; by their opponents, in thousands. After retreating from street-barriers, the Social Democrats, some of whom were in uniform, had taken up defensive positions in a block of workers' flats in Heiligenstadt, the Neunzehnte Bezirk. Their chief defensive position was the Karl-Marx-Hof, a massive building over half a mile long; and the noise I had mistaken for thunder was the sound, muted by distance, of a battle settling down into a siege. The besiegers, unable to make a frontal attack across an open space under machine-gun fire from the besieged building, had brought up mortars, howitzers and field guns; but they were firing solid shot, as opposed to the normal and much more destructive high explosive shells. The command of the besieging troops and the Heimwehr were much blamed afterwards for using artillery. By cutting off water and supplies, it was held, the besieged could finally have been induced to surrender with many less casualties. Before the surrender, the Social Democrat leaders fled to Czecho-slovakia; and Vienna, except for bitterness and recrimination, returned, more or less, to normal. Or rather, to a resumption of the briefly interrupted Nazi subversion.

Robbed of their historical context, these were the purely physi-cal circumstances. At the time, one had only a confused inkling of events. Immediately afterwards, these were blurred, in con-versations and newspapers, by conflict of versions and rumour and recrimination. And then, most surprisingly – at least, so it seemed to a stranger in the city – the whole topic vanished from the air as though it had never happened and, with amazing speed, ordinary life resumed its course.

It was a desperate time for Austria. All through 1933, the country had been shaken by disturbances organized by the Nazis and their Austrian sympathizers. During one outbreak, they had attempted to assassinate Dr Dollfuss. Soon after these February troubles, similar activities started again. They culminated five months later in a Nazi *coup d'état*. It failed, but not without bloodshed and heavy fighting and the murder of Dr Dollfuss. Afterwards there was ostensible quiet until the final disaster of the Anschluss in 1938, when Austria disappeared as an inde-pendent nation until the destruction of the Third Reich.

We seemed to have been walking for miles in this dim wilder-ness. At last, not far, I think, from the Danube Canal, we reached a quarter full of sidings and warehouses, and tramlines running over cobblestones glimmered amid dirty snow, and broken crates

were scattered about. Under the lee of a steep ramp, a lighted
doorway opened at the foot of a large building whose windows
were bright in the murk. The policeman left me and I went in.

A large antechamber was filled with a moving swarm of tramps.
Each one had a bundle; their overcoats flapped like those of scarecrows and their rags and sometimes their footgear were held
together by rusty safety-pins and string. There were Guy Fawkes
beards and wild or wandering eyes under torn hat brims. Many of
them seemed to have known each other for years. Social greetings
and gossip combined in an affable manner and a vague impulse
kept them on the move in a shuffling ebb and flow.

A door opened, and a voice shouted '*Hemden!*' – 'Shirts!' – and
everyone stampeded towards the door of the next room, elbowing
and barging and peeling off their upper clothes as they went. I did
the same. Soon we were all naked to the waist, while a piercing
unwashed smell opened above each bare torso like an umbrella.
Converging wooden rails herded us in a shuffling, insolvent
swarm towards a circular lamp. As each newcomer came level
with it, an official took his shirt and his under-linen, and, stretching them across the lamp, which was blindingly bright and a yard
in diameter, gazed searchingly. All entrants harbouring vermin
were led away to be fumigated, and the rest of us, after giving our
names at a desk, proceeded into a vast dormitory with a row of
lamps hung high under the lofty ceiling. As I wriggled back into
my shirt, the man who had taken my name and details led me to
an office, saying that a Landsmann of mine had arrived that evening, called Major Brock. This sounded strange. But when we entered the office, the mystery was solved and the meaning of the
word *Heilsarmee* as well. For on the table lay a braided and shiny-
peaked black forage-cap with a maroon strawberry growing from
the centre of the crown. The words 'Salvation Army' gleamed in
gold letters on a maroon band. The other side of the table, drinking cocoa, sat a tired, grey-haired figure in steel-rimmed glasses
and a frogged uniform jacket unbuttoned at the neck. He was a
friendly-looking man from Chesterfield – one could tell he was
from The North – and his brow was furrowed by sober piety and
fatigue. Breaking his journey on a European inspection tour of
Salvation Army hostels, I think he had just arrived from Italy. He

was leaving next day and knew as little about events as I. Too
exhausted to do much more than smile in a friendly way, he gave
me a mug of cocoa and a slice of bread. When he saw how quickly
they went down, a second helping appeared. I told him what I was
up to – Constantinople, etc. – and he said I could stay a day or
two. Then he laughed and said that I must be daft. I untied
Trudi's eggs and arranged them on his desk in a neat clutch. He
said 'Thanks, lad,' but looked nonplussed about what to do with
them.

I lay on my camp bed fully dressed. A dream feeling pervaded
this interior; and soon the approach of sleep began to confuse the
outlines of my fellow-inmates. They flitted about, grouping and re-
grouping in conversation, unwinding foot-cloths and picking over
tins of fag ends. One old man kept putting his boot to his ear as
though he were listening to sea-sounds in a shell and each time his
face lit up. The noise of talk, bursting out in squabbles or giggles
on a higher note and then subsiding again to a universal collusive
whisper, rippled through the place with a curious watery resonance. The groups were reduced in scale by the size and the height
of the enormous room. They seemed to cluster and dissolve like
Doré figures swarming and dwindling all over the nave of some
bare, bright cathedral – a cathedral, moreover, so remote that it
might alternatively have been a submarine or the saloon of an
airship. No extraneous sound could pierce those high bare walls.
To those inside them, everyday life and the dark strife of the city
outside seemed equally irrelevant and far away. We were in
Limbo.

SEVEN

Vienna

AN arresting figure in blue-striped pyjamas was sitting up reading in the next bed when I awoke. The fleeting look of Don Quixote in his profile would have been pronounced if his whiskers had been springier but they drooped instead of jutting. His face was narrow-boned and his silky, pale brown hair was in premature retreat from his brow and thin on top. His light blue eyes were of an almost calf-like gentleness. Between the benign curve of his moustache and a well-shaped but receding chin the lower lip drooped a little, revealing two large front teeth, and his head, poised on a long neck with a prominent Adam's apple, was attached to a tall and gangling frame. No appearance could have tallied more closely with foreign caricatures of a certain kind of Englishman; but instead of the classical half-witted complacency – *Un Anglais à Mabille* – a mild, rather distinguished benevolence stamped my neighbour. When he saw that I was awake, he said, in English, 'I hope your slumbers were peaceful and mated with quiet dreams?' The accent, though unmistakably foreign, was good, but the turn of phrase puzzling. No trace of facetiousness marred an expression of sincere and gentle concern.

His name was Konrad, and he was the son of a pastor in the Frisian Islands. I hadn't read *The Riddle of the Sands* and I wasn't sure of their whereabouts but I soon learnt that they follow the coasts of Holland and Germany and Denmark in a long-drawn-out archipelago from the Zuider Zee to the Heligoland Bight where they turn north and die away off the Jutish coast. Tapered by tides and winds, interspersed with reefs, always crumbling and changing shape, littered with wrecks, surrounded by submerged villages, clouded with birds, and heavily invaded, some of them, by summer bathers, the islands scarcely rise above sea-level. Konrad belonged to the German central stretch. He had learnt English at school and had continued his studies, during his spare time from a multiplicity of jobs, almost exclusively by reading

Shakespeare and this sometimes gave his utterances an incongruous and even archaic turn. I can't remember what mishaps had brought him, in his late thirties, into such low water and he didn't dwell on them. He was not a dynamic personality. The quiet good humour, the poise and the mild but unmistakable dignity of bearing that glowed from him, were strikingly at odds with the feckless morning hubbub of the enormous room. Holding up a distintegrating volume, he told me he was re-reading *Titus Andronicus*. When I realized that the book was a complete Shakespeare, I begged for it and turned to *The Winter's Tale* in high excitement. We know the results. He was deeply sympathetic with my dashed hopes.

We shared some of his bread and cheese at one of the scrubbed tables down the middle of the room and, as we ate, I learnt that his feelings for the English language – and for England in general – sprang from a theory about his native archipelago. Before they were driven to the islands, the Frisians had been a powerful and important mainland race and it seems that they and their language were more akin to the ultimate English than any of the other Germanic tribes that invaded Britain. He was convinced that Hengist and Horsa were Frisians. (Where was the polymath? As Konrad spoke, I began to see the two invaders in a new light: instead of meaty, freckled and tow-haired giants barging their berserker way into Kent, I now saw two balding, slightly equine and Konrad-like figures wading ashore with diffident coughs.) He cited a further proof of the closeness of the two nations: a couple of centuries after Hengist, when the shipwrecked St Wilfred of York began to preach to the still heathen Frisians, no interpreter was needed. It was the same when St Willibrord arrived from Northumbria. I asked him to say something in the Frisian dialect. I couldn't understand his answer, but the short words and flat vowels sounded just as English must to someone who doesn't know the language.

I drew him as he talked, and it came out well – one couldn't go wrong! He gazed at the result with thoughtful approval and offered to guide me to the British Consulate, where I hoped salvation lay. We left our effects, as he called them, in the office. 'We must beware,' he said. 'Among good and luckless men there is no lack of base ones, footpads and knaves who never shrink from purloining. Some love to filch.' Tall and bony in a long, threadbare overcoat and a rather wide-brimmed trilby, he looked serious and imposing, though something in his bearing and in his wide, soft gaze lent a touch of absurdity. His stylish and well brushed hat was on the point of disintegration. With unexpected worldliness, he showed me the maker's name inside: 'Habig,' he said. 'He is the most renowned of the hatters of Vienna.'

The surroundings were even more depressing by daylight. The Hostel* lay in the Kolonitzgasse in the Third District between the loading bays of the Customs House and the grimy arches of a viaduct and an overhead railway track, silent now like the whole derelict quarter. Rubbish seemed to cover everything. Our track took us over the Radetzky Bridge and beside the Danube Canal through a dismal scene of sad buildings and dirty snow under a cloudy sky. We turned up the Rotenturmstrasse and, as we made our way into the Inner city, things began to change. We passed St Stephen's Cathedral and its single gothic spire. The barriers and the road-blocks of the day before were still there, but passage was free and for the moment no gunfire sounded in the distance. The city seemed to have returned to normal. Palaces began to assemble, fountains rose, and monuments with fantastical elaboration. We crossed the Graben to the Am Hof-Platz: passing a tall pillar with a statue of the Virgin, we headed for a street the other side, where a flagpole and a tin oval with the lion and the unicorn indicated the British Consulate. The clerk inside looked in all the pigeon holes for a registered letter. There was nothing.

If Vienna had looked grim and overcast before, it was doubly so as I joined Konrad below in the Wallnerstrasse. A few drops of sleety drizzle were falling. 'Be not downcast, my dear young,' Konrad said, when he saw me. 'We must take counsel.' We walked down the Kohlmarkt. At the other end a great archway opened into the courtyard of the Hofburg and zinc-green domes assembled over rows of windows. We turned left into the Michaelerkirche. It was dark inside and after the classical surroundings,

---

* It was closed years ago and a new hostel was opened in the Schiffgasse, in the Second District.

unexpectedly gothic and empty except for a beadle who was lighting candles for an impending Mass. We settled in a pew, and after
perfunctory prayers for the beadle's benefit, Konrad said: 'Hark,
Michael! All is not lost. I have been ripening a plan. Have you
your sketch-block by you?' I tapped the pocket of my greatcoat,
and he unfolded his plan, which was that I should sketch pro-
fessionally from house to house. I was appalled, firstly from tim-
idity, secondly out of very well-founded modesty. I protested that
my drawing of him had been a lucky exception. Usually they
were very amateurish; putting his suggestion into practice would
almost be taking money under false pretences. Konrad quickly
overrode these objections. Think of wandering artists at fairs!
Where was my spirit of enterprise? His siege was mild but firm.

I gave in and soon I began to feel rather excited. Before we left, I
thought of lighting a candle to bring us luck, but we hadn't a
single coin between us. We headed for the Mariahilf Quarter.
Falling into step, he said: 'We will commence with the small
buggers' – to my surprise, for his usual discourse was rather prim. I
asked him: what small buggers? He stopped dead, and a blush
began to spread until it had entirely mantled his long face. 'Oh!
dear young!' he cried. 'I am sorry! Ich meinte, wir würden mit
Kleinbürgern anfangen – with little burghers! The rich and the
noble here,' he waved his hand round the old city 'have always
lackeys, many and proud, and sometimes they are not deigning to
vouchsafe.' As we walked, he rehearsed me in what to say. He
thought I should ask for five schillinge a picture. I said it was too
much: I would ask for two: a bit more than an English shilling, in
fact. Why didn't he keep me company for the first few times? 'Ah,
dear young!' he said, 'I am of ripe years already! I would be always
frightening them! You, so tender, will melt hearts.' He told me
that Viennese front doors were pierced by peepholes at eye level,
through which the inhabitants always surveyed prospective visitors before they unlatched. 'Never cast your eye on it,' he advised
me: 'Ring, then gaze upward at the Everlasting with innocence
and soul.' He took my walking stick, and advised me to carry my
coat folded over my arm and to hold my sketching book and pencil
in the other hand. My outfit looked a little odd, but it was still
clean and tidy: boots, puttees, cord breeches, leather jerkin and a

grey shirt and a pale blue hand-woven and rather artistic tie. I combed my hair in a shop window, and the closer we got to our field of action, the more I felt we must have resembled Fagin and the Artful Dodger. We shook hands earnestly in the hall of an old-fashioned block of flats and I mounted and rang the first bell on the mezzanine floor.

The little brass peep-hole gleamed cyclopically. I pretended not to notice that an eye had replaced the lid on the other side but bent my gaze on vacancy; and when the door opened and a little maid asked me what I wanted, I spoke up on cue: 'Darf ich mit der Gnä' Frau sprechen, bitte?' ('Please may I speak to the gracious lady?') She left me in the open doorway, and I waited, eagerly poised for my next utterance, which was to be: 'Guten Tag, Gnä' Frau! Ich bin ein englischer Student, der zu Fuss nach Konstantinopel wandert, und ich möchte so gern eine Skizze von Ihnen machen!'* But it remained unuttered, for the maid's embassy to the drawing-room, almost before she could have opened her mouth, produced results that neither Konrad nor I could have foreseen. A man's shrill voice cried: 'Ach nein! Es ist nicht mehr zu leiden!' 'It's not to be borne! I must make an end!'; and, hot-foot on these words, a small bald figure in a red flannel dressing-gown came hurtling down the passage with the speed of a cannon ball. His head was averted and his eyes were tight shut as though to exclude some loathed vision and his palms were repellingly spread at the ends of his arms. 'Aber nein, Helmut!' he cried. 'Nein, nein, nein! Not again, Helmut! Weg! Weg! Weg! Weg! Away, away, away!' His hands by now were against my chest and thrusting. He carried me before him like snow before a snowplough and the two of us, one advancing and one retreating, flowed out through the door and across the landing in a confused and stumbling progress. Meanwhile the little maid was squeaking 'Herr Direktor! It's not Herr Helmut!' Suddenly he stopped; and his re-opened eyes sprang from their sockets. 'My dear young man!' he cried aghast. 'A thousand times, my apologies! I thought you were my brother-in-law! Come in! Come in!' Then he shouted to the room

---

* 'Good morning, Madam! I am an English student walking to Constantinople on foot, and I would so much like to do a sketch of you.'

we had left, 'Anna! It's not Helmut!' and a woman in a dressing-
gown was soon at hand and anxiously seconding her husband's
apologies. 'My dear sir!' he continued, 'please come in!' I was
whirled into the drawing-room. 'Gretl! Bring a glass of wine and a
slice of cake! There! Sit down! A cigar?' I found myself in an
armchair, facing the man and his wife, who were beaming at me.
His rosy face was adorned with one of those waxed and curled
moustaches that are kept in position overnight by a gauze ban-
dage. His eyes sparkled and his fingers drummed arpeggios in
double time on his knees as he talked. His wife murmured something and he said: 'Oh yes! Who are you?' I slipped into my
second phase: ('Student', 'Constantinople', 'sketch', etc.). He
listened intently and I had barely finished before he shot into his
bedroom. He emerged two minutes later in a stand-up collar, a
speckled bow tie and a velvet jacket trimmed with braid. His
moustache had a fresh twist to it and two carefully trained strands
of hair were arranged across his scalp with great skill. Sitting on
the edge of his chair, he folded his hands palm to palm on his
joined knees with a challenging jut to his elbows, and, gazing
nobly into the middle distance with one toe tapping at high speed,
froze into a bust. I got to work, and his wife poured out another
glass of wine. The sketch didn't seem very good to me, but when it
was finished, my sitter was delighted. He sprang to his feet and
flew buoyantly about the room with the sketch at arm's length,
the forefinger and thumb of the other hand joined in con-
noisseurship. 'Ein chef d'oeuvre!' he said – 'Ein wirkliches Mei-
sterstück!' They declared themselves astonished at the low fee
demanded. I graciously accepted a handful of cigars as well, and
did a sketch of his wife. He persisted as she sat in using the bun on
the crown of her head as a pivot for swivelling her face to more
telling angles; and when this was finished they led me across the
landing to do a sketch of a retired lady singer who in her turn
passed me on to the wife of a music-publisher. I was launched!
When I found Konrad again, he was patiently mooning about the
pavement. I approached him as though I had just slain the Jab-
berwock, and was suitably acclaimed. In a few minutes, we were
in a snug Gastzimmer, toying with Krenwurst, ordering delicious
Jungfernbraten and geröstete potatoes and wine. Thanks to

Trudi, Major Brock and, that morning, Konrad and my recent sitter, body and soul had been kept firmly together; but it was the first actual meal since dinner at the castle two days earlier. It seemed a long time ago. For Konrad, I think, it was the first real spread for much longer. A little flustered at first, he professed to deplore all this extravagance. My attitude, from a phrase in the *Winter's Tale* which we had been looking at earlier, was ' 'Tis fairy gold, boy, and 'twill prove so'; and, as we clinked glasses, my elation affected him. 'You see, dear young, how boldness is always prospering?' After this feast, I went back to work, leaving Konrad in a café reading *Venus and Adonis*.

These drawings were neither better nor worse than those which an average half-taught knack turns out. Occasionally, when dealing with very marked features, or with traits that constituted natural caricatures, I got a likeness in a few lines, but they usually took at least a quarter of an hour and sometimes much longer. It was a laborious process involving much erasure and eked out with the spreading of shadow with a stealthy finger-tip. But my sitters were not an exacting public; many people love being drawn, and it is wonderful what even worse practitioners than I can get away with. My lucky break was due, I knew, to kind Viennese hearts and though I felt a fleeting touch of guilt, it was not enough to extinguish the intoxicating thought that I could earn a more or less honest penny in an emergency. Also, I had become utterly absorbed by these sudden plunges into the unknown and my early shyness was soon replaced by nerves of brass.

A card in a metal frame under the doorbell usually revealed the householder's identity. The high proportion of foreign names demonstrated the inheritance of the Habsburg Empire at its widest expansion.* Many subjects of alien race, finding their regional

---

* Florence, Milan, Venice, Trieste, Fiume, Lubljana, Zagreb, Ragusa, Sarajevo, Budapest, Clausenburg, Csernovitz, Lvov, Brno, Prague ... all of them, for varying periods, were part of the Empire. The influx of their citizens to Vienna is the other side of the medal from endemic irredentism and sporadic revolt. (Habsburg absolutism, backed by Metternich's secret police and the dread Moravian fortress-prison of Spielberg were the villains of much nineteenth-century literature: Browning, Meredith and Stendhal spring to mind.)

capitals too narrow a stage for them, streamed to the glittering Kaiserstadt: Czechs, Slovaks, Hungarians, Rumanians, Poles, Italians, Jews from the whole of Central and Eastern Europe and every variety of southern Slav. In one flat there was even a genial old gentleman from Bosnia, probably of Islamized Bogomil descent, Dr Murad Aslanovic Bey who, in spite of Sarajevo, had remained firmly Austrophile. A little framed flag on the wall still showed a combination of the Austrian double eagle and the Crescent and a paperweight on his desk was a little bronze figure of a soldier charging with fixed bayonet and fez-tassel flying, a memento of the First K.u.K. Bosniak Infantry Regiment. (These fierce mountain troops had wrought havoc all along the Italian Front from the Dolomites to the Isonzo.) He had long ago abandoned the fez for a grey jäger hat and a blackcock's tail-feather, and, he hinted, slack observance during Ramadan. A white spade beard made him an easy sitter. In many dwellings, a solitary emblem would strike a note as clear as a tuning fork: Franz Josef, Archduke Otto in a fur-trimmed Hungarian magnate's costume; a crucifix, a devotional oleograph, an image, a photograph of Pius X under the tiara and crossed keys; a star of David enclosing the Ineffable Tetragrammaton. Because of their frequency in books of magic, the interlocking triangles and the Hebrew symbols always seemed mysterious and arcane. There were faded blazons, framed citations, medals and diplomas and the collapsed-concertina shakos of students with embroidered cyphers on the crown and tri-coloured sashes and fencing gauntlets; photographs of Marx and Lenin, a star and a hammer and sickle or two. If there are no swastikas or snapshots of Hitler in my memory, it was not through lack of Nazis: there were plenty; but at that moment, I think, the display of these emblems was an indictable offence. There were death masks of Beethoven and plaster busts, tinted like old ivory, of Mozart and Haydn. This scattered iconology ran parallel with another, where Garbo, Dietrich, Lilian Harvey, Brigitte Helm, Ronald Colman, Conrad Veidt, Leslie Howard and Gary Cooper re-affirmed their universal sway.

There was not much room to move in the first flat I tried that afternoon. The floors were blocked with trunks, crates and con-

tainers of varied and enigmatic shapes, with THE KOSHKA
BROTHERS stencilled over them in scarlet letters. Multilingual
posters displayed the masked and hooded Brothers crossing gorges
on tight-ropes, shooting each other out of cannon, flying through
the air to clasp hands in a criss-cross of spotlights, piling up in
precarious and many layered pagodas and thundering round the
insides of giant barrels on motor bicycles. There were Koshka
sisters too, and white-haired ancestors and crawling descendants,
all talking volubly in Czech. They were athletic, smiling, handsome, slightly stunned-looking and nearly identical figures who
continued flexing their knees and feeling their biceps as they
spoke, or slowly rotating alternate shoulder blades. I was lost for
several minutes in this crowd. At last, with sinking heart, I approached a muscle-bound patriarch and mumbled my set proposal
about doing a sketch. He spoke no German, but he gave me a
friendly pat and dispatched a descendant into the next room, who
returned carrying a glossy photograph of the whole tribe. It
showed all the Koshkas balanced in a vertiginous grande finale of
which he was the supporting Atlas at the base. He signed it with
a friendly message and a flourish and led me politely from Koshka
to Koshka and each of them, from the seasoned grandsire to the
minutest of unbreakable tots, added a signature with a kind word
or two and a fringe of exclamation marks. When all the signatures
had been garnered, I again murmured something about doing a
sketch, but in a strangled voice, for my nerve had long gone. There
was a pause, then they all burst out in a joyful deprecating
chorus: No! No! No! Iss a present! For de Picture, ve take not vun
groschen! Not vun! Iss free!' But they were sincerely touched at
the idea of my pilgrimage.

In the next flat, someone had just died.

In a third, the maid said 'Ssh!' as she let me into a little softly-lit
hall. After a moment a pretty ash-blonde girl tiptoed out of a pink
bathroom on pink mules trimmed with swan's down, tying the
sash of a turquoise dressing-gown. She too laid her forefinger col-
lusively across a pursed cupid's bow, enjoining silence, and whispering 'I'm busy now, schatzili!'; she pointed significantly at the
closed door next to the one she had come in by. There was a shako
on the table and a greatcoat and a sabre had been flung across an

armchair: 'Come back in an hour!' Then, with a smile and a friendly pat on the cheek, she tiptoed away again.

But in the fourth flat was a music teacher with a free period between lessons, and we were off.

Konrad and I had a snug and cheerful dinner in one of the lanes of the old Town. Then we went to a cinema, and into a bar for a final drink. We talked about Shakespeare and England and the Frisian Islands as we puffed away at two more of the Herr Direktor's cigars (Director of what, we wondered?) like two bookies after a lucky day at the races.

Our way back took us along the Graben and the Kärntnerstrasse. About lamplighting time, I had noticed a small, drifting population of decorative girls who shot unmistakable glances of invitation at passers-by. Konrad shook his head. 'You must beware, dear young,' he said in a solemn voice. 'These are wenches and they are always seeking only pelf. They are wanton, and it is their wont.'

We drew blank at the Consulate again next morning; but this time it didn't seem to matter. Emboldened by yesterday's progress, Konrad thought we might lay siege to a more ambitious quarter, nearer the heart of the town, but still outside the dread zones where the proud lacqueys held sway. The tall buildings didn't look very different to me, but, as a concession to our richer prospective sitters, I let him persuade me into charging three *schillinge* instead of two.

The preliminary moment, standing in the hall with a score of unpressed doorbells and all the tiers of mystery piling up overhead, on the edge, as it were, of a still undrawn cover rife with quarry, was filled with a tremor of excitement. There was no sound, except someone practising the violin somewhere.

In answer to the first peal, a bearded man in a smock and a Lavallière tie ushered me into a room full of stacked and hanging canvases. There were mountain ranges showing pink in the afterglow, country inns with vine-trellises, cloisters under cascading wisteria, oases and sphinxes and pyramids and caravans casting long sunset shadows over the dunes. An easel in the middle of the room displayed a damp and half-finished atoll at daybreak, plumey with palm trees. He stroked his beard as he led me from picture to picture as though to aid me in my choice. I was embarrassed when I had to explain that I was a kind of *cher confrère*. He seemed rather vexed, though we both sent up jovial and insincere peals of laughter; but the glint in his eye and the gnash of his splendid teeth grew fiercer, and I felt that, had the exit corridor been longer, they might have detached a bit, like a bite out of a muffin.

The second call was a surprise. I was let in by a wild-eyed Englishwoman from Swindon with bobbed iron-grey hair. She didn't want to be drawn but she talked without stopping as she poured out tea and plied me with short-cake and Edinburgh Rock from an old Huntley and Palmers tin. She had come to Vienna many years ago as a lady's companion and they had both become converts to the Catholic faith and when her employer died, my hostess had inherited the little flat where she now gave English lessons. It was plain to see, and to hear, that she was in the throes of an acute and rather disturbing religious passion that was chiefly fixed on the church of the Franciscans hard by. She took me down a floor to draw an Indian friend who was a Syrian Jacobite Christian from Travancore. Voluminous in a mauve and gold-edged sari under a black fur coat, she overflowed from a rocking chair beside a roaring stove. From her I graduated to a flat that was decorated in white suède and corduroy and many cushions. Here a burly, golden-haired and Anglophil baron in a white polo jersey allowed me to draw him and then insisted on sketches of three cheerful and ornate young men in similar jerseys but of different colours while they put on Cole Porter records and gave me a Manhattan cocktail from a huge electro-plated shaker. The baron reminisced with enjoyment about London and parties and the Chelsea Arts Ball. As for Lady Malcolm's Servants Ball, he declared that words failed him. It was a familiar London atmosphere, and I felt a bit homesick. Beyond the next door a terrible row was going on and I wished I hadn't rung. A figure stamped down the hall shouting at someone in the depths of the flat. Jerking the door open, he glared at me with hatred and disgust, slammed it shut, and resumed his interrupted quarrel.

Shed evening clothes scattered the floor of the next flat – tails, a white tie, an opera hat, gold high-heeled shoes kicked off, a black

skirt twinkling with sequins, spirals of streamers and a hail-drift
of those multicoloured little papier-maché balls that are sometimes
flung at parties. The face of the tousled and pyjama-clad young
man who had crept to the door displayed familiar symptoms of
hangover. His bloodshot eyes signalled helpless appeal. 'I'm sorry!'
he said. 'Can't speak . . .', then: '*Kopfweh!*' pointing to his head.
Headache . . . A woman's voice moaned expiringly in the background, and I stole away. (There were similar signs in many faces
and flats; it was the end of carnival, which political upsets had
failed to damp. Shrove Tuesday was only a few days off.) In an
armchair in a large drawing-room on another floor, inert as an
aardvark or a giant ant-eater and moving his head slowly from
side to side with the puzzled expression of a ruminant, sat a
middle-aged man, wide-eyed. Beyond the negative and slow-
motion rocking of his head, he returned no answer to my awe-
struck overtures. Again, there was nothing for it but retreat. But
the last sitters of the morning were a jolly retired Admiral and his
wife surrounded by Biedermeier and Sezession furniture. He declared, with a breezy quarterdeck laugh, that he was still an *active*
Admiral from whom, with the loss of Trieste and Fiume – his
navy had retired. His midshipman's dirk and his dress-sword hung
on the wall. There were enlarged photographs of the gun-decks of
warships in those lost ports. One of these illustrated a tour of
inspection by Archduke Franz Ferdinand, his whiskers twisted up
fiercely under his cocked hat.

It had been a splendid morning. Konrad and I agreed, unfolding
and shaking out our napkins. He tucked his prudently into his
collar as some cutlets of young lamb arrived. They were delicious;
he declared it a lamb unparalleled. On our fourth evening, when I
picked him up in a café at the end of the afternoon's toil, we
decided it had been another bumper day but we both had the
feeling, I didn't quite know why, that it might turn out to be the
last. Over dinner, which we had ordered earlier – a delicious roast
chicken, of the classical sort that sizzles enclouded in the strip-
cartoon dreams of slumbering tramps – we talked of our plans. I
outlined roughly what I thought my itinerary would be. But what
about him? He had been hanging about, he had told me earlier,
waiting with rather Micawber-like optimism for something – I've

forgotten what – which persistently failed to turn up. 'But I am
fostering a deep plan,' he said earnestly at last. 'It is a plan that
leads on to fortune. It was divulged to me by a well-versed and
thoughtful one. But it has need of capital . . .' We both looked
glum: no hopes there. I asked him out of curiosity how much. He
named the sum and we both nodded sadly at our wine glasses.
Then – it was literally a double-take – I asked him to repeat it.
'Twenty *schillinge*,' he said. 'Twenty *schillinge*? But Konrad,
that's easy! We've probably got it already! If not, we'll get it
tomorrow morning!' I had been handing over half of the takings,
but Konrad had looked on himself as my custodian and now insisted on handing them all back, knotted in a handkerchief.
'There, dear young,' he said, 'it is the moiety of your guerdon.'
After paying for dinner, we were only two schillings short of the
needed capital. I asked him what kind of enterprise he had in
mind.

'For many moons, dear young,' he said, looking at me gravely
with wide blue eyes, 'I have been longing to become a smuggler. A
saccharine smuggler, dear young! No, do not laugh!' Ever since
Czechoslovakia – or was it Austria or Hungary? – had placed an
exorbitant tax on saccharine, the secret import of this innocent
commodity made great profits – all one needed was the initial
outlay: 'And there are people – wise, daring and nimble ones,'
Konrad said, 'who, on nights when the moon lacks, scull across
the Danube in barques.' They were never caught. Austrians,
Hungarians and Czechs were engaged in this traffic: 'serious folk,
of a gentlemanly cast of mind'. After all, it was an unjust law,
much more honoured in the breach than the observance. 'And this
breach of the law is meaning succour to persons that ail,' he said.
'It enables those of great girth to become once again slender.' I
hoped he wouldn't be involved in the frontier-crossing part. 'No,
no! I shall be an envoy, dear young, a stately negotiator! They
think that I have a dignified bearing,' he said, straightening his tie
with a cough. 'I hope I have, dear young, in spite of all!' His eyes
kindled happily at the thought of his prospects.

The night before, we had been looking at the photograph of the
Koshka Brothers when the proprietor had brought the bill. As a
great admirer of the Brothers, he had been much struck by the

picture. I had made him a present of it, and his delight had found expression in two glasses of Himbeergeist. Now the photograph had been pinned on the wall; and two more tulip-shaped glasses had appeared at the same time as coffee. Sustained by the glow of future hopes, we now ordered two more, and lit the last of the Direktor's cigars. At Konrad's request, we spent the rest of the evening reading aloud from Shakespeare. As more Himbeergeist appeared, my renderings, in the battle-smoke of flourished cigars, became more impassioned and sonorous. 'Noble words!' Konrad kept interjecting, 'noble words, dear young!' We sang and recited on the long trudge back to the Heilsarmee. Both of us felt a touch of guilt about occupying our two cots there, in the midst of our affluence; it was another prompting towards departure. We were fairly tipsy; Konrad, I noticed, as he bumped into a lamp-post with a faint giggle, a little more so than I was. We both stumbled slightly going upstairs. We were anxious lest our places had been taken, but there they were, side by side at the far end and both empty still.

It was late and all was silent except for the haunting involuntary chorus that spans the watches of the night in these dormitories. As we tiptoed down the long row Konrad bumped into the foot of a bed and a bearded face like a black hedgehog shot out of the other end of a cocoon of blankets and fired off a torrent of abuse. Konrad stood murmuring and rooted to the spot, his hat lifted in a chivalrous posture of apology. The noise woke several sleepers on either side, who launched a rumbling crescendo of blasphemy and anathema at Konrad's protesting victim. I led him by the elbow to our corner, as though on wheels and with his hat still lifted, while the altercation waxed louder until it reached a noisy climax and then very slowly waned into near-silence. Konrad sat down on the edge of his cot, murmuring, as he unlaced his boots: 'He was chafed by mishap and choler unsealed their lips.'

'Let us regain our fardels,' Konrad said next morning. We bade good-bye to the people in the office and to a few fellow-inmates with whom we were on hobnobbing terms, and I hoisted on my rucksack. Konrad's fardel – a wicker creel slung diagonally across his torso on a long baldric of canvas and leather – turned him into a lanky urban fisherman. For the fourth time we set off for the Wallnerstrasse. It was a bright, blowy morning; and we had been right to be optimistic; the moment I entered the Consulate, the clerk held up from afar a registered envelope crossed with blue chalk, and some others. The good news, which would have spread delight four days before, was something of an anti-climax now. We headed for a coffee-house in the Kärntnerstrasse called Fenstergucker. Settling at a corner table by the window near a hanging grove of newspapers on wooden rods, we ordered Eier im Glass, then hot Brötchen and butter, and delicious coffee smothered in whipped cream. It was a morning of decisions, separations, departures; and they weighed on us both. Konrad was determined to set off at once and smite while the iron was hot, determination high and the capital still intact. He became gently excited and the Harfleur spirit was beating its wings in the air; but I felt anxious about him and hoped his associates had as gentlemanly a cast of mind as he thought. He, in his turn, was filled with concern about me. It was true that we had been ripping rather fast through the fairy gold; but he built up a headstrong Sir Harry Scattercash kind of picture that I rather liked. 'Husband all lucre when you are in squandering vein, dear young,' he said, and 'Do not dog *bona robas*.'

I accompanied him to the junction of the Kärntnerstrasse and the Ringstrasse by the Opera House. He was going to catch a tram to the Donaukai Bahnhof and then continue eastwards by rail along the Danube. He was rather arch and secretive about place names; I don't think he wanted to involve me, even remotely, in these illicit doings. He climbed on the tram, sat down, then immediately gave his seat to an elderly and almost spherical nun with a carpet bag. As it clattered off, I could see him towering head and shoulders above the other passengers, strap-hanging with one hand, holding up his Habig hat between the two long first fingers of the other, smiling and slowly rotating it in valediction, while I waved until the tram clashed across the points and swung left into the Schubertring and out of sight.

I felt very lonely as I wandered back to the café. He had promised to write and tell me how things were going. (I got a postcard

from him in Budapest soon after Easter, saying that the Future
was smiling. But he gave no address, so I had no further news
until I got to Constantinople, eleven months later. There I found a
fat letter, franked in Norderney, Konrad's home island in the Frisian Archipelago. The first things to emerge from the envelope
were several enormous sheets of German postage stamps whose
value amounted not only to the pound note that I had thrust on
Konrad much against his will – one of the four I had picked up at
the Consulate – but the fairy gold as well; and I saw, as I counted
up the scores of Bismarck's heads, that he had sent half as much
again. The stamps were accompanied by a long, affectionate, and
deeply touching letter, which I read in a café above the Golden
Horn. The smuggling, to which he guardedly referred as 'haz-
ardous trading, dear young', had become ancient history by then.
All had gone well; he was back in the islands and teaching English; and there was a coy hint that he might be getting married to
a lady teacher . . . Apart from everything else, I was overjoyed by
the idea that his English idiom might not be wholly lost. Perhaps it
would spread among Frisian disciples like the words of St Wilfred.)

But as I walked back to the Fenstergucker, I was troubled by the
idea that with only three pounds to last the month, I might be in a
fix; especially with a stretch of town life ahead. Of course, in the
light of the last days' windfalls, I could get some more . . . Yet,
with Konrad gone, the zest had vanished too. What had appeared
an escapade now seemed, alone and in cold blood, hideously for-
bidding.

Back at our café table, I took out the rest of my letters. The first,
with an Indian stamp and Calcutta postmark, was from my father,
the first since I had set out from England, re-forwarded from
Munich. It was in answer to a letter of mine from Cologne in
which I had broken the news of the fait accompli. I opened it with
foreboding. But neatly folded inside the letter, was a birthday-
cheque for a fiver! I had cast my bread upon the waters and it had
returned to me in a quarter of an hour and, so to speak, with
knobs on.

During the days with Konrad, our own preoccupations had
selfishly taken precedence over everything else. Intermittently

rumbling in the distance like stage thunder, the sounds of strife
had gradually diminished and then ceased. Among the flat-dwell-
ers these offstage noises had prompted deprecating clicks of the
tongue and deep fatalistic sighs, but not for very long: hard times
had induced a stoic attitude to trouble. The revolution vanished
from the front pages of the foreign press and the headlines describing it in the café newspapers were less lurid each morning. As
everything in the mood of the city conspired to reduce the scale of
the events, it was easy to misunderstand them and I bitterly re-
gretted this misappraisal later on: I felt like Fabrice in *La Chart-
reuse de Parme*, when he was not quite sure whether he had been
present at Waterloo.

Outside the café, meanwhile, I hastened to join a one-way population drift along the Kärntnerstrasse. Everyone was heading for
the Ring and I soon found myself jammed in the crowd not far
from the point where I had parted from Konrad. All eyes were
gazing the same way and in a little while a procession advanced
out of the distance: it was to solemnize the end of the emergency.
At the head, on a grey horse and carrying his sabre at the slope,
rode the Vice-Chancellor, Major Fey, who had commanded the
government forces: a grim-looking man with a jutting chin and a
stahlhelm. An army contingent followed: then a column of the
Heimwehr with Prince Starhemberg marching in front in a képi
like a ski-cap and a long grey overcoat of martial cut, mildly
waving; his face and his tall figure were immediately recognizable
from his photographs. A black-clad group of ministers came next,
led by the Chancellor himself. Dressed in a morning coat and
carrying a top-hat, Dr Dollfuss was hurrying to keep up. At the
approach of Major Fey, the intermittent ripple of clapping remained unchanged; Starhemberg induced a slight rise in volume;
but Dollfuss was hailed with something approaching an ovation.
Another column of troops formed the rearguard and the procession was over.

There was something cheerful and engaging about the Chancellor, but in spite of all the anecdotes, his small stature came as a
surprise. As the crowd broke up, a fellow-bystander told me yet
another. One of the soldiers in the recent siege, pointing to some-

thing on the pavement, had exclaimed: 'Look! Fancy seeing a tortoise in the streets of Vienna!' 'That's not a tortoise,' his companion had said, 'that's Doktor Dollfuss in his stahlhelm;' and, for an outsider, that was the last of it.

I hadn't arrived in Vienna totally unprepared. There were a few inhabitants on whom I could stake a shadowy claim. But, for the sake of morale, prompted by a sort of vagrant's amour-propre, I hadn't wanted to launch myself on them when I was absolutely broke. Now that this problem was solved, I dumped my stuff at the cheapest lodging house I could find and sought out a telephone. If I were asked to a meal it would be best, I felt, to turn up unburdened; a rucksack would have been too broad a hint. Unfounded though they had been, my qualms at the last castle had implanted the uncharacteristic notion in my mind that the appearance on the doorstep of an affable tramp with all his possessions on his back might possibly be considered a nuisance. (I shudder to think of the scourge I must have been. The idea that they are always welcome is a protective illusion of the young. Dangerously untroubled by doubts, I rejoiced in these changes of fortune with the zest of an Arabian beggar clad and feasted by the Caliph or the crapulous tinker who is picked up snoring and spirited to splendour in the first scene of *The Taming of the Shrew*.)

In Vienna, the brunt fell on compatriots and Austrians almost equally. Robin Forbes-Robertson Hale, the sister-in-law of an old friend, put me up in a large flat which was always teeming with guests. It was perched in a gaunt and fascinating rookery in a street of the Inner City called the Schreyvogelgasse, or Shriekbird Lane. Tall and striking, she was just back, with two Austrian friends, from a wintry stay in Capri: they belonged to a small half-native and half-expatriate Bohemian set which seemed perfect from the first moment I became involved in it. With the end of the political troubles, the last days of Carnival were given over to music and dancing and dressing up. Wildish nights and late mornings set in, and after a last climactic fancy dress party, I woke in an armchair with an exploding head still decked with a pirate's eyepatch and a cut-out skull and crossbones. At the first strokes of noon from the tower of the nearby Schottenkirche, the shuttered

penumbra began to stir with groans; a concerted croaking for
Alka-Seltzer broke out. A pierrot, a Columbine, a lion and a sleeping lioness with her moulting tail over the back of a sofa were
disposed about the drawing-room like damaged but still just articulate toys.

The recollection of the days that followed is blurred by the
penitential onslaughts of snow, rain, sleet and hail which
scourged the city with all the rigours of February and Shrovetide
and Ash Wednesday. It was a wild winter; but the angry skies
and the wind make the fires and the lamplight glow all the
brighter in retrospect. With the first days of March, the Lenten
ferocity flagged a little. I was living in a state of exaltation. I
couldn't quite believe I was there; and as though to put it beyond
question, I often repeated 'I'm in Vienna' to myself when I woke
up in the night or as I wandered about the streets.

Some of this small society lived in old houses in the Inner City,
others in the gently decaying fragments of subdivided palaces still
adorned by swirls of wrought iron and leafy arabesques and moulded ceilings and the shutters and the double doors opened with
intricately flourished handles. One of these new friends, Basset
Parry-Jones, was a teacher – of English literature, I think – at the
Konsularakademie, a sort of extension for older students of the
Theresianum, the celebrated school founded by Maria Theresa.
(Like students at St Cyr and Saumur and the grim institution in
Young Törless, the boys once wore cocked hats and rapiers which
turned them into miniature French Academicians. It was the most
famous place of its kind in the country and only rivalled by the
Jesuit foundation at Kalksburg.) The Konsularakademie used to
train candidates for the Diplomatic Service of the old Dual Monarchy and it still trailed some clouds of this k. und k. glory. Basset
– half-sardonic, half-enthusiastic, always beautifully dressed and a
staunch guide and companion for noctambulism – lent me books
and got permission for me to consult the Akademie library.
Another new friend was an American girl called Lee, who was
recuperating from some minor illness under the same roof. Good-
looking, solemn and gentle, she was the daughter of the United
States military attaché in a neighbouring capital. Surprisingly, or
half-inevitably, she was a convinced pacifist. She applauded my

reluctance to become a professional soldier but when I told her that I was only shy of peace-time soldiering, this excellent first impression was ruined. We often argued, and once or twice, in spite of her convalescence, until long after dawn. She was as little qualified as I for such debates: emotion and a kind heart were her guides; the arguments grew blurred on either side as the protracted but unacrimonious hours advanced, and ended in concord.

A colleague of Basset's called Baron von der Heydte and known as Einer, was a great friend of everyone, and soon of mine. In his middle twenties, civilized, quiet, thoughtful and amusing, he belonged to a family of Catholic landowners and soldiers in Bavaria, but his style and manner were far removed from what foreigners consider the German military tradition; and with the Nazi movement he had still less in common. (A few years later, I heard he had returned to Germany. Out of family atavism, and to avoid politics and the party activities which were swallowing up the whole of German civilian life, he had become a regular cavalry officer, rather like *ancien régime* Frenchmen, I think, who followed the profession of arms in spite of their hatred of the government.)

On the first day of the battle of Crete, the memory of these Vienna weeks leapt back to my mind.

Shortly after the first wave of German parachutists had dropped, a captured enemy document was brought to our battle H.Q. in the rocks outside Herakleion, where I was a junior officer. The paper contained the entire enemy order of battle, and, as I was thought to know German, it was handed to me: the spearhead of the attack, it disclosed, was under the command of a Captain von der Heydte: his battalion had been dropped near Galata, at the other end of the island, between Canea and Maleme aerodrome: close to where I had been stationed until a few days before. A German officer who was taken prisoner soon after cleared up any doubt. It was Einer, beyond question: he had transferred from the cavalry to a parachute unit some time before.

The noise and the fighting died down at sunset. The short May night was illuminated by destroyed planes burning fitfully among the olive-trees and during these hours of respite, I couldn't stop thinking of this strange coincidence. Chaos broke out again at dawn; and, all through the mortal blind-man's-buff of the next eight days, I thanked my stars that we were loose, as it were, in different parts of the wood, for battles had degenerated during the last eighty-seven years. No chance now, like Cardigan and Radziwill recognizing each other from London ballrooms, of exchanging brief and ceremonious greetings through the smoke of the Russian guns. Again and again, in those whistling and echoing ravines, where a new and unknown smell was beginning to usurp the scents of spring, my thoughts flew back to the winter of 1934 and the tunes and jokes and guessing games, the candlelight and the scent of burning pine-cones when nothing was flying through the air more solid than snowflakes.*

Surrounded by maps and atlases in the Akademie library, I discovered that, as the crow flies between Rotterdam and Constantinople, I was a little less than half-way. But no crow would have flown in the enormous loop that I had followed, and when I plotted the route and stepped it out with dividers, the total came to a great deal more than half; not that this meant much: the rest of the journey was sure to take an equally tortuous course. I knocked off the miles for the trip on the Rhine-barge and the lifts I had taken in bad weather and found that the distance I had actually slogged on my two feet was seven hundred and fifty miles. The journey had lasted sixty-two days, and when I had struck out

---

* I only learnt with certainty that Einer had survived the battle when his admirable book about it came out. *Daedalus Returned* (Hutchinson, 1958) gives a thoughtful, sympathetic and compelling picture of the anxieties and dangers of those days. He was awarded the Knight's Cross of the Iron Cross after the battalion he commanded had been the first to enter Canea. Following many operations on the Russian front, he was taken prisoner in 1944 during the Ardennes counter-offensive. I. Mc. D. G. Stewart, in his *The Struggle for Crete*, says: 'Von der Heydte's ... barely disguised distaste for the leaders of the regime was said to have blocked his promotion.' He is now a professor of International Law at Würzburg University, and in a recent letter posted during a journey across Ethiopia, he writes: 'I hope we may meet soon and wander once more along the silver streets of our youth.'

the halts of more than one night and divided the distance by the time, the average worked out at twelve miles a day. Bearing in mind a few marches from daybreak till long after dark, but conveniently forgetting the times I had merely strolled to the next village, I was a little disappointed. I had imagined it was far more. But I was delighted with everything else. I never tired of recapitulating the journey. I had crossed three parallels of latitude and eleven meridians and moved over from the North Sea – still called 'the German Ocean' on old maps – to a minute-line of longitude running from the Baltic to the south-east Adriatic. Even looked at from the moon – so the terrestrial and celestial globes suggested – the distance covered would have been as discernible as the Great Wall of China.

Back among the maps, and conscious all at once of the accessibility of the Mediterranean, I was assaulted by a train of thought which for a moment set the expedition in jeopardy. It is a famous hazard. All dwellers in the Teutonic north, looking out at the winter sky, are subject to spasms of a nearly irresistible pull, when the entire Italian peninsula from Trieste to Agrigento begins to function like a lodestone. The magnetism is backed by an unseen choir, there are roulades of mandoline strings in the air; ghostly whiffs of lemon blossom beckon the victims south and across the Alpine passes. It is Goethe's Law and is ineluctable as Newton's or Boyle's. I had felt twinges of its power as I crossed the Inn between Augsburg and Munich during a snowstorm: *why not follow the river upstream to the Brenner*, soft voices had seemed to whisper, *and swoop down on Lombardy?* And, sitting as restlessly as a fifth-century Goth and gazing at the cartographic defiles that cross the atlas page to Venice, I felt it now; but not for long. Thank heavens the fit passed. Venice, after all, was on the edge of familiar territory: Italy could wait. Just in time, the windings of the Middle and the Lower Danube began to reassert their claims and the Carpathians and the Great Hungarian Plain and the Balkan ranges and all these mysterious regions which lay between the Vienna Woods and the Black Sea brought their rival magnetisms into play. Was I really about to trudge through this almost mythical territory? How would it compare to the lands I had already crossed? I would have been amazed had I known how circuitous it would be, and how much further than I had thought.

Meanwhile, there was Vienna.

I had always enjoyed museums and picture galleries, but it was firmly established here that no stranger could let any of the city's wonders elude him – 'I suppose you've seen the Harrach collection? Have you looked at Habsburg tombs in the Kapuzinerkirche yet? What about the Belvedere?' – that I was shamed into exploring Vienna with unusual thoroughness. I found a companion now and then. One, much too briefly, was a funny, extremely vague and marvellously beautiful girl who was being finished in Vienna, called Ailsa McIver. She had the sort of radiant high spirits that made everyone turn round and smile. But usually I was alone.

Few delights could compare with these wintry days: the snow outside, the bare trees outlined by the frost, the muted light, and, indoors, the rooms following each other filled with the spoils, the heirlooms and the dowries of a golden age. The galleries of the hibernating city retreated and grew smaller in the distance like vistas along dim rectangular telescopes. I had heard someone say that Vienna combined the splendour of a capital with the familiarity of a village. In the Inner City, where crooked lanes opened on gold and marble outbursts of Baroque, it was true; and, in the Kärntnerstrasse or the Graben, after I had bumped into three brand-new acquaintances within a quarter of an hour, it seemed truer still, and parts of the town suggested an even narrower focus. There were squares as small and complete and as carefully furnished as rooms. Façades of broken pediment and tiered shutter enclosed hushed rectangles of cobble; the drip of icicles eroded gaps in the frozen scallops of the fountains; the statues of archdukes or composers presided with pensive nonchalance; and all at once, as I loitered there, the silence would fly in pieces when the initial clang from a tower routed a hundred pigeons crowding a Palladian cornice and scattered avalanches of snow and filled the geometric sky with wings. Palace succeeded palace, casemented arches sailed across the streets, pillars lifted their statues; ice-fettered in their pools, tritons floundered beneath a cloudy heaven and ribbed cupolas expanded by the score. The greatest of these, the dome of the Karlskirche, floated with a balloon's lightness in its enclosing hemisphere of snow and the friezes that spiralled the shafts of the two statue-crowned guardian columns – free-standing and as heavily wrought as Trajan's – gained an added impromptu spin when they vanished half-way up in a gyre of flakes.

A hint of touchy Counter-Reformation aggression accompanies some ecclesiastical Baroque. There is a dash of it here and there in Vienna, and St Stephen's – steep and streamlined and Gothic – springs up unchallenged in the heart of it as though the balance needed redress. Bristling with finials and unloosing its gargoyles, the cathedral lifts a solitary and warning steeple which dominates every dome and cupola and bell-tower in the city. (Styles of architecture become an obsession in this town. They played a great part in the circle I had strayed into. In a game of analogies, someone had suggested a murex shell, with its spines and its centrifugal asymmetry and its flaky and crusted surfaces, as the epitome of Rococo. Likewise, the symmetrical convolutions and the balancing arabesques of Baroque could be symbolized by a violin. A crosier hit off the brackeny helix and the exfoliation of Flamboyant; and Gothic could be a mitre – in the case of a cathedral, a whole Council of them piled like a card house until they vanished tapering in the clerestory shadows where void and solid change places and turn to stone.) In the rank of fiacres outside the south door of St Stephen's, cabbies in bowlers conversed in the Vienna dialect while they straightened the blankets on their horse's quarters and gave them their feed in buckets. Some of these were as heavily whiskered as their masters. They steamed and fidgeted between the shafts, scattering their oats over the caked snow and the cobbles and sending an agreeable stable-yard whiff across the fumes of the hot coffee and the fresh cakes in the pastrycooks' shops. Joining in my memory with the cold edge of the frost, the combination of these scents conjure up the city in a second.

'When the right vertuous E.W. and I were at the Emperour's court togither, wee gave our selves to learne horsemanship of Ion Pietro Pugliano.' It was the opening sentence of Sir Philip Sidney's *Defense of Poesie*; he was talking of Vienna in the winter of his twentieth year – 1574 – when he and Edward Wotton were on some unexacting mission from Elizabeth to Maximilian II. Their duties left them plenty of free hours for the riding school and for listening to the fertile Italian wit of their friend and instructor. 'He said ... horsemen were the noblest of soldiers ... they were the maisters of war, and ornaments of peace, speedie goers, and strong abiders, triumphers both in Camps and Courts: nay, to so unbleeved a point he proceeded, as that no earthly thing bred such wonder to a Prince, as to be a good horseman. Skill of government were but a Pedanteria, in comparison; then would he adde several praises, by telling what a peerless beast the horse was, the only serviceable Courtier without flattery, the beast of most bewtie, faithfulnesse, courage, and such more, that if I had not beene a peece of a Logician before I came to him, I think he would have perswaded mee to have wished my selfe a horse.' Basset Parry-Jones had read the passage aloud to show that Vienna had always been a temple for the cult of horsemanship. It had been an imported Italian skill in Renaissance times, like fencing, sonnet-writing, building loggias and the technique of foreshortening; but in later centuries the passion rioted like a native growth all over the Empire and there were still plenty of Austrians with a horsy gait and bearing – and of Hungarians, even more, as I was to learn during the coming months – who had a soft spot for the British Isles on purely equestrian grounds. There, they felt, lay the central shrine: not of dressage and haute école, but of speed and huge fences and broken necks, and their eyes would cloud over at the memory of antediluvian seasons in the shires. Hard-bitten centaurs from both parts of the Dual Monarchy recalled with just pride how their great-uncle Kinsky had won the Grand National on Zoedone in 1883. Among these earnest experts omniscience in horse-genealogy ran neck and neck with mastery of the Almanach of Gotha, and they fondly cherished the many equine links between the two countries. Why, an Austrian affirmed, three Turkish mares, seized from the rout of the Turkish cavalry at the relief of Vienna, had been sent to England in 1684, several years before any of the famous founding sires of English bloodstock had set a hoof in the kingdom. Where was the Godolphin Barb then, or the Byerly Turk, and where the Darley Arabian? That was nothing, a grizzled Hungarian would protest, his brows beetling: what about the Lister Turk, the stallion the Duke of Berwick had captured from the Ottomans at the siege of Buda a couple of years later, and taken back to James II's stables?

It was our visit to the Spanish Riding School that had given rise to all this. (The beautiful wing of the Hofburg was built a century and a half later than the oval where Sidney and Wotton must have practised, but Maximilian's stables were up already; they are resonant still with whinnying and munching.) We had lolled over the balcony like Romans at the games while virtuosi in glistening jackboots and brown frock-coats – the scarlet was kept for Sundays – evolved beneath us. They wore their bicornes sideways like Napoleon and sat erect and still as tin horsemen in the saddles of their Lippizaner greys. These horses were traditionally derived from the noblest Spanish or Neapolitan strains – which probably means they were Arabs, like the godlike Barbs and Arabians and Turks we were talking about – and they used to be bred at Lippiza, in the Slovenian hills and oak-woods to the northeast of Fiume.* Slightly darker in hue when young, they get paler as they grow and the juvenile dappling fades from their quarters like freckles from children's cheeks. Fully grown, they are snow white creatures of great beauty, strong, elegant, compact and mettlesome, wide-eyed under their taciturn riders and with manes and tails as sleekly combed and as rippling as the tresses of Rhinemaidens.

They moved with grace and precision about the glaucous concavity of the school: caracoling across the raked and muffling tan, rhythmically changing step, passaging, advancing as though double-jointed, flicking out their forelegs as straight as matchsticks, slewing over the manège in side-stepped hesitation waltzes, pawing the air as they backed slowly on their haunches and taking to the air at last like Pegasus and seeming to remain there for long moments of suspension and stasis. Except when a recondite feat evoked a crackle of applause, the sequence unfolded in a

---

* It is in Yugoslavia now. When I went there two years ago, it was a soaking day, so I could only catch a glimpse of the lovely spectres through a film of rain.

stilly hush. Learned writers derive the style from the classical school of the seventeenth century and, in particular, from the principles elaborated in the Duke of Newcastle's great work. He wrote and published it during the Commonwealth when he was a Royalist general in exile at Antwerp. Anyone turning over the plates in the splendid folio, especially when he gazes on engravings of the author himself in action, will notice the kinship at once. (The dales and the queer rusticated façade of Bolsover sweep across the background and the solitary cavalier, periwigged, ribanded and plumed and as cool as a cucumber, is levitated in patrician aloofness astride a mount with its mane tied in neat bows and curvetting in mid-air with the resilience of a dolphin. Watching his lavoltas and corantos, expert hidalgos from Castille with rowels the size of Michaelmas daisies would make the sign of the cross and cry '¡Miraculo!') These later Viennese evolutions were as precise and as complex and as unhastening as the Spanish etiquette which, so the survivors say, constricted the Habsburg court till the end. Poker-faces froze the riders' features into masks which were symbolic of the arcane and introvert madness which pervades all haute école; and a spell-bound aura, as of four-footed zombies, clothed their neurotic and ravishing steeds. A vision of haunting wonder.

There was much talk of this obsolete Spanish etiquette. It is hard to imagine when one is surrounded by the easy-going charm of present-day Austrian ways, but portraits are lavish with hints. It is clear that something new and strange was planted in the Habsburg Empire at the marriage of Philip the Handsome to Joan the Mad. She brought Castille and Aragon and all Spain and an array of new kingdoms as a dowry, and Sicily and half Italy and a slice of North Africa and nearly all the new-found Americas; and ceremoniousness as well, and black clothes and the high Spanish punctilio. With the lapse of generations, when lantern jaws and pendulous underlips held sway in both capitals and infantas and archduchesses were almost interchangeable, sombre capes with the scarlet crosses of Santiago and Calatrava began to mingle with the gaudy plumes and slashes of the Landsknecht captains; Escurial solemnity threw the shadows of ritual postures along the Hofburg flagstones and the Holy Roman Empire and the Most Catholic

Kingdom were fused. Was Don John a Spanish or an Austrian hero? Above the cavernous bends of the Tagus, hewn or picked out in coloured scales on the barbicans of Toledo, the great double-headed eagle of the Empire opens its feathers wider, even today, than any kindred emblem by the Danube or in Tyrol. Crossing the Atlantic with its wings heraldically spread on the sails of his fleets, the same bird was emblematic of the sudden expanse of Charles V's amazing inheritance. Cut in volcanic stone and crumbling among the lianas, that display of stone feathers still puzzles the Quetzal-conscious Maya; four centuries of earthquakes have spared them from ruin by Lake Titikaka. Charles was the epitome of the double heritage, a living symbol of the Teutonic and the Latin compound and the whole age. Darkly clad against a dark background, wearied with governing and campaigning, standing with one hand resting on his dog's head, how thoughtfully and sombrely the great Emperor looks out from Titian's picture! When he retired after his abdication, it fitted the prevailing duality that he should settle neither in Melk nor Göttweig nor St Florian nor in any of the famous Austrian abbeys, but in a small royal annexe which he attached like a limpet to the walls of the little Hieronymite monastery of Yuste, among the beech and ilex woods of Estremadura.

I had never understood till now how near the Turks had got to taking Vienna. Of the first siege in Tudor times there were few mementoes in the museums. But the evidence of the second, more than a century later, and of the narrow escape of the city, was compellingly laid out. There were quivers and arrows and quarrels and bow-cases and tartar bows; scimitars, khanjars, yatagans, lances, bucklers, drums; helmets damascened and spiked and fitted with arrowy nasal-pieces; the turbans of janissaries, a pasha's tent, cannon and flags and horsetail banners with their bright brass crescents. Charles of Lorraine and John Sobiesky caracoled in their gilded frames and the breastplate of Rüdiger v. Starhemberg, the town's brave defender, gleamed with oiling and burnishing. (When John Sobiesky of Poland met the Emperor on horseback in the fields after the city was saved, the two sovereigns conversed in Latin for want of a common tongue.) There, too, was the mace of

Suleiman the Magnificent, and the skull of Kara Mustafa, the Grand Vizir strangled and decapitated at Belgrade by Suleiman's descendant for his failure to take Vienna; and beside it, the executioner's silken bowstring. The great drama had taken place in 1683, eighteen years after the Great Fire of London; but all the corroborative detail, the masses of old maps, the prints and the models of the city, turned it into a real and a recent event.

A huge wall encircled the roofs of the city. Eagle banners fluttered from the gables and the battlements and above them loomed many of the towers and steeples I could see when I looked out of the windows. The trenches and the mines of Turkish sappers, all heading for the two key bastions, wriggled across mezzotints like a tangle of wormcasts; the moats, the glacis, the ruins, and the bitterly contested ravelins had all been tilted by the engravers as though for the convenience of a studious bird. Hundreds of tents encompassed the walls; spahis and janissaries pressed forward; the wild cavalry of the Khan of Krim Tartary scoured the woods and bristling regiments of lancers moved about like counter-marching cornfields. Tethered beyond the fascines and the gabions and the stacked powder-kegs, a score of camels that had padded all the way from Arabia and Bactria gazed at the scene and then at each other, while turbaned gunners simultaneously plied their linstocks and clouds of smoke burst out of the cannon. And lo! even as I looked, the same guns, captured and melted down and recast as bells when the Moslems were driven downstream, were peacefully chiming the hour from the steeple of St Stephen's.

It had been a close run thing. What if the Turks had taken Vienna, as they nearly did, and advanced westward? And suppose the Sultan, with half the east at heel, had pitched his tents outside Calais? A few years before, the Dutch had burnt a flotilla of men-of-war at Chatham. Might St Paul's, only half re-built, have ended with minarets instead of its two bell-towers and a different emblem twinkling on the dome? The muezzin's wail over Ludgate Hill? The moment of retrospective defeatism set off new speculations: that wall – fortifications two and a half miles in length and sixty yards wide – had once enclosed the Inner City with a girdle of rampart and fosse. Like the fortifications of Paris which gave way to the outer boulevards in the last century, they were pulled down and replaced by the leafy thoroughfare of the Ring. Very much in character, the Viennese of the late fifties whirled and galloped about their ballrooms to the beat of Strauss's new 'Demolition-Polka', composed in celebration of the change. But, for as long as it stood, that massive wall of defensive masonry, twice battered by the Turkish guns and twice manned by the desperate Viennese, had been, for all its additions, materially the same as the great wall of the thirteenth century; and the cost of building it, I learnt with excitement, had been paid for by the English ransom of Richard Coeur de Lion. So the King's fury on the battlements of Acre had been the first link in a chain which, five centuries later, had helped to save Christendom from the paynims! The thought of this unconscious and delayed-action crusading filled me with keen delight.

Martial spoils apart, the great contest has left little trace. It was the beginning of coffee-drinking in the West, or so the Viennese maintain. The earliest coffee houses, they insist, were kept by some of the Sultan's Greek and Serbian subjects who had sought sanctuary in Vienna. But the rolls which the Viennese dipped in the new drink were modelled on the half-moons of the Sultan's flag. The shape caught on all over the world. They mark the end of the age-old struggle between and hot-cross-bun and the croissant.

Waking one morning, I saw that it was 3 March. It was impossible to believe that I'd been in Vienna three weeks! The days had sped by. They had simultaneously spun themselves into a miniature lifetime and turned me into a temporary Viennese. (Unlike halts in summer, winter sojourns bestow a kind of honorary citizenship.) There is little to account for this long lapse of days; there seldom is, in the towns on this journey. I had met many people of different kinds, had eaten meals in a number of hospitable houses, above all, I had seen a lot. Later, when I read about this period in Vienna, I was struck by the melancholy which seems to have impressed the writers so strongly. It owed less to the prevailing political uncertainty than to the fallen fortunes of the old imperial city. These writers knew the town better than I, and they must have been right; and I did have momentary inklings of this sadness. But my impression of infinite and glowing charm is probably the result of a total immersion in the past coupled with joyful dissipation. I felt a touch of guilt about my long halt; I had made friends, and departure would be a deracination. Bent on setting off next day, I began assembling my scattered gear.

What was the name of the village on that penultimate morning, and where was it? West of Vienna, and certainly higher; but all the other details have gone. It was Saturday; everybody was free; we drove there in two motor-cars and feasted in an inn perched on the edge of a beech forest. Then, tingling with glühwein and himbeergeist, we toiled in high spirits and with the snow half-way up our shanks down a long forest ride. We halted in clouds of our own breath and looked north-east and across Vienna towards Czechoslovakia and the dim line of the Little Carpathians; and, just as the sun was beginning to set, we came on a tarn in a ghostly wood of rime-feathered saplings as two-dimensional and brittle-seeming as white ferns. The water was solid, like a rink. Breaking icicles off the trees, we sent the fragments bounding across the surface and into the assembling shadows with an eerie twittering sound and an echo that took half a minute to die away. It was dark when we drove back, talking and singing with the prospect of a cheerful last evening ahead. How different it seemed from my first arrival, under the tarpaulin with Trudi! *Where was Konrad?* It might have been a year ago. Prompted by my recent preoccupations, perhaps, the conversation veered to Charles V's grandfather, the first Maximilian: The Last of the Knights, as he was called, half Landsknecht, and, until you looked more carefully at Dürer's drawing, half playing-card monarch. Someone was describing how he used to escape from the business of the Empire now and then by retiring to a remote castle in the Tyrolese or Styrian forests. Scorning muskets and crossbows and armed only with a long spear, he would set out for days after stag and wild boar. It was during one of these holidays that he composed a four-line poem, and inscribed it with chalk, or in lampblack, on the walls of the castle cellar. It was still there, the speaker said.

Who told us all this? Einer? One of the Austrian couple who were with us? Probably not Robin or Lee or Basset ... I've forgotten, just as I've forgotten the place we were coming from and the name of the castle. Whoever it was, I must have asked him to write it out, for here it is, transcribed inside the cover of a diary I began a fortnight later – frayed and battered now – with the old Austrian spelling painstakingly intact. There was something talismanic about these lines, I thought.

> Leb, waiss nit wie lang,
> Und stürb, waiss nit wann
> Muess fahren, waiss nit wohin
> Mich wundert, das ich so frelich bin.*

They have a more hopeful drift than the comparable five lines by an earlier Caesar, especially the last line. I preferred Maximilian's end to Hadrian's desolating

> Nec ut soles dabis jocos.

---

* Live, don't know how long,
  And die, don't know when;
  Must go, don't know where;
  I am astonished I am so cheerful.

Stop press! I've just discovered that the castle is called Schloss Tratzberg. It is near Jenbach, still standing, and not very far from Innsbruck.

EIGHT

The Edge of the Slav World

THE friend who had driven me through the eastern suburbs of Vienna drew up under the barbican of Fischamend: 'Shall we drive on?' he asked. 'Just a bit further?' Unawares, we had gone too far already. The road ran straight and due east beside the Danube. It was very tempting; all horsepower corrupts. But rather reluctantly, I fished out my rucksack, waved to the driver on his return journey to Vienna and set off.

Trees lined the road in a diminishing vista. The magpies that flew to and fro in the thin yellow sunshine were beyond all joy-and-sorrow computation and all other thoughts were chased away, as I approached the little town of Petronell, by wondering what a distant object could be that was growing steadily larger as I advanced. It turned out to be a Roman triumphal gateway standing in the middle of a field like a provincial version of the Arch of Titus; alone, enormous and astonishing. The vault sprang from massive piers and the marble facings had long fallen away, laying bare a battered and voluminous core of brick and rubble. Rooks crowded all over it and hopped among the half-buried fragments that scattered the furrows. Visible for miles, the arch of Carnuntum must have amazed the Marcomanni and the Quadi on the opposite bank. Marcus Aurelius wintered here three years, striding cloaked across the ploughland amid the hovering pensées, alternately writing his meditations and subduing the barbarians on the other side of the Danube. His most famous victory – fought in a deep canyon and celestially reinforced by thunder and hail – was known as the Miracle of the Thundering Legions. It is commemorated on the Antonine Column in Rome.

The Marchfeld – the moss-land and swamp on the other shore – was another region that history has singled out for slaughter: wars between Romans and the Germanic tribes at first, dim clashes of Ostrogoths, Huns, Avars and the Magyars later on, then great medieval pitched-battles between Bohemia and Hungary and the

Empire. Archduke Charles, charging flag in hand through the reeds, won the first allied victory over Napoleon at Aspern, a few miles upstream and the field of Wagram was only just out of sight.

In the late afternoon I knocked on the gate of Schloss Deutsch-Altenburg – a wooded castle on the Danube's bank. Friends in Vienna had asked the owner to put me up for the night and old Graf Ludwigstorff, after a kind welcome, handed me over to his pretty daughter Maritschi. We gazed at the Roman tombstones in the museum and the marble and bronze busts. There were fragments of a marble maenad and a complete shrine of Mithras, companion to all the others that scattered the Roman frontier from Hadrian's Wall to the Black Sea.

Snowdrops were out along the tow-path. We played ducks and drakes, sending the pebbles skimming among the floating ice until it was too dark to see them. Then, stepping through the driftwood, we got back in time for tea. The windows were only separated from the river by a clump of trees, and any lingering pangs for lost Vienna soon dissolved in the friendly lamplight.

I was through the barbican in the old walled town of Hainburg early next day. Castled hills rose from the shore, and soon, under the ruins of Theben, the battle-haunted fens came to an end on the other side of the river. Below this steep rock, the March – which is the Czech Morava – flowed into the Danube from the north, marking the Czechoslovak border. The Wolfstal, the narrow trough between the two spurs that rose on either side of the Danube, was the immemorial sally-port that led to Hungary and the wild east: the last bastion to be stormed by Asian invaders before laying siege to Vienna.

I was excited by the thought that the frontiers of Austria and Czechoslovakia and Hungary were about to converge. Though separated from it by the river, I was opposite Czechoslovakian territory already; I planned to wheel left into the Republic and attack Hungary later on from the flank. In reality I was even closer than that: I was wandering across a field when a man in uniform began shouting from the dyke-road overhead. Where the devil did I think I was going? It was the Austrian frontier post.

'You were walking straight into Czechoslovakia!' the official said reproachfully as he stamped my passport. I left the eagles and the red-white-red road barrier behind. The next frontier, after a stretch of no man's land, was closed by a barrier of red, white and blue. Another rubber-stamp was smacked down by a broad-faced Czechoslovak official with the Lion of Bohemia on his cap. 'My fourth country,' I thought exultantly.

In a little while I got to an enormous bridge. Its great frame, the masts and trees and old buildings congregated at the further bridgehead and the steep ascending city above them had been visible for miles. It was the old city of Pressburg, re-baptized with the Slav name of Bratislava when it became part of the new Czechoslovak Republic. The climbing roofs were dominated by a hill and the symmetry of the huge gaunt castle and the height of its corner-towers gave it the look of an upside-down table.

. I reached the middle of the bridge at the same moment as a chain of barges and leaned over to watch them nose their way upstream through the flotsam. The ice-fragments were beginning to get furry at the edges. Colliding with them softly, the vessels disappeared under the bridge one by one and emerged the other side in the wake of a sturdy tug. It flew the Yugoslav colours and the name *Beograd* was painted along the sooty bows in Cyrillic and Latin characters. The long-drawn-out wail of the siren gave way to the coughing staccato of the engine. The funnel puffed out a non-stop sequence of smoke balloons that lingered on the still air as the procession grew smaller in the distance, in a slowly-dissolving dotted line. The barges toiled against the current, sunk to their gunwales under a tarpaulined cargo. But in a day or two – I thought with sudden envy – they would be stealing into the Wachau and waking the two-noted echo of Dürnstein.

Listening to the unfamiliar hubbub of Slovak and Magyar the other side, I realized I was at last in a country where the indigenous sounds meant nothing at all; it was a relief to hear some German as well. I managed to find my way to the Bank where my friend Hans Ziegler held minor sway and ask if the Herr Doktor was in his office; and that evening I was safe under a roof which was to be my haven for days.

Hans and I had made friends in Vienna. He was nine years older than I. His family lived in Prague and, like many Austrians at the break-up of the Empire, they had found themselves citizens of the new-born Republic, tied there beyond uprooting by old commitments; in this case, by a family bank. Hans helped to run the branch of an associate establishment in Bratislava – or Pressburg, as he still firmly called it, just as ex-Hungarians stubbornly clung to Pozony* – and felt rather cut off from life. Vienna was his true home. Apart from this, England was his favourite. He had many friends there and happy memories of college lawns and country sojourns. His fondness for architecture coincided with my early fumblings in the same direction; and it was from him, I am certain, that I first heard the great names of Fischer von Erlach and Hildebrandt and the Asam family. 'Come and stay on your way to Hungary and cheer me up,' he had said. 'I get so bored there.'

To my uncritical eye Bratislava didn't seem too bad. Anyway, Hans's humorous gift turned the society of the place into a comic and entertaining scene. Whenever he had a free moment, we explored the surviving relics of the town, plunging through arched barbicans and along twisting lanes in our search; journeys which ended with cakes stuffed with nuts and poppy-seeds in a wonderful Biedermeier café called the Konditorei Maier, or sipping stronger stuff in a little vaulted bar hard by. At certain hours, all that was dashing in the town assembled there like forest creatures gathering at their water-hole.

Hans wasn't alone in his critical feelings about Bratislava. Most of the people we saw would have agreed – a few worldly-wise Austrians, that is, some breezy Hungarian squires from nearby estates, the amusing Jewish manager of the brewery, a Canon of the Cathedral chapter expert in Magyar history, and the local eccentrics and a few of the local beauties. 'You should have seen it before the War!' – this was the general burden of those who were old enough to remember. The great days of the city were long past. During the centuries when all Hungary south of the Danube

* The word is pronounced as though it were French and spelt Pôjogne, with a heavy stress on the first syllable.

was occupied by the Turks, the city was the capital of the un-conquered remainder of the Kingdom on the north side of the river: the modern province of Slovakia, that is to say. The Kings of Hungary were crowned here in the gothic Cathedral from 1536 to 1784: Habsburgs by then, thanks to the able marriage policy of the dynasty, by which the Hungarian crown had become an appanage of the Austrian ruling house. When the Turks were flung back, the accumulated splendours of the city flowed downstream. The palaces remained, but their incumbents settled in rival mansions that sprang up on the slopes of reconquered Buda. In 1811, as though immolating itself in protest, the great royal castle – the upturned table on the hill – caught fire and burned to a cinder. It was never rebuilt, and the enormous gutted shell, which still looked intact from a distance, sulked on its hilltop as a memento of fled splendour. For its old Hungarian overlords the city's recent change of nationality and name and nature seemed the ultimate sorrow.

'Östlich von Wien fängt der Orient an.'* I had picked up this phrase of Metternich's somewhere, and it kept reminding me that the crescent moon of the Turks had fluttered along the southern bank of the river for nearly two centuries. But there was another feeling in the air as well, unconnected with the vanished Otto-mans, which was new and hard to define. Perhaps it had some-thing to do with the three names of the city and the trilingual public notices and street names: the juxtaposition of tongues made me feel I had crossed more than a political frontier. A different cast had streamed on stage and the whole plot had changed.

Except for balalaika-players in night-clubs, the Slovak and the occasional Czech in the streets were the first Slav sounds I had ever heard. I learnt all I could about how they had come here but even so, there was something mysterious about that vast advent. It was so quiet: a sudden Dark Ages outflow, in the twilight regions between the Vistula and the Pripet Marshes, from a staunchless spring of tribes. The noisy upheavals of the Germanic races and their famous *Drang* westwards must have muffled other

---

* 'East of Vienna, the Orient begins.'

sounds while the Slavs flowed south through the Carpathians.
The settlements of the Czechs and the Slovaks were no more than
early landmarks in this voluminous flux. On it went: over the
fallen fences of the Roman Empire; past the flat territories of the
Avars; across the great rivers and through the Balkan passes and
into the dilapidated provinces of the Empire of the East: silently
soaking in, spreading like liquid across blotting paper with the
speed of a game of Grandmother's Steps. Chroniclers only noticed
them every century or so and at intervals of several hundred miles.
They filled up Eastern Europe until their spread through the barbarous void was at last absorbed by the greater numbers and the
ancient and ailing realm of Byzantium.* Their eastward expansion and hegemony only stopped at the Behring Straits.

There was no ambiguity about the events that split the Slav
world in two. The Magyars, at the end of their journey from
faraway pastures a thousand miles north-east of the Caspian,
broke through the Carpathian passes in 895. Although they had
been some centuries on the way, it was a demon-king entrance –
the flames and the thunder were accompanied by shouts from
saddle to saddle in the Ugro-Finnish branch of the Ural-Altaic
languages – and everything went down before it. The desert tract
east of the Danube, abruptly cleared of the newly arrived Bulgars
and the last of the shadowy Avars, became the Great Hungarian
Plain at last; and the Slav kingdom of Great Moravia, the vital link
between the northern and the southern Slavs, broke up for ever
under the newcomers' hoofs. Their arrival had followed the well-
known pattern of barbarian invasions. Indeed, the analogy between the Huns of Attila and the Magyars of Arpád was close
enough for the West to misname not only the new arrivals, but
the land where they took root. But, after a few decades of spirited
havoc all over western and southern Europe, the pattern changed.
Within a century, the conquests of these heathen horsemen had

---

* But by no means at once. Even in the Mani, the southern tip of
Europe where I am writing these pages, there are traces of their progress: the names of hill villages a couple of miles from my table,
incomprehensible here, would be understood at once on the banks of
the Don.

turned into one of the most powerful and resplendent of the western states, a realm with enormous frontiers and a saint for a king. From the very first, the kingdom included all the lands of the Slovaks and the frontier remained unchanged for the ten centuries that separate Arpád from President Wilson. A few years ago, they had been detached from the crown of St Stephen and given to the new Republic of Czechoslovakia. If the transferred province had contained only Slovaks, it would have been painful to the Hungarians, but ethnologically just. Unfortunately it contained a wide strip of land to the north of the Danube whose inhabitants were Magyars: a fierce amputation for Hungary, a double-edged gift for Czechoslovakia, and rife with future trouble. The German-speakers were descendants of the Teutonic citizens who had helped to populate most of the cities of Central Europe.

Few readers can know as little about these new regions as I did. But, as they were to be the background for the next few hundred miles of travel, I felt more involved in them every day. All at once I was surrounded by fresh clues – the moulding on a window, the cut of a beard, overheard syllables, an unfamiliar shape of a horse or a hat, a shift of accent, the taste of a new drink, the occasional unfamiliar lettering – and the accumulating fragments were beginning to cohere like the pieces of a jigsaw puzzle. Meanwhile, further afield, the shift of mountains and plains and rivers and the evidence of enormous movements of races gave me the feeling of travelling across a relief map where the initiative lay wholly with the mineral world. It evicted with drought and ice, beckoned with water and grazing, decoyed with mirages and tilted and shifted populations, like the hundreds-and-thousands in a glass-topped balancing game; steering languages, breaking them up into tribes and dialects, assembling and confronting kingdoms, grouping civilizations, channelling beliefs, guiding armies and blocking the way to philosophies and styles of art and finally giving them a relenting shove through the steeper passes. These thoughts invested everything with drama. As I listened to the muffled vowels of the Slovaks and the traffic-jams of consonants and the explosive spurts of dentals and sibilants, my mind's eye automatically suspended an imaginary backcloth of the Slav heartlands behind the speakers: three reeds on a horizontal line, the map-makers' symbol for a swamp, infinitely multiplied; spruce and poplar forests, stilt houses and fish-traps, frozen plains and lakes where the ice-holes were black with waterfowl. Then, at the astonishing sound of Magyar – a dactylic canter where the ictus of every initial syllable set off a troop of identical vowels with their accents all swerving one way like wheat-ears in the wind – the scene changed. For some reason I surveyed this from above – prompted, perhaps, by a sub-conscious hint from *Sohrab and Rustam?* – as though I were a crane migrating across Asia. League upon league of burnt-up pasture unfurled. The glaciers of the Urals or the Altai hung on the skyline and threads of smoke rose up from collapsible cities of concertina-walled black felt pavilions while a whole nation of ponies grazed. Everything seemed to corroborate these inklings. Wandering in the back-lanes on the second day I was there, I went into a lively drinking-hall with the Magyar word VENDEGLÖ painted in large letters across the front pane and bumped into a trio of Hungarian farmers. Enmeshed in smoke and the fumes of plum-brandy with paprika-pods sizzling on the charcoal, they were hiccupping festive dactyls to each other and unsteadily clinking their tenth thimblefuls of palinka: vigorous, angular-faced, dark-clad and dark-glanced men with black moustaches tipped down at the corners of their mouths. Their white shirts were buttoned at the throat. They wore low-crowned black hats with narrow brims and high boots of shiny black leather with a Hessian notch at the knee. Hunnish whips were looped about their wrists. They might have just dismounted after sacking the palace of the Moravian kral.

My next call, only a few doors away, was a similar haunt of sawdust and spilt liquor and spit, but, this time, KRČMA was daubed over the window. All was Slav within. The tow-haired Slovaks drinking there were dressed in conical fleece hats and patched sheepskin-jerkins with the matted wool turned inwards. They were shod in canoe-shaped cowhide moccasins. Their shanks, cross-gartered with uncured thongs, were bulbously swaddled in felt that would only be unwrapped in the spring. Swamp-and-conifer men they looked, with faces tundra-blank and eyes as blue and as vague as unmapped lakes which the plum-brandy was misting over. But they might just as well have been swallowing hydromel a thousand years earlier, before setting off to track the cloven spoor of the aurochs across a frozen Trans-Carpathian bog.

Liquor distilled from peach and plum, charcoal-smoke, paprika, garlic, poppy seed – these hints to the nostril and the tongue were joined by signals that addressed themselves to the ear, softly at first and soon more insistently: the flutter of light hammers over the wires of a zither, glissandos on violin strings that dropped and swooped in a mesh of unfamiliar patterns, and, once, the liquid notes of a harp. They were harbingers of a deviant and intoxicating new music that would only break loose in full strength on the Hungarian side of the Danube.

In the outskirts of the town these hints abounded: I felt myself drawn there like a pin to a magnet. Half-lost in lanes full of humble grocers' shops and harness-makers and corn-chandlers and smithies, I caught a first glimpse of Gypsies. Women with chocolate-coloured babies were begging among the pony-carts and a brown Carpathian bear, led by a dancing-master dark as sin, lumbered pigeon-toed over the cobbles. Every few seconds, his leader jangled a tambourine to put the animal through his paces; then he laid a wooden flute to his lips and blew an ascending trill of minims. Sinuous and beautiful fortune-tellers, stagily coifed and ear-ringed and flounced in tiers of yellow and magenta and apple-green, perfunctorily shuffled their cards and proffered them in dog-eared fans as they strolled through the crowds, laying soft-voiced and unrelenting siege to every stranger they met. Sinking flush with the landscape, the town quickly fell to pieces and gave way to an ambiguous fringe of huts and wagons and fires and winter flies where a tangle of brown children scampered and wrestled in the mud among the skirmishing and coupling dogs. I was soon sighted. This far-off glimpse launched a pattering of small feet and a swarm of snot-caked half-naked Mowglis who pummelled each other for precedence as they raced on their quarry. Clambering over each other, they patted and pulled and wheedled in Hungarian and reviled each other in Romany. An old blacksmith, bronze-hued as an Inca, egged them on under the semblance of rebuke in a stream of words from beyond the Himalayas. (His anvil, with a row of horse-nails laid out, was stapled to a tree-stump and one brown foot worked the bellows of a little forge.) I gave a small coin to the nearest. This wrought the onslaught of his rivals to a frenzy and their shrill litanies rose to such a pitch that I scattered my small change like danegeld and retreated. At last, when they saw there was nothing left, they trotted back to the huts, exchanging blows and recriminations. All except one, that is, a hardy chestnut-coloured boy about five years old wearing nothing at all except a black trilby that must have been his father's. It was so big for him that, though he constantly wriggled his head from side to side as he plucked and pleaded, the hat remained stationary. But there was nothing left. Suddenly giving up, he pelted downhill to join the others.

Pincers in hand, the old blacksmith had watched all this with the mare's near-fore hoof cupped in his lap while her colt tugged thirstily. A hush had spread among the wagons and the twinkling fires when I last looked back. The Gypsies were settling down to their evening hedgehog and dusk was beginning to fall.

Bratislava was full of secrets. It was the outpost of a whole congeries of towns where far-wanderers had come to a halt, and the Jews, the most ancient and famous of them, were numerous enough to give a pronounced character to the town. In Vienna, I had caught fleeting glimpses of the inhabitants of the Leopoldstadt quarter, but always from a distance. Here, very early on, I singled out one of the many Jewish coffee houses. Feeling I was in the heart of things, I would sit rapt there for hours. It was as big as a station and enclosed like an aquarium with glass walls. Moisture dripped across the panes and logs roared up a stove-chimney of black tin pipes that zigzagged with accordion-pleated angles through the smoky air overhead. Conversing and arguing and con-tracting business round an archipelago of tables, the dark-clad cus-tomers thronged the place to bursting point. (Those marble squares did duty as improvised offices in thousands of cafés all through Central Europe and the Balkans and the Levant.) The minor hubbub of Magyar and Slovak was outnumbered by voices speaking German, pronounced in the Austrian way or with the invariable Hungarian stress on the initial syllable. But quite often the talk was in Yiddish, and the German strain in the language always made me think that I was going to catch the ghost of a meaning. But it eluded me every time; for the dialect – or the language, rather – though rooted in medieval Franconian German, is complicated by queer syntax and a host of changes and diminutives. Strange gutturals, Slav accretions and many words and formations remembered from the Hebrew have contributed to its idiosyncrasy. The up-and-down, rather nasal lilt makes it more odd than harmonious to an outsider but it is linguistically of enormous interest: a vernacular in which the history of the Jews of northern Europe and the centuries of their ebb and flow between the Rhine and Russia are all embedded. (Two years later, in London, when I felt I knew German a little better, I went twice to the Yiddish Theatre in Whitechapel; but I found the dialogue on the stage more fugitive than ever.) There were rabbis in the café now and then, easily singled out by their long beards and beaver hats and by black overcoats down to their heels. Occasionally they were accompanied by Talmudic students of about my age, some even younger, who wore small skullcaps or black low-crowned hats with the wide brims turned up, and queer elf-locks trained into corkscrews which hung beside their ears. In spite of these, pallor and abstraction stamped some of these faces with the beauty of young saints. They had a lost look about them as if they were permanently startled when they were away from their desks. Their eyes – bright blue, or as dark as midnight oil – were expanded to the innocent width of the eyes of gazelles. Sometimes they had a nearly blind expression; years of peering at texts seemed to have put their gaze out of focus for a wider field. I had visions of them, candle-lit behind sealed and cobwebbed windows, with the thick lenses of their spectacles gleaming close to the page as they re-unravelled Holy Writ: texts that had been commented on, recensed, annotated and bickered over in Babylon, Cordova, Kairouan, Vilna, Troyes and Mainz and Narbonne by fourteen centuries of scholiasts. Mists of dark or red fluff blurred a few of those chins that no razor touched, and their cheeks were as pale as the wax that lit the page while the dense black lettering swallowed up their youth and their lives.*

---

* These days marked the resumption of an old obsession with alphabets. The back pages of a surviving notebook are full of Old Testa-

I longed to attend a religious service, but without the guidance of some initiate friend, didn't dare. This diffidence was broken many years later by Dr Egon Wellesz' book on Byzantine plainsong. In apostolic times, he writes, the Psalms formed the backbone of the Christian liturgy, chanted just as they were in the great temples of Jerusalem and Antioch. The same music is the common ancestor of the Jewish service, the chants of the Greek Orthodox Church and Gregorian plainsong; of the last, the *cantus peregrinus*, which appropriately accompanies the chanting of *In exitu Israel*, is considered the closest. Spurred by this, I ventured into the magnificent Carolean Portuguese-Dutch Synagogue in Artillery Row. By good luck, a visiting Sephardic choir of great virtuosity was singing, and I thought, perhaps rather sanguinely, that I could detect a point of union between the three kinds of singing. It was like singling out familiar notes faintly carried by the breeze from the other side of a dense forest of time. There was a comparably moving occasion many years later. Wandering about north-western Greece, I made friends with the Rabbi of Yannina, and he invited me to attend the Feast of Purim. The old, once

ment names laboriously transliterated into Hebrew characters, complete with their diacritics. There are everyday words copied down as well, for the ancient script was also used in the Yiddish vernacular on shop-fronts and in the newspapers I saw in cafés. (There are even words, similarly transliterated on later pages, from the old Spanish Ladino of the Constantinople and Salonica Jews.) Next, symptoms from the final stages of this journey, come Cyrillic and Arabic: Arab letters were still used among the unreformed Turks in Bulgaria and in Greek Thrace. There are struggles with obsolete Glagolitic and bold attempts at the twisted pothooks and hangers of the Armenians who scattered the Balkans like little colonies of toucans. The brief catalogue ends with a flood of Greek. The magic of all these letters largely depended on their inscrutability: when I learnt a bit of Bulgarian, Cyrillic lost some of its *mana*. But Arabic and Hebrew retain theirs to the last. Even today, a toothpaste advertisement in Arabic suggests the *Thousand and One Nights*, a message in Hebrew over a shop window – 'Umbrellas Repaired on the Spot', or 'Daniel Kisch, Koscher Würste und Salami' – is heavy with glamour. The symbols carry a hint of the Kabala, an echo of Joshua's ram's horns and a whisper from the Song of Songs.

crowded Sephardic Jewish quarter inside Ali Pasha's tremendous walls was already falling to ruin. The rabbi had assembled the little group which was all that had survived the German occupation and come safe home. Cross-legged on the low-railed platform and slowly turning the two staves of the scroll, he intoned the book of Esther – describing the heroine's intercession with King Ahasuerus and the deliverance of the Jews from the plot of Haman – to an almost empty synagogue.

The Schlossberg, the rock which dominates the town with its colossal gutted castle, had a bad name, and I hadn't climbed many of the steps of the lane before understanding why. One side of the path dropped among trees and rocks, but on the other, each of the hovels which clung to the mountain was a harlot's nest. Dressed in their shifts with overcoats over their shoulders or glittering in brightly-coloured and threadbare satin, the inmates leaned conversationally akimbo against their door-jambs, or peered out with their elbows propped on the half-doors of their cells and asked passers-by for a light for their cigarettes. Most of them were handsome and seasoned viragos, often with peroxided hair as lifeless as straw and paint was laid on their cheeks with a doll-maker's boldness. There were a few monsters and a number of beldames. Here and there a pretty newcomer resembled a dropped plant about to be trodden flat. Many sat indoors on their pallets, looking humble and forlorn, while Hungarian peasants and Czech and Slovak soldiers from the garrison clumped past in ascending and descending streams. During the day, except for the polyglot murmur of invitation, it was rather a silent place. But it grew noisier after dark when shadows brought confidence and the plum-brandy began to bite home. It was only lit by cigarette ends and by an indoor glow that silhouetted the girls on their thresholds. Pink lights revealed the detail of each small interior: a hastily tidied bed, a tin basin and a jug, some lustral gear and a shelf displaying a bottle of solution, pox-foiling and gentian-hued; a couple of dresses hung on a nail. There would be a crucifix, or an oleograph of the Immaculate Conception or the Assumption, and perhaps a print of St Wenceslas, St John Nepomuk or St Martin of Tours.

Postcards of male and female film stars were stuck in the frames of the looking-glasses, and scattered among them snapshots of Mas-zaryk, Admiral Horthy and Archduke Otto declared the al-legiance of the inmates. A saucepan of water simmered over charcoal; there was little else. The continuity of these twinkling hollows was only broken when one of the incumbents charmed a stooping soldier under her lintel. Then a dowsed lamp and the closing of a flimsy door, or a curtain strung from nail to nail, masked their hasty embraces from the passers-by. This staircase of a hundred harlots was trodden hollow by decades of hobnails, and the lights, slanting across the night like a phosphorescent diag-onal in a honeycomb, ended in the dark. One felt, but could not see, the huge battlemented ruin above. At the lower end, the diffused lights of the city cataracted downhill.

This was the first quarter of its kind I had seen. Without know-ing quite how I had arrived, I found myself wandering there again and again, as an auditor more than an actor. The tacit principle to flinch at nothing on this journey quailed here. These girls, after all, were not their Viennese sisters, who could slow up a bishop with the lift of an eyelash. And even without this embargo, the retribution that I thought inevitable – no nose before the year was out – would have kept me safely out of doors. The lure was more complicated. Recoil, guilt, sympathy, attraction, *romantisme du bordel* and *nostalgie de la boue* wove a heady and sinister garland. It conjured up the abominations in the books of the Prophets and the stews of Babylon and Corinth and scenes from Lucian, Juvenal, Petronius and Villon. It was aesthetically astonishing too, a Jacob's ladder tilted between the rooftops and the sky, crowded with shuffling ghosts and with angels long fallen and moulting. I could never tire of it.

Loitering there one evening, and suddenly late for dinner, I began running downhill and nearly collided in the shadows with a figure that was burlier than the rest of us and planted like a celebrity in the centre of a dim and respectful ring. When the bystanders drew to one side, it turned out to be the brown Car-pathian bear, unsteadily upright in their midst. His swart companion was at hand, and as I sped zigzagging among my fellow-spectres, I could hear the chink of a tambourine, the first choreographic trill of the wooden flute and the clapping hands and the cries of the girls.

A few minutes later, safe in the brightly-lit anticlimax of the central streets, the stairs and their denizens and the secret pandemic spell that reigned there were as bereft of substance as figments from a dream in the small hours, and as remote. It was always the same.

Hans's rooms, after all these mild forays, were a charmed refuge of books and drinks and talk. He was illuminating on the questions and perplexities I came home with and amused by my reactions, especially to the Schlossberg. When I asked him about the Czechs and Austrians, he handed me an English translation of Hašek's *Good Soldier Švejk* – or Schweik, as it was spelt in this edition – which had just come out.* It was exactly what I needed. (Thinking of Czechoslovakia, I was to remember it much later on, when the horrors of occupation from the West were followed by long-drawn-out and still continuing afflictions from the East; both of them still unguessed at then, in spite of the gathering omens.) It was rather broadminded of Hans, as the drift of the book is resolutely anti-Austrian. Though he was a dutiful citizen of the successor state, his heart, I felt, still lay with the order of things that had surrounded his early childhood. How could it be otherwise?

At last, with a sigh, I began to assemble my gear, making ready to plunge into Hungary. I climbed to the castle for a final chance to spy out the land.

Two nuns were gazing over the blowy void. They stood on the terrace exactly where an engraver would have placed them to balance his composition and give the castle scale. One, with a voluminous sleeve and a dynamically pointing forefinger outstretched, was explaining the vast landscape while her static companion listened in wonder. Their survey ended, they passed me, stooping into the wind with a rustle of their habits and a clash of beads, each with a hand across the crown of her head to

---

* Superseded by Sir Cecil Parrott's fine translation a few years ago.

steady the starch of her coif and her swirling veils. Their glances
were lowered in the custody of the eyes that their rule enjoins. As
they vanished downhill through a tall gateway of late gothic
ashlars, I hoped they had found the more conventional of the two
descending flights. Except for a throng of jackdaws perching in
the chinks and sliding about noisily in the wind, I was alone.

In the west, a narrow vista of the Marchfeld, which the Wolfstal enclosed between the two tower-crowned headlands of the
Porta Hungarica, brought the uncoiling Danube on the scene. It
flowed under the great bridge; Hungary replaced Austria on its
southern strand; then the plains to the south and the east spread
the water in a shallow fan. These sudden lowlands, the antechamber to the puszta, had seduced the river into breaking loose.
Flood and marsh expanded and streams wandered away in branching coils which an invisible tilt of the plain always guided back to
their allegiance; and at each return, as though to atone for their
truancy, the deserting streams brought a straggle of new tributaries with them. The flat islands of meadow and pasture retreated into the distance with the ampleness of counties. Snow
striped the landscape still and the patches of grass between the
stripes were beginning to revive again in sweeps of green. Brooks
divided field from field and the trees that marked their windings
were feathery with a purplish haze of buds. Spinneys of mist surrounded the barns and the manor-houses, and the copper domes of
faraway parishes flashed back the light above these changing
woods. The ice had all but thawed. The gleam beyond the film of
rushes on the river had grown scarce. But the retreat of the racing
cloud-shadows turned the streams from lead to steel and from steel
to bright silver.

On the south side, so far downstream that they were hard to
discern, a blur of low mountains marked the end of all this watery
disintegration. On my side, as I climbed among the burnt-out
fortifications and looked inland, I could follow the advance of
another range, the Little Carpathians, of which I was standing on
the smallest and southernmost spur. They flowed eastwards, rising
gently out of the plain, the merest wave of the land at first. Then
they slowly turned, as the shallow buttresses ascended, into the
great range itself, steepening like a warning roll of thunder to soar

into the distance, snow-covered and out of sight beyond the fur-
thest ceiling of cloud. The invisible watershed shares its snowfalls
with the Polish slopes and the tremendous Carpathian barrier,
forested hiding-place of boars and wolves and bears, climbs and
sweeps for hundreds of miles beyond the reach of even memory's
eye. It towers above southern Poland and the Ukraine and the
whole length of Rumania in a thousand-mile-long boomerang-
shaped curve until it retreats west again, subsides and finally
drops into the lower Danube at the Iron Gates for its underwater
meeting with the Great Balkan Range.

From the foot of the castle's north-western tower, a ravine saun-
tered towards Moravia. Then, as I rotated the beam of my glance
westward, the valley-framed fragment of the Marchfield – penultimate glimpse of Maria Theresa's kind world – wheeled back
into view. The western edge of the plain melted into the Leitha
mountains of Lower Austria and the glimmering Neusiedlersee.
This was the Burgenland, taken from Hungary two decades earlier
to compensate Austria for the loss of the South Tyrol. It was once
the most southern region of the vanished kingdom of Great Moravia, the last connecting filament which still united the North and
the South Slavs when the Magyars sundered them for ever.

Craning from these ramparts and peering beyond the long
and winding lake that was just out of sight, a giant with a tele-
scope could have spotted the Italianate palace of the Eszterházys
at Eisenstadt. He could also have picked out the chapel and the
private theatre and the tiled roof under which Haydn had lived
and composed for thirty years. A few miles further on, this giant
would have pin-pointed the dairy-farm where Liszt was born – his
father was a steward in the same music-loving family. A group of
local noblemen subscribed for the young composer to study in
Paris. Later on, they presented him with a sword of honour to cut
a dash with in the courts of the West. It was just a thousand
years since their pagan ancestors, who could only count up to
seven, had drawn rein here. I liked to think of those country
dynasts, with their theatres and their sword of honour and
their passion for music. The memory of the two great composers
hallowed the region and seemed to scatter the southern skyline
with notes.

My glance, having completed its circle, veered over the Hungarian border again and followed the eastward rush of the clouds. I should be on the march there next day.

Or so I thought.

NINE

Prague under Snow

BUT next evening, when I should have been finding somewhere to sleep after the first day's march in Hungary, Hans and I were unfolding our napkins under the pink lampshades of the dining-car while the night train to Prague whirled us full tilt in the opposite direction. Hans, who had taken my Central European education in hand, said it would be a shame to go gallivanting further east without seeing the old capital of Bohemia. I couldn't possibly afford the trip but he had abolished all doubts by a smile and a raised hand enjoining silence. I had been gaining skill, when involved in doings above my station, at accepting this tempering of the wind to the shorn lamb. The banknote I flourished in restaurants, like Groucho Marx's dollar-bill on a length of elastic, grew more tattered with each airing. I strove to make my protests sound sincere, but they were always brushed aside with amiable firmness.

Falling asleep after dinner, we woke for a moment in the small hours as the train came to a halt in a vast and silent station. The infinitesimal specks of snow that hovered in the beam of the station lamps were falling so slowly that they hardly seemed to move. A goods train at another platform indicated the sudden accessibility of Warsaw. PRAHA – BRNO – BRESLAU – LODZ – WARZAVA. The words were stencilled across the trucks; the momentary vision of a sledded Polack jingled across my mind's eye. When the train began to move, the word BRNO slid away in the opposite direction then BRNO! BRNO! BRNO! The dense syllable flashed past the window at decreasing intervals and we fell asleep again and plunged on through the Moravian dark and into Bohemia.

At breakfast time, we climbed down into the awakening capital.

Stripped of the customary approach on foot, Prague remains distinct from all the other towns of this journey. Memory encircles it with a wreath, a smoke-ring and the paper lattice of a valentine. I might have been shot out of a gun through all three of them and landed on one of its ancient squares fluttering with the scissor-work and the vapour and the foliage that would have followed me in the slipstream. The trajectory had carried Hans and me back into the middle of winter. All the detail – the uprush of the crockets, the processions of statues along the coping of bridges and the levitated palaces – were outlined with snow; and, the higher the buildings climbed, the more densely the woods enfolded the ancient town. Dark with nests, skeleton trees lifted the citadel and the cathedral above the tops of an invading forest and filled the sky with cawing and croaking.

It was a bewildering and captivating town. The charm and the kindness of Hans's parents and his brothers were a marvellous enhancement of it, for an articulate enthusiasm for life stamped them all; and, in borrowed evening plumage that night, among the candle-lit faces of an animated dinner party, I first understood how fast was the prevailing pace. Hans we know. Heinz, the eldest brother, a professor of political theory at the University, looked more like a poet or a musician than a don and the ideas he showered about him were stamped with inspiration. Paul, the youngest and a few years older than me, was touched by the same grace. Those candles, rekindled now for a moment, also reveal their kind parents, and Heinz's dark and beautiful wife. There is also a remarkable relation-in-law of hers, a man of great age and originality, called Pappi, or Haupt zu Pappenheim. His talk, rooted in a picaresque life all over the world, emerged in a headlong rush of omniscience and humour. (My seventeenth-century obsession connected the name at once with the great cavalry commander in the Thirty Years War, one who had sought out Gustavus Adolphus at Lützen, as Rupert had sought out Cromwell at Marston Moor, to be struck down at the same moment as the King in another part of the field. His relation's discourse had some of the same dash.)

Much later the scene shifted from these candles to a cave-like nightclub where silhouettes floated past on a tide of cigarette smoke, and the talk – abetted by syphon-hiss and cork-pop, and encouraged rather than hindered by the blues and the muted cymbals and the wailing saxophone – flowed unstaunchably on. It culminated in marvellously abstruse and inventive theories, launched by Heinz, about Rilke and Werfel and the interrelation of Kafka's *Castle* – as yet unread by me – and the actual citadel that dominated the capital. When we emerged, the great pile itself was still wrapped in the dark, but only just.

As I followed Hans's zigzag and switchback course all over the steep city, it occurred to me that hangovers are not always harmful. If they fall short of the double-vision which turns Salisbury Cathedral into Cologne they invest scenery with a lustre which is unknown to total abstainers. Once we were under the lancets of St Vitus's Cathedral, a second conviction began to form. Prague was the recapitulation and the summing-up of all I had gazed at since stepping ashore in Holland, and more; for that slender nave and the airy clerestory owed spiritual allegiance far beyond the Teutonic heartland, and the Slav world. They might have sprung up in France under the early Valois or in Plantagenet England.

The last of the congregation were emerging to a fickle momentary sunlight. Indoors the aftermath of incense, as one might say with a lisp, still floated among the clustered piers. Ensconced in their distant stalls, an antiphonal rearguard of canons was intoning Nones.

Under the diapered soffits and sanctuary lamps of a chantry, a casket like a brocaded ark of the covenant enclosed the remains of a saint. Floating wicks and rows of candles lit up his effigy overhead: they revealed a mild medieval sovereign holding a spear in his hand and leaning on his shield. It was Good King Wenceslas, no less. The confrontation was like a meeting with Jack the Giant Killer or Old King Cole . . . English carol-singers, Hans told me as we knelt in a convenient pew, had promoted him in rank. The sainted Czech prince – ancestor of a long line of Bohemian kings, however – was murdered in 934. And there he lay, hallowed by his countrymen for the last thousand years.

Outside, except for the baroque top to the presiding belfry, the cathedral itself might have been an elaborate gothic reliquary. From the massed upward thrust of its buttresses to the stickleback ridge of its high-pitched roof it was spiked with a forest of perpendiculars. Up the corner of the transepts, stairs in fretted polygonal cylinders spiralled and counter-spiralled, and flying buttresses enmeshed the whole fabric in a radiating web of slants. Borne up in its flight by a row of cusped and trefoiled half-arches, each of them carried a steep procession of pinnacles and every moulding was a ledge for snow, as though the masonry were perpetually unloosing volleys of snow-feathered shafts among the rooks and the bruise-coloured and quicksilver clouds.

A spell hangs in the air of this citadel – the Hradčany, as it is called in Czech; Hradschin in German – and I was under its thrall long before I could pronounce its name. Even now, looking at photographs of the beautiful lost city, the same spell begins to work. There was another heirloom of the old Bohemian kings hard by the cathedral: the church of St George, whose baroque carapace masked a Romanesque church of great purity. The round arches that we call Norman plunged through bare and massive walls, flat beams bore up the ceiling; and a slim, gilt medieval St George gleamed in the apse as he cantered his charger over the dragon's lanced and coiling throes. He reminded me of that debonair stone banneret at Ybbs. It was the first Romanesque building I had seen since those faintly remembered Rhenish towns between Christmas and the New Year.

And, at this very point, confusion begins. The city teems with wonders; but what belongs where? Certainly that stupendous staircase called the Riders' Steps, and all that lay beyond them, were part of the great castle-palace. The marvellous strangeness of the late gothic vaults enclosing this flight must have germinated in an atmosphere like the English mood which coaxed fan-tracery into bloom. The Winter Queen, in her brief snowy reign, was equally astonished, perhaps; her English renaissance upbringing – those masques and their fantastic stage-sets by Inigo Jones – may have been a better preparation. I kept thinking of her as I peered up. These vaults are almost impossible to describe. The ribs burst straight out of the walls in V-shaped clusters of springers. Grooved like celery stalks and blade-shaped in cross section with the edge pointing down, they expanded and twisted as they rose. They separated, converged again and crossed each other and as they sped away, enclosed slender spans of wall like the petals of tulips; and when two ribs intersected, they might both have been obliquely notched and then half-joggled together with studied carelessness. They writhed on their own axes and simultaneously followed the curve of the vault; and often, after these contorted intersections, the ribs that followed a concave thrust were chopped off short while the convex plunged headlong and were swallowed up in the masonry. The loose mesh tightened as it neared the rounded summit and the frantic reticulation jammed in momentary deadlock. Four truncated ribs, dovetailing in rough parallelograms, formed keystones and then broke loose again with a wildness which at first glance resembled organic violence clean out of control. But a second glance, embracing the wider design, captured a strange and marvellous coherence, as though petrifaction had arrested this whirling dynamism at a chance moment of balance and harmony.

Everything here was strange. The archway at the top of these shallow steps, avoiding the threatened anticlimax of a flattened ogee, deviated in two round-topped lobes on either side with a right-angled central cleft slashed deep between the cusps. There had been days, I was told, when horsemen on the way to the indoor lists rode in full armour up these steps: lobster-clad riders slipping and clattering as they stooped their ostrich-plumes under the freak doorway, gingerly carrying their lances at the trail to keep the bright paint that spiralled them unchipped. But in King Vladislav's vast Hall of Homage the ribs of the vaulting had further to travel, higher to soar. Springing close to the floor from reversed and bisected cones, they sailed aloft curving and spreading across the wide arch of the ceiling: parting, crossing, re-joining, and – once again – enclosing those slim subdivided tulips as they climbed. Then they cast their intertwining arcs in wider and yet wider loops with the looseness and the overlap of lassoes kept perpetually on the move, accelerating, as they ascended, to the speed of coiling stockwhips . . . Spaced out along the wide ridge of the vault, their intersections composed the corollas of marguerites and then fled away once more into wider patterns that needed another shift of focus to apprehend. Travelling the length of that arched vista of ceiling, the loops of the stone ribs expanded and crossed and changed partners, simultaneously altering direction

and handing on the succession of arcs until the parabolas, reaching the far limit of this strange curvilinear relay-race, began to
swing back. Nearing home and completing the journey in reverse, they rejoined their lost companions at their starting point
and sank tapering and interlocked. The sinuous mobility entranced
the eye, but it was not only this. Lit by the wintry chiaroscuro of
the tall windows, the white tulip-shaped expanses that these
stone ribs enclosed so carelessly seemed to be animated by an even
more rapid and streamlined verve. Each of these incidental and
sinuous facets reflected a different degree of white, and their
motion, as they ascended the reversed half-cones of the vault and
curled over into the ceiling, suggested the spreading and upward-
showering rush of a school of dolphins leaping out of the water.

It was amazing and marvellous. I had never seen anything like
it. One can imagine a draughtsman twiddling arcs and marguerites with his compass and elaborating them for fun in vast
symmetrical tangles – only to push them aside with a sigh. It is
the high-spirited audacity of their materialization that turns
everything to wonder. Hans was telling me as I gazed how Count
Thurn and a party of Protestant nobles had tramped under these
vaults on the way to their fateful meeting with the councillors of
the Holy Roman Emperor, all in full armour: the word 'armour'
suddenly offered a solution. It seemed, all at once, the apt analogy
and the key to everything here. The steel whorls and flutings,
those exuberant wings of metal that adorned the plate-armour of
Maximilian's Knights! Carapaces which, for all their flamboyance
and vainglory, withstood mace-blows and kept out arrows and the
points of swords and lances. In the same way the flaunting halls
and the seven hundred rooms of this castle have maintained thousands of labyrinthine tons of Kafka masonry against fire and siege
for centuries. These vaults and these stairways were concave three-
dimensional offshoots of the Danubian breakout, and shelter for
Landsknechts. Altdorfer's world!

Heraldry smothered the walls and the vaults that followed.
Shield followed painted shield and aviaries and zoos and aquaria
supplied the emblems that fluttered and reared and curvetted
among the foliage on the helmets. We were in the very heart of
the Landsknecht century. Reached by a spiral, the last of these

castle-interiors was an austere and thick-walled room, roofed with dark beams and lit by deeply embrased leaded windows; a sturdy old table was set on the waxed flag-stones. It was in this Imperial aulic council chamber, on 23 May 1618, that Thurn and those mail-clad Czech lords had pressed their claims on the Imperial councillors and broken the deadlock by throwing them out of the window. The Defenestrations of Prague were the penultimate act before the outbreak of the Thirty Years War. The last was the arrival of the Elector Palatine and his English Electress to be crowned.*

It was time to seek out one of the wine cellars we had noticed on the way up.

I climb about the steep city in retrospect and rediscover fragments one by one. There are renaissance buildings, light arcaded pavilions and loggias on slim Ionic pillars that could have alighted here from Tuscany or Latium, but the palaces on the squares and the citadel and the steep wooded slopes belong to the Habsburg afternoon. Troops of Corinthian pillars parade along half-façades of ashlars rusticated like the nail-head patterns on decanters, and symbols and panoplies overflow the pediments. Branching under processions of statues, shallow staircases unite before great doorways where muscle-bound Atlantes strain under the weight of the lintels, and the gardens underneath them are flocked by marble populations. Nymphs bind their collapsing sheaves, goddesses tilt cornucopias, satyrs give chase, nymphs flee, and tritons blow fanfares from their twirling shells. (The snow in the folds of their flying garments and the icicles which seal the lips of the river gods are there till spring.) Terraces climb the hillside in a giant staircase and somewhere, above the frosty twigs, juts a folly like a mandarin's hat; it must have been built about the time when *Don Giovanni* was being composed a mile away. Looking-glass regions

---

* They lost their kingdom for ever when the Bohemian army was routed by Maximilian of Bavaria, Chief of the Catholic League, at the battle of the White Hill – only a mile from the citadel – on 8 November 1620.
Question: Who is the most unexpected private soldier to be fighting as a volunteer in Maximilian's army? Answer: Descartes.

succeed each other inside the palaces – aqueous reaches under vernal and sunset pastorals where painters and plasterers and cabinet-makers and glaziers and brasiers have fused all their skills in a silence that still seems to vibrate with fugues and passacaglias and the ghosts of commiserating sevenths.

Where, in this half-recollected maze, do the reviving memories of the libraries belong? To the Old University perhaps, one of the most ancient and famous in Europe, founded by the great King Charles IV in 1384. I'm not sure. But I drive wedge-shaped salients into oblivion nevertheless and follow them through the recoiling mists with enfilading perspectives of books until bay after bay coheres. Each of them is tiered with burnished leather bindings and gold and scarlet gleam on the spines of hazel and chestnut and pale vellum. Globes space out the chessboard floors. There are glass-topped homes for incunables. Triangular lecterns display graduals and antiphonals and Books of Hours and coloured scenes encrust the capitals on the buckled parchment; block-notes and lozenges climb and fall on four-line Gregorian staves where the Carolingian uncials and blackletter spell out the responses. The concerted spin of a score of barley-sugar pillars upholds elliptic galleries where brass combines with polished oak, and obelisks and pineapples alternate on the balustrades. Along the shallow vaulting of these chambers, plasterwork interlocks triangular tongues of frosty bracken with classical and allegorical scenes. Ascanius pursues his stag, Dido laments the flight of Aeneas, Numa slumbers in the cave of Egearia and all over the ceiling draped sky-figures fall back in a swoon from a succession of unclouding wonders.

Floating downhill, memory scoops new hollows. Churches, echoing marble concavities dim as cisterns in this cloudy weather, celebrate the Counter-Reformation. Plinths round the floor of rotundas hoist stone evangelists aloft. With robes spiralling in ecstasy and mitres like half-open shears, they hover half-way up the twin pillars from whose acanthus-tops the dome-bearing semicircles fly. In one of these churches, where the Tridentine fervour had been dulled by two centuries of triumph, there were saints of a less emphatic cast. The figure of St John the Divine – imberb, quizzically smiling, quill in hand and at ease in a dressing-gown with his hair flowing loose like an undress-wig, he might be setting down the first line of *Candide* instead of the Apocalypse; perhaps the sculptor has confused his Enlightenments. Seen from a fountain-square of the Hradčany, the green copper domes, where each snow-laden segment is pierced with a scrolled lunette, might belong to great Rome itself. The pinnacles on all the cupolas are tipped with monstrances shooting rays like golden fireworks; and when these and the gold balls on the tips of the other finials are touched by a rare sunbeam, the air glitters for a moment with a host of flying baubles.

A first glance, then, reveals a baroque city loaded with the spoils of the Austrian Caesars. It celebrates the Habsburg marriage-claims to the crown of Bohemia and reaffirms the questionable supersession of the old elective rights of the Bohemians; and alongside the Emperor's temporal ascendancy, this architecture symbolizes the triumph of the Pope's Imperial champion over the Hussites and the Protestants. Some of the churches bear witness to the energy of the Jesuits. They are stone emblems of their fierce zeal in the religious conflict. (Bohemia had been a Protestant country at the outbreak of the Thirty Years War. It was Catholic once more at its close and as free of heresy as Languedoc after the Albigensian crusade, or the sea-shore of oyster-response at the end of 'The Walrus and the Carpenter'.)*

But in spite of this scene, a renewed scrutiny of the warren below reveals an earlier and a medieval city where squat towers jut. A russet-scaled labyrinth of late medieval roofs embeds the baroque splendours. Barn-like slants of tiles open their rows of flat dormers like gills – a medieval ventilation device for the breeze to dry laundry after those rare washing-days. Robust buildings join each other over arcades that are stayed by the slant of heavy buttresses. Coloured houses erupt at street corners in the cupola-topped cylinders and octagons that I had first admired in Swabia

---

* These were bad decades for religious toleration in Europe. They include the massacres of Drogheda and Wexford, the expulsions beyond the Shannon and Cromwell's resolute attempts to stamp out the Catholic Church in Ireland.

and the façades and the gables are decorated with pediments and scrolls and steps; teams of pargetted men and animals process solemnly round the walls; and giants in high relief look as though they are half immured and trying to elbow their way out. Hardly a street is untouched by religious bloodshed; every important square has been a ceremonious stage for beheadings. The symbolic carved chalices, erased from strongholds of the Utraquist sect of the Hussites – who claimed communion in both kinds for the laity – were replaced by the Virgin's statue after the re-establishment of Catholicism. Steel spikes, clustered about with minor spires, rise by the score from the belfries of the older churches and the steeples of the riverside barbicans, flattened into sharp wedges, are encased in metal scales and set about with spikes and balls and iron pennants. These are armourers' rather than masons' work. They look like engines meant to lame or hamstring infernal cavalry after dark. Streets rise abruptly; lanes turn the corners in fans of steps; and the cobbles are steep enough to bring down dray-horses and send toboggans out of control. (Not now; the snow has been heaped in sooty banks, deep and crisp but uneven; the real Wenceslas weather was over.)

These spires and towers recalled the earlier Prague of the Wenceslases and the Ottokars and the race of the Přemysl kings, sprung from the fairy-tale marriage of a Czech princess with a plough-boy encountered on the banks of the river. The Czechs have always looked back with longing to the reigns of the saintly sovereign and of his descendants and to the powerful and benevolent Charles IV – a golden age when Czech was the language of rulers and subjects, religious discord unknown and the rights of crown and nobles and commons and peasants all intact. These feelings gained strength during the Czech revival under the last hundred years of Habsburg ascendancy. Austrian rule fluctuated between unconvinced absolutism and liberalism soon repented and it was abetted by linguistic pressures, untimely inflexibility and all of the follies that assail declining empires, for knavery was not to blame. These ancient wrongs must have lost much of their bitterness in the baleful light of modern times when the only evidence to survive is an heirloom of luminous architectural beauty.

It took me a little time to realize that the Vltava and the

Moldau were the Czech and the German names for the same river.
It flows through the capital as majestically as the Tiber and the
Seine through their offspring cities; like them, it is adorned with
midstream islands and crossed by noble bridges. Among crowding
churches and a mist of trees, two armoured barbicans prick their
steeples like gauntlets grasping either end of a blade and between
them flies one of the great medieval bridges of Europe. Built by
Charles IV, it is a rival to Avignon and Regensburg and Cahors
and a stone epitome of the city's past. Sixteen tunnelling spans
carry it over the flood. Each arc springs from a massive pier and the
supporting cutwaters advance into the rush of the current like a
line of forts. High overhead and every few yards along either
balustrade stand saints or groups of saints and as one gazes
along the curve of the bridge, the teams unite in a flying population; a backward glance through one of the barbicans reveals the
façade of a church where yet another holy flock starts up from a
score of ledges. At the middle of one side and higher than the rest,
stands St Johannes Nepomuk. He was martyred a few yards away
in 1393 – he is said to have refused, under torture, to betray a
confessional secret of Queen Sophia. When the henchmen of Wenceslas IV carried him here and hurled him into the Vltava, his
drowned body, which was later retrieved and entombed in the
Cathedral, floated downstream under a ring of stars.*

It was getting dark when we crossed the bridge. Leaning on the
balustrade, we gazed upstream and past an eyot towards the
river's source; it rises in the Bohemian forest somewhere north of
Linz. Then, looking over the other side, we pieced together the
river's itinerary downstream. If we had launched a paper boat at
the quay she would have joined the Elbe in twenty miles and
entered Saxony. Then, floating under the bridges of Dresden and
Magdeburg, she would have crossed the plains of Old Prussia with
Brandenburg to starboard and Anhalt to port and finally, battling
on between Hanover and Holstein, she would have picked her

---

* Other versions exist. There are several instances of defenestration
in Czech history, and it has continued into modern times. The Martyrdom of St Johannes is the only case of depontication, but it must
be part of the same Tarpeian tendency.

way between the ocean liners in the Hamburg estuary and struck
the North Sea in the Bight of Heligoland.

We shall never get to Constantinople like this. I know I ought
to be moving on; so does the reader. But I can't – not for a page or
two.

Prague seemed – it still seems, after many rival cities – not only
one of the most beautiful places in the world, but one of the
strangest. Fear, piety, zeal, strife and pride, tempered in the end by
the milder impulses of munificence and learning and *douceur de
vivre*, had flung up an unusual array of grand and unenigmatic
monuments. The city, however, was scattered with darker, more
reticent, less easily decipherable clues. There were moments when
every detail seemed the tip of a phalanx of inexplicable phantoms.
This recurring and slightly sinister feeling was fortified by the
conviction that Prague, of all my halts including Vienna itself,
was the place which the word *Mitteleuropa*, and all that it implies,
fitted most aptly. History pressed heavily upon it. Built a hundred
miles north of the Danube and three hundred east of the Rhine, it
seemed, somehow, out of reach; far withdrawn into the conjectural hinterland of a world the Romans never knew. (Is there a
difference between regions separated by this ancient test? I think
there is.) Ever since their names were first recorded, Prague and
Bohemia had been the westernmost point of interlock and conflict
for the two greatest masses of population in Europe: the dim and
mutually ill-disposed volumes of Slavs and Teutons; nations of
which I knew nothing. Haunted by these enormous shadows, the
very familiarity of much of the architecture made Prague seem
more remote. Yet the town was as indisputably a part of the
western world, and of the traditions of which the West is most
justly vain, as Cologne, or Urbino, or Toulouse or Salamanca – or,
indeed, Durham, which – on a giant scale, *mutatis mutandis*, and
with a hundred additions – it fleetingly resembled. (I thought
about Prague often later on and when evil times came, sympathy,
anger and the guilt which the fate of Eastern Europe has justly
implanted in the West, coloured my cogitations. Brief acquaintance in happier times had left me with the vision of an actual city
to set against the conjectural metamorphosis and this made later

events seem both more immediate and more difficult to grasp.
Nothing can surprise one in the reported vicissitudes of a total
stranger. It is the distant dramas of friends that are the hardest to
conjure up.

I was glad Hans had given me *The Good Soldier Švejk* to read,
but I only realized its importance later on. After *Don Quixote*,
Švejk is the other fictitious figure who has succeeded in represent-
ing – under one aspect and in special circumstances – a whole
nation. His station in life and his character have more in common
with Sancho Panza than with his master, but the author's ironic
skill leaves it doubtful whether ruse or innocence or merely a
natural resilience under persecution, are the saving talisman of his
hero. Jaroslav Hašek was a poet, an anti-clerical eccentric and a
vagabond full of random learning and his adventures paralleled
the picaresque wanderings of his creation. In and out of jail, once
locked up as insane and once for bigamy, he was an incessant
drinker and his excesses killed him in the end. He had a passion
for hoaxes and learned journals. Until he was found out, his description of imaginary fauna in the *Animal World* attained wild
heights of extravagance; and his fake suicide, when he jumped off
the Charles Bridge, at the point where St John Nepomuk was
thrown in, set all Prague by the ears.

Some of Hašek's compatriots disliked his fictional hero and
disapproved of the author. In the rather conventional climate
of the new Republic, Švejk seemed an unpresentable travesty
of the national character. They needn't have worried. The
forces that Švejk had to contend with were tame compared to the
mortal dangers of today. But it is the inspiration of his raffish and
irrefragable shade that has come to the rescue.

In this late attempt to recapture the town, I seem to have
cleared the streets. They are as empty as the thoroughfares in an
architectural print. Nothing but a few historical phantoms survive; a muffled drum, a figure from a book and an echo of Ut-
raquists rioting a few squares away – the milling citizens, the
rushing traffic vanish and the voices of the bilingual city sink to a

whisper. I can just remember a chestnut-woman in a kerchief stamping beside a brazier to keep warm and a hurrying Franciscan with a dozen loaves under his arm. Three cab-drivers nursing their tall whips and drinking schnapps in the outside-bar of a wine cellar materialize for a moment above the sawdust, their noses scarlet from the cold or drink or both, and evaporate again, red noses last, like rear lamps fading through a fog.

What did Hans and I talk about in the cask-lined cave beyond? The vanished Habsburgs for sure, whose monuments and dwelling-places we had been exploring all day. My Austrian itinerary had infected me long ago with the sad charm of the dynasty. I felt that this comforting grotto, with its beams and shields and leaded windows and the lamplight our glasses refracted on the oak in bright and flickering discs, might be the last of a long string of such refuges. We were drinking Franconian wine from the other side of the Bohemian-Bavarian border. *In what glasses?* The bowls, correctly, were colourless. But by the Rhine or the Mosel, as we know, the stems would have ascended in bubbles of amber or green, and tapered like pagodas. Perhaps these stalks were ruby alternating with fluted crystal, for these, with gentian blue and underwater green and the yellow of celandines, are the colours for which the Prague glass-makers have always been famous ... We had gazed with wonder at the astronomical instruments of Emperor Rudolf II. A celestial globe of mythological figures in metal fretwork turned in a giant foliated egg-cup of brass. Chased astrolabes gleamed among telescopes and quadrants and compasses. Armillary spheres flashed concentrically, hoops within hoops ... More of a Spanish Habsburg than an Austrian, Rudolf made Prague his capital and filled it with treasures; and, until the horrors of the Thirty Years War began, Prague was a Renaissance city. Deeply versed in astronomical studies, he invited Tycho Brahe to his Court and the great astronomer arrived, noseless from a duel in Denmark, and lived there until he died of the plague in 1601. Kepler, promptly summoned to continue Brahe's work on the planets, remained there till the Emperor's death. He collected wild animals and assembled a court of mannerist painters. The fantasies of Arcimboldi, which sank into oblivion until they were unearthed again three centuries later, were his discovery. Moody and unbalanced, he lived in an atmosphere of neo-platonic magic, astrology and alchemy. His addiction to arcane practices certainly darkened his scientific bent. But Wallenstein, who was one of the ablest men in Europe, was similarly flawed. In fact, an obsession with the supernatural seems to have pervaded the city. A whole wing of the Italianate palace which Wallenstein inhabited with such mysterious splendour was given over to the secret arts; and when Wallenstein inherited Kepler from Rudolf, the astronomer took part in these sessions with an ironic shrug.*

As well as astrology, an addiction to alchemy had sprung up, and an interest in the Cabala. The town became a magnet for charlatans. The flowing robes and the long white beard of John Dee, the English mathematician and wizard, created a great impression in Central Europe. He made the rounds of credulous Bohemian and Polish noblemen and raised spirits by incantation in castle after castle. He arrived in Central Europe after being

---

* The Waldstein Palace (as I learnt that it was more correctly called) was still owned by the family, and it harboured, among more usual heirlooms, the stuffed charger which had carried Wallenstein at Lützen. An eighteenth-century descendant befriended Casanova, who spent his last thirteen years as librarian composing his memoirs in Waldstein's Bohemian castle. Another descendant was the friend to whom Beethoven dedicated the Waldstein Sonata. He was the most interesting figure of the Thirty Years War. Suspected by the Emperor of intriguing with the Swedes before actually changing sides – and perhaps planning, it was rumoured, to seize the Bohemian crown – he fled to a snow-bound castle near the Bavarian border. Four soldiers of fortune from the British Isles – Gordon, Leslie, Devereux and Colonel Butler of Butler's Irish regiment of Dragoons – cut down Wallenstein's henchmen over the dinner table. Then they sought out the great duke and Devereux ran him through with a pike. By far the best and most exciting book on the whole period is C. V. Wedgwood's *Thirty Years' War*. Dame Veronica delivers an adverse verdict on the last part of Wallenstein's career; ruthlessness and megalomania and increasing trust in astrology had dimmed his earlier genius. He was tall, thin and pale with reddish hair and eyes of a remarkable brilliance.

stripped of his fellowship at Cambridge.* (One wonders how the
Winter Queen, arriving a few decades later, reacted to this odd
atmosphere; we have mentioned, earlier on, her contacts in Heidelberg with the early Rosicrucians.) The Jews, who had been settled
in Prague since the tenth century, fell victims in the eighteenth to
a similar figure called Hayan. He was a Sephardic Jew from Sarajevo, a Cabalist and a votary of the false Messiah Sabbatai Zevi;
he convinced the trusting Ashkenazim. With Elijah's guidance,
he proclaimed in private séances that he could summon God, raise
the dead, and create new worlds.

Our wanderings had ended under a clock tower in the old
Ghetto, where the hands moved anti-clockwise and indicated the
time in Hebrew alphabetic numbers. The russet-coloured synagogue, with its steep and curiously dentated gables, was one of
the oldest in Europe; yet it was built on the site of a still older fane
which was burnt down in a riot, in which three thousand Jews
were massacred, on Easter Sunday, 1389. (The proximity of the
Christian festival to the Feast of the Passover, coupled with the
myth of ritual murder, made Easter week a dangerous time.) The
cemetery hard by was one of the most remarkable places in the
city. Thousands of tombstones in tiers, dating from the fifteenth to
the end of the eighteenth century, were huddled under the elder
branches. The moss had been scoured from the Hebrew letters and
the tops of many slabs bore the carved emblems of the tribes
whose members they commemorated: grapes for Israel, a pitcher
for Levi, hands raised in a gesture of benediction for Aaron. The
emblems on the other stones resembled the arms parlant which
symbolize some family names in heraldry: a stag for Hirsch, a carp
for Karpeles, a cock for Hahn, a lion for Löw; and so on. A
sarcophagus marked the resting place of the most famous bearer of

---

* The cause of his downfall was a public demonstration of the
device by which Trygaeus, the hero of The Peace of Aristophanes,
flew to the crest of Olympus to beg the Gods to end the Pel-
oponnesian War. As this vehicle was a giant dung-beetle from Mount
Etna which the protagonist refuelled with his own droppings on the
long ascent, the exhibition may well have caused a stir. I would like
to have seen it.

the name of Löw. He was Rabbi Jehuda ben Bezabel, the famous scholar and miracle-worker who died in 1609. His tomb is the most important memento of Prague's involvement with the super-natural, for it was the Rabbi Löw who constructed the many-legended robot-figure of the Golem, which he could secretly endow with life by opening its mouth and inserting slips of paper on which magic formulae were inscribed.

My last afternoon was spent high above the river in the library of Heinz Ziegler's flat. I had had my eye on those book-covered walls for a couple of days and this was my chance. I was in pur-suit of links between Bohemia and England, and for a specific reason: I had taken my disappointment over the topography of *The Winter's Tale* very hard, and it still rankled: Shakespeare *must* surely have known more about Bohemia than to give it a coast ... So I stubbornly muttered as I whirled through the pages. He needn't have known much about Peter Payne, the York-shire Lollard from Houghton-on-the-Hill who became one of the great Hussite leaders. But he was full of knowledge about my second Anglo-Bohemian figure, Cardinal Beaufort. He was not only John of Gaunt's son and Bolingbroke's brother and Bishop of Winchester, but one of the chief characters in the first and second parts of *Henry VI*. Before completing his cathedral and being buried there, Beaufort took part in a crusade against the Hussites and slashed his way across Bohemia at the head of a thousand English archers. A third connection, John of Bohemia, must have been equally well known, for he was the blind king who fell in the charge against the Black Prince's 'battle' at Crécy. (His putative crest and motto – the three silver feathers and *Ich dien* – were once thought – wrongly, it appears – to be the origin of the Prince of Wales's badge.) This remarkable man, famous for his Italian wars and his campaigns against the Lithuanian heathen, was married to the last of the Přemysl princesses and one of his children was the great Charles IV, the builder of bridges and universities and, almost incidentally, Holy Roman Emperor as well; and here the connecting thread with England suddenly thickens; for another child was Princess Anne of Bohemia, who became Queen of Eng-

land by marrying the Black Prince's son, Richard of Bordeaux.*
But my last discovery clinched all. Sir Philip Sidney's brief passage
across the sixteenth century glowed like the track of a comet: he
seemed unable to travel in a foreign country without being offered
the crown or the hand of the sovereign's daughter, and his two
sojourns in Bohemia – once after his Viennese winter with
Wotton and a second time at the head of Elizabeth's embassy to
congratulate Rudolf II on his accession – must have lit up the
Bohemian Kingdom, for even the most parochial of his distant
fellow countrymen, with a flare of reality.† Ten years younger
than Sidney, Shakespeare was only twenty-three and quite unknown when his fellow poet was fatally wounded at Zutphen.
But Sidney's sister was married to Lord Pembroke and Pembroke's
Players were the most famous acting company in London: they
must have been friends of the playwright. Their son William
Herbert could not – as some critics used rashly to maintain – have
been Mr W.H., but when the posthumous First Folio was published, he and his brother were the dedicatees; their cordial links
with the poet are carefully stressed by the publishers. Shakespeare

---

* She died young and her tomb is in Westminster Abbey. It is her
successor, the French Princess Isabelle, who, in *Richard II*, overhears
the gardeners talking of the King's fall as they bind up the dangling
apricocks. She was only eleven when Richard was murdered. Back in
France as a Queen Dowager, she married her cousin, the poet Charles
d'Orléans, who was later captured at Agincourt by Henry V and held
prisoner in England for a quarter of a century. She was only nineteen
when she died.

† Edmund Campion was also in Prague at the time, teaching at a
Jesuit seminary. The two had long meetings and they liked and respected each other. Once, in honour of a state occasion, Campion
wrote a long tragedy on the theme of Saul and the city produced it at
vast expense; it was produced with great magnificence and although
it lasted six hours, Rudolf ordered a special repeat performance. In
England four years later, secretly ministering to harried recusants
under the new penal laws, Campion was captured and after the customary tortures and a rushed trial, condemned to die at Tyburn. He
endured the barbarous penalty with the courage of a saint.

must have known everything about Sir Philip Sidney. It became plainer every minute that Bohemia can have held no secrets for him.

This was the point I had reached when Heinz came into the room. He was amused by the earthwork of books which the search had flung up on the carpet, and I explained my perplexity. After a thoughtful pause, he said: 'Wait a moment!' He shut his eyes for a few seconds – they were grey with a hazel ring round the pupil – tapped his forehead slowly once or twice with a frowning effort of memory, opened them again and took down a book. 'Yes, I thought so!' he said in an eager and cheerful voice as he turned the pages, 'Bohemia *did* have a coast line once' – I jumped up – 'but not for long . . .' He read out the relevant passages: 'Ottokar II . . . Yes, that's it . . . Victory over Béla II of Hungary in 1260 . . . enlarged the frontiers of Bohemia . . . Kingdom expands over all Austria . . . yes, yes, yes . . . *southern border extended to both sides of the Istrian peninsula, including a long stretch of the north Dalmatian shore* . . .! Failed to become Emperor, perhaps owing to anti-Slav prejudice among the Electors . . . Yes, yes . . . Defeated and slain by Rudolf of Habsburg at Dürnkrut in 1273, when the country shrank once more to its old frontiers . . .' He shut the book. 'There you are!' he said kindly. 'A coast of Bohemia for you! But only for thirteen years.'

It was a moment of jubilation! There was no time to go into detail, but it looked as though my problems were solved. (The lack of time was a boon; for, once again, disappointment lay in wait. None of the historical characters, even by the boldest feat of literary juggling, could be made to fit. Worse, I discovered that when Shakespeare took the story of *The Winter's Tale* from Robert Greene's *Pandosto, or the Triumph of Time*, he light-heartedly switched the names of Sicily and Bohemia! It was total defeat. I felt as though the poet himself had reached from the clouds to checkmate me by castling the pieces in a single unorthodox move. I understood at last what I should have divined at the outset: punctiliously exact in the historical plays, Shakespeare didn't care a fig for the topography of the comedies. Unless it were some Italian town – Italy being the universal lucky dip for Renaissance playwrights – the spiritual setting was always the same. Woods and

parkland on the Warwickshire, Worcestershire and Gloucestershire borders, that is; flocks and fairs and a palace or two, a mixture of Cockayne- and Cloud-Cuckoo- and fairyland with stage
mountains rather taller than the Cotswolds and full of torrents
and caves, haunted by bears and washed, if need be, by an ocean
teeming with foundering ships and mermaids.)

But it was an instant of seeming triumph in which Heinz and
his wife and Paul and Hans all joined. Heinz was soon filling
glasses of celebration from a decanter cut in a nail-head pattern as
bold as the façade of the Czernin palace. It was a valedictory
drink as well, for the night train was taking Hans and me back to
Bratislava and I planned to cross the Danube into Hungary next
day.

The windows of the flat looked down on the whole of Prague.
Towards the end of my search, the pale sun had set among those
silver and purplish clouds and at lighting-up time all the lamps of
the city had leapt simultaneously to life. Now, though the towers
and pinnacles and the snow-covered domes were swallowed by the
night, their presence was reaffirmed by the city-wide collusion of
bells. Picked out by the embankment lights and the rushing head-
lamps of the traffic, the river was a curving band of darkness
crossed by the many-beaded necklaces of the bridges. Directly
below, between clusters of baroque lamp-brackets, the grouped
statues dimly postured along the balustrades of the Charles
Bridge. The lights grew scarcer as they climbed the citadel and
dispersed round the steep dark wastes where the rooks had assembled for the night in the invading woods. It was a last glimpse
of Prague which has had to last me from that evening to this.

TEN

Slovakia: A Step Forward at Last

MY original scheme, on leaving Bratislava, had been to cross the Danube, strike south-east to the Hungarian frontier and then follow the right bank to the old town of Győr. This itinerary, which would have led across those beginnings of the puszta I had spied out from the castle, was the traditional entrance to Hungary.

But the plan had been changed at the last moment by friends of Hans. Gerti v. Thuroczy, who was married to one of the breezy Hungarian country-gentlemen I mentioned two chapters ago, suggested I should change my route and stay with her brother, Philipp Schey, on the way. The Barons Schey v. Koromla, to give them their full style, were an extremely civilized Austrian-Jewish family – friends of artists, poets, writers and composers and with kinsmen and ramifications in half a dozen countries – that had played an important part in the life of Central and Western Europe. They had once been very rich, but, like everyone else, they were less so now. I had met Pips Schey (as he was universally called) but only for a moment. He was a fascinating and many-legended figure and he lived about forty miles east of Bratislava. Telephones had rung and I was expected in two days.

So I headed north-east instead of south. I was still on the wrong side of the Danube and getting further from the river with every step and deeper into Slovakia. My new plan was to make a wide Slovakian loop, strike the Danube again about a hundred miles downstream and cross into Hungary by the Parkan-Esztergom bridge.

Meanwhile, an important change has come over the raw material of these pages.

Recently – after I had set down all I could remember of these ancient travels – I made a journey down the whole length of the Danube, starting in the Black Forest and ending at the Delta; and in Rumania, in a romantic and improbable way too complicated to recount, I recovered a diary I had left in a country house there in 1939.

I must have bought the manuscript book in Bratislava. It is a thick, battered, stiffly-bound cloth-backed volume containing 320 closely-written pages in pencil. After a long initial passage, the narrative breaks off for a month or two, then starts up again in notes, stops once more, and blossoms out again in proper diary form. And so it goes on, sporadically recording my travels in all the countries between Bratislava and Constantinople, whence it moves to Mount Athos and stops. In the back of the book is a helpful list of overnight sojourns; there are rudimentary vocabularies in Hungarian, Bulgarian, Rumanian, Turkish and Modern Greek and a long list of names and addresses. As I read these, faces I had forgotten for many years began to come back to me: a vintner on the banks of the Tisza, an innkeeper in the Banat, a student in Berkovitza, a girl in Salonica, a Pomak hodja in the Rhodope mountains ... There are one or two sketches of the details of buildings and costumes, some verses, the words of a few folk-songs and the alphabetical jottings I mentioned two chapters back. The stained covers are still warped from their unvarying position in my rucksack and the book seemed – it still seems – positively to smell of that old journey.

It was an exciting trove; a disturbing one too. There were some discrepancies of time and place between the diary and what I had already written but they didn't matter as they could be put right. The trouble was that I had imagined – as one always does with lost property – that the contents were better than they were. Perhaps that earlier loss in Munich wasn't as serious as it had seemed at the time. But, with all its drawbacks, the text did have one virtue: it was dashed down at full speed. I know it is dangerous to change key, but I can't resist using a few passages of this old diary here and there. I have not interfered with the text except for cutting and condensing and clearing up obscurities. It begins on the day I set out from Bratislava.

'*March 19th 1934.*
'... The sky was a lovely blue with big white clouds, and I

walked along a twisting avenue of elm trees. The grass is a
brilliant green and Spring has begun! Looking back, I could see
all the chimney pots of Pressburg and the grey castle on the
mountain and hear the bells over the fields. I wandered on,
smoking contentedly, and at noon sat on a log and looked at the
sun shining on the Little Carpathian mountains to the left of
the road as I ate my brioches, speck and a banana. A troop of
Czechoslovak cavalry were exercising in a field nearby. Their
horses were lovely long-legged creatures, about sixteen hands,
with undocked tails and uncobbed manes. The soldiers rode very
well. Their shaven heads made them look tough and Kossack-
like.

'I felt very drowsy sitting in the sun. My path ran through a
hazel-wood where young roedeer bounced nimbly away, their
white rumps twinkling in the undergrowth. Later, I must have
been wandering along in a sort of trance, as by four o'clock I
had no idea where I was, and whenever I stopped peasants and
asked the way to Baron Schey's at Kövecsespuszta, they ges-
ticulated helplessly, saying "Magyar" or "Slovenski", and I realized the difficulty I was going to have about languages. I must
learn some Hungarian! I was miles off my way, close to a little
town called Senec and about as far from Kövecses as Kövecses
is from Pressburg. A country postman speaking a little German
said I should head for Samorin, about twenty kilometres off; so I
set out along a dismal track over an absolutely flat plain with a
few white farmhouses dotted about. Occasionally I came on an
old bent woman gathering catkins and pussy-willows. (Next
Sunday's Palm Sunday.) They must be frightfully devout
people. I've never seen anything like the reverence with which
they knelt on the earth before wayside crucifixes, crossing themselves and laying sprigs of palm on the ledge. At last I came to a
tributary of the Danube winding through water meadows and
shaded by willows. It's called the Kleine Donau, or in Magyar,
Kish* Duna. I walked till I came to a ferry, and shouted across.
An old man showed up and got in the boat and pulled it over by

---

* *Kis*, little.

tugging at a taut rope stretched shoulder-high. I was on the edge of that marshy country, full of rivers and brooks, that I looked down on from the castle before we went to Prague.

'On the other side, I was walking through utterly flat fields again. The sun was setting in a soft pink sky with a few strands of lighted cloud. *The gold bar of heaven!* Everything was quiet and windless and high above the green fields larks were fluttering. I watched them soaring about the sky, hovering and sinking and ascending. It was lovely and it made me think of Spring in England.

'Soon, as the sky began to fade into twilight, I reached a little place called Nagy-Magyar,* a collection of white-washed houses thatched with long reeds, unkempt and desolate, with roads of rutted mud and no pavements or garden fences. The whole village teemed with swarthy black-haired children in coloured blankets. There were dark-skinned hags with strands of greasy hair hanging out of their headcloths and tall, dark, loose-limbed and shifty-eyed young men. *Zigeunervolk!* Hungarian Gipsies, like the ones I saw in Pozony. Amazing! *Östlich von Wien fängt der Orient an!*

'I found the Burgomaster's house, I don't know how, with all these people surging about. He was a splendid man, a typical Hungarian with a handsome hatchet-face, speaking German in the Hungarian way with the accent always on the first syllable and half the a's turning to o. He at once said he would put me up, and we talked all the evening by the fire, smoking his very strong Hungarian tobacco and drinking golden wine. Wine is *sor* (pronounced *shor*); tobacco, *dohányi*; a light or matches, *gyufa*; "Good night", "jó étszokát kivánok", and "I kiss your hand", "*kezeit csokolom!*" I know this because the old crone who brought in our supper said this and did it in a ceremonious and stately way. I was nonplussed, but it seems it's usual, even to a tramp like me, if he is a stranger and a guest. (Only one word of Slovak so far: *selo* = village, like the Russian

---

* I can't find this tiny village (which means 'Big Hungarian') in any map. There is a much larger place called Nagy Megyer some distance off, but it can't be the same. It's rather confusing.

Tsarskoë Selo, the Tsar's or Imperial village.) There are no boards on the floor, only earth stamped flat and so hard it seems to do as well. The house is thatched with rushes like the others. I went to bed in his spare room and, pulling the eiderdown over me, was soon asleep.

'I've just had breakfast, after scribbling the foregoing rot at high speed. I must say good-bye to the burgomaster and set out for Kövecsespuszta. It's a lovely morning with a light wind.'

In for a penny, in for a pound! I will let my nineteen-year-old forerunner carry on till we get to Kövecses* and then stop.

'*Kövecsespuszta, March 20th*
'I was hardly out of Nagy Magyar this morning, when I saw swarms of tiny tots on the warpath, khaki or darker and later on, three Gipsy women walking towards me down the dusty road. They wore silk and cotton draperies of scarlet, green and purple. I've never seen anything so marvellous. One had a brown baby slung round her waist like a squaw's papoose, but the other two were young and beautiful with brown cheeks and very large, very dark eyes and black, black hair. As we passed each other, they all three shouted something very matey in Magyar or Romany and I made cheerful noises back and beamed a bit. They were without any bashfulness. *I will take some savage woman, she shall rear my dusky race.*

'I soon got to Samorin. Here, to my horror and surprise they told me I was going completely wrong for Sopornya (?) and that it was 30 miles away! It was getting late and I had promised to be at Kövecses by five or six – tea time, in fact; so I asked if I could get there by train. The only way was to go back to Bratislava by bus, they said, and take the train from there. There was nothing else for it.

'The bus was packed. As usual, there were two nuns with bulgy umbrellas, peasants in high boots, sheepskin caps and fleece jerkins, two fat, urban-looking men with gladstone bags on their laps and *grey* bowler hats, and a country gendarme, dripping with sweat in a thick greatcoat; his belt, with revolver

---

* Pronounced Követchesh.

and truncheon and a sword which was more like a cutlass hung swinging from the rack. It took an hour to get back to Pressburg and luckily there was a train leaving for Sered at once, the nearest station to Kövecsespuszta. We passed through Senec once again, then Galanta and Diosegh. In Sered I learnt it was a 10 kilometre march via Sopornya to Kövecses, which would make me two hours late. So I went to the Post Office and tried to telephone, but learnt that the nearest Post Office to Kövecses — a place called Sala-nad-Vahom, I think — closed at six. The boy at the office, though he didn't speak a word of German, was frightfully helpful. He got someone round from the grocer's who did, and this chap took me to the shop. His boss, a big jovial man, said he would send me in his car, with the boy at the wheel. The road got worse and worse. It was dark now and the headlights lit up the trees and the bushes and started a few rabbits, their eyes shining in the dark. At last we got there. The Schloss — the *Kastély* (pronounced *koshtey*) as the boy called it in Magyar — stood in a clump of trees. Only a few windows were lit. The baron's housekeeper Sari let us in and gave the boy a drink. She was a dear old thing with a kerchief tied under her chin. Hand kissed for second time! I found Baron Schey in his library in a leather armchair and slippers reading Marcel Proust.'

The house had the charm of a large and rambling rectory occupied by a long line of bookish and well-to-do incumbents torn between rival passions for field sports and their libraries. 'It's not a *Schloss*,' Baron Pips said when he was showing me my room, 'though they call it that. It's a shooting-box really. But it's also Liberty Hall.' His English was so good that I never heard a single mistake during my whole stay, though he occasionally used an Edwardian turn of phrase that might have fallen into disuse in England a few decades earlier. He was spending the winter there. Except for his own bedroom and a couple of others in case friends turned up and the delightful library where I had found him, most of the rooms had been shut up.

The library was so crammed that most of the panelling was hidden and the books, in German and French and English, had overflowed in neat piles on the floor. The surviving area of wall was filled by antlers and roebuck horns, a couple of portraits and a Rembrandt etching. There was an enormous desk covered with photographs, a box of cigars with a cutter made out of a deer's slot and, beside them, a number of silver cigarette cases laid in a neat row, each of them embossed with a different gold monogram. (This, I noticed later on, was an invariable item in Central European country houses. particularly in Hungary. They were presents exchanged on special occasions, and always between men: for standing godfather, being best man at a wedding, second in a duel, and so on.) There were shaded lamps and leather arm-chairs beside a huge open stove, a basket of logs and a spaniel asleep in front of it.

'I'm on the last volume,' Baron Pips said, lifting up a French paper-bound book. It was *Le Temps Retrouvé* and an ivory paper-knife marked the place three quarters of the way through. 'I started the first volume in October and I've been reading it all winter.' He put it back on the table by his chair. 'I feel so involved in them all, I don't know what I'll do when I've finished. Have you ever tried it?'

As one can guess from the tone of my diary, I had only just heard of Proust, but always mentioned in tones of such respect that I was flattered by his question. I took the first volume to bed that night; but it was too dense a wood. When I tried again in Rumania next year, the wood lightened and turned into a forest whose spell has been growing ever since: so, in spite of this hesi-tant start, Baron Pips was my true initiator. Perhaps because of this, some perverse process of the subconscious for a long time associated him in my mind's eye with the figure of Swann. Beyond one or two haphazard points in common, the resemblance was not close. Certainly not physically, if Swann is to be identified with photographs of Charles Haas in Mr Painter's book. Nevertheless the confusion persisted for years.

He was fifty-two years old and tall and slim and his extra-ordinary good looks were marked by a kind of radiant distinction. I remember them all the more lucidly – the rather pale, high fore-head, the chiselled lines of brow and nose and jaw, the clear blue eyes and the straight silver hair – from making a careful sketch a couple of days later. There was a cast of wisdom and kindness in his face and something about the mouth which suggested an artist or a musician, and his features often lit up with humour and amusement. He wore a very old tweed shooting jacket, soft leather breeches of the kind I had envied in Austria, and thick ribbed green stockings, and his slippers replaced some muddy brogues I had seen in the hall. From his demeanour and the excellence of his English I think a stranger in a railway carriage would have taken him for an Englishman but of a half-patrician, half-scholarly kind which even then seemed threatened with extinction. I knew that his life had been full of movement and adventures, quite apart from his two marriages, the first to a charming and highly suitable member of a similar dynasty, the other to a famous actress in Max Reinhardt's Deutsches Theater in Berlin. There existed, at the time we met, a great attachment between him and a beautiful and poetic-looking white Russian I had met in Bratislava, I think on her way from Kövecses.*

On the evening I arrived, Sari laid dinner on a folding table in the library. When it was cleared away, we went back to the armchairs and the books with our brandy glasses and, undeterred by a clock striking midnight somewhere in the house, talked until nearly one o'clock†

These days at Kövecses were a sojourn of great delight and an

---

* They were married soon after.

† I learnt later on that the eponymous hero (though not the plot) of Wassermann's two-volume novel *Christian Wahnschaffe* – 'World's *Illusion*' in translation – was based on Baron Pips as a young man: and hastened to read it. It's an extraordinary book, written before the first World War; rather turgid and very melodramatic. The hero is a young patrician of dazzling looks, brilliant talents and great wealth. Through idealism and some not very clearly expounded philosophy he gradually divests himself of all his friends, his money and his goods in order to live a life of Franciscan poverty and unworldliness among the poor and the criminals and the whores of a great city. There is a touch of resemblance, I think; with the exception that the saintly fictional figure is without a flicker of the humour of his living prototype.

important private landmark. The delight is plain sailing – the kindness and charm of Baron Pips, and all the erudition, worldly wisdom, reminiscence and humour squandered on someone a third of his age; but the importance as a landmark is more complex. Being told by someone much older to stop calling him Sir may have had something to do with it. It was a sort of informal investiture with the *toga virilis*. I seemed to be getting the best of every world. The atmosphere at Kövecses was the culmination of a change which had been taking place ever since my departure from England. In the past, I had always arrived on any new scene trailing a long history of misdeeds and disasters. Now, the continuity was broken. Somewhere between the Dogger Bank and the Hook of Holland the scent had gone cold; and, for a quarter of a year there had been no rules to break except ones I had chosen. Things were on the mend! No wonder I looked on life with a cheerful glance.

It is hard to think of anyone less didactic than my host. Yet, without any effort, he exerted an emancipating and de-barbarizing influence similar to the mood that radiates from a few exceptionally gifted dons: liberators, that is, whose tact, insight, humour and originality clear the air and store it with new oxygen. He resembled a much-travelled Whig aristocrat – a friend of Voltaire and Diderot, perhaps – who, after enjoying and exhausting the intrigues and frivolities of half a dozen European courts, had retired to his books in some remote and well wooded shire.

I could never tire of hearing about the frivolous aspects of Central European life and it was my curiosity, not his choice, that often led his reminiscences into these worldly channels. He had spent several years in England at the beginning of the century and he recalled those long-fled seasons with all their gleaming details intact: feasts and regattas, race-meetings and house-parties and summer nights when a young bachelor could go to several balls in the same evening. 'I used to, often,' he said, 'it seems too extraordinary to think of. Night after night, getting back to my cousin's house in broad daylight. I remember, just about dawn, seeing a flock of sheep streaming out of Knightsbridge and into the Park at Albert Gate.' He remembered, for my benefit, anecdotes about Edward VII, Mrs Keppel, Lily Langtry, Rosebery, Balfour, Sir Ernest Cassel and Ellen Terry and recalled the conversation of the young Mrs Asquith. The names of the Benson brothers, of Anthony Hope and Frank Schuster came to the surface – but in what connection? I've forgotten. The re-discovered diary is to blame for this sudden profusion.

As he spoke, fashionable Europe at the turn of the century rose like an emanation of absurd and captivating splendour. Sovereigns and statesmen confabulated in a rose-coloured, dove-grey mist. Ambassadors, proconsuls and viceroys, winking with jewelled stars, postured in colloquy. The scene was scattered with uniforms of scarlet and sky-blue; it was afloat, above all, with women of almost supernatural radiance. In Rotten Row or the Bois de Boulogne or the Prater or the Borghese Gardens, they cantered with cockaded grooms in attendance through the sliding leaf-shadows and a ripple of lifted toppers. Under hats which were ibises swerving round corners, they twirled like figures in a dream down perspectives of pleached hornbeam in a retinue of cloth-topped boots. After dark, rainbowed in chandelier-refracting tiaras, with swan-throats clasped in cylinders of pearl, they gyrated through a cloud of sighs to the tunes of *Fledermaus* and *Lily of Laguna*. Paris, he said, had been dazzling in a different and even more complex style. 'Rather like this,' he went on, touching the volume at his side. 'It was still recovering from the Dreyfus case when I first knew it.' He told me how he had listened to older people, just as I was listening to him, describing an anterior France of the Second Empire, the Franco-Prussian War and the Siege of Paris.

'The Kaiser and Little Willie sound pretty dreadful,' I wrote in my diary, 'though Baron Pips is very fair about them.' I asked him about the von Moltke circle and the Eulenburg scandal with its exotic Wildean parallels. He had been much in Germany; but the thought of the new régime was poisoning his memory of them retrospectively. 'Not only on race grounds,' he said, 'though of course that counts.' He had had many German friends, but few had survived the recent changes. How could they? It was as if an entire civilization were sliding into calamity and taking the world with it. We talked much of these things and once, as we were walking to our rooms late at night, he stopped in the passage and said 'I feel I ought to set out like a kind of Don Quixote,' then added with a sad laugh, 'but of course I won't.'

Austria was a rich mine for reminiscence. The familiar figures of Franz Josef and the Empress Elizabeth led to Pauline Metternich, Frau Schratt, the tragedy of Mayerling, the axioms of Taaffe, the misadventures of Bay Middleton. An entire mythology unfolded and I felt glad that Vienna had recently become a real background, in my mind, both for these shadows and for the newer *dramatis personae* I was meeting at one remove: Hofmannsthal, Schnitzler, Kokoschka, Musil and Freud and a galaxy of composers whose importance I didn't really take in till years after. (I wished I had gone to the Opera! I might have broken into an unknown field of delights a decade earlier than I did.) Hölderlin, Rilke, Stefan George and Hofmannsthal were the poets I remember him taking down from the bookshelves when I asked how they sounded. Apropos of Lewis Carroll and Lear and nonsense poetry in general, he introduced me to Christian Morgenstern.* I developed an immediate passion for the characters in his poems and for the vague and hallucinating world they inhabit: a world in which unprincipled architects steal and make off with the empty spaces between the uprights of a railing; where unclassified creatures, followed by their young, stalk on the scene on their multiple noses; and where the legs of two boys, side by side in the cold, begin to freeze, one boy centigrade, the other fahrenheit … An inventor, in one poem, after building a smell-organ, composes music for it – triplets of eucalyptus, tuberose and alpine flowers are followed by hellebore scherzos; and later on, the same inventor creates a giant wicker trap into which he lures a mouse by playing the violin, in order to set it free in the solitudes of a distant forest. Dreamland.

We were sitting in front of the house in the shade of two ancient and enormous poplars and Baron Pips, to illustrate the reckless frequency of French words in pre-war Austrian conversations, told me that when he was a small boy, he had overheard the Emperor ·saying to a Princess Dietrichstein at a garden-party at

---

* He died in 1914.

Bad Ischl, 'Das ist ja *incroyable*, Fürstin! Ihr Wagen scheint ganz *introuvable* zu sein.'† Similar surroundings were the scene of another tale. Friedrich-August, the last King of Saxony, a fat, easy-going and proverbially good-natured man, loathed all court functions and especially the midsummer garden party at Dresden. Once, in liquefaction after a heat-wave afternoon, he was escaping, his duty done, to a cool drink in his study when he spotted, at the other side of the park under a tree, two aged and dismal-looking professors he had forgotten to greet. Hating to hurt anyone's feelings he toiled all the way over to them and shook their hands limply. But the afternoon's output had been too much for him: he just managed to croak 'Na, ihr beide' – 'Well, you two' – and tottered away again.*

I loved these stories. Another, prompted by a mention of Frederick the Great, cropped up while we were walking through the woods at the other end of the demesne. As I've never heard or read it anywhere else, here it is.

Learning that one of his officers had fought with great bravery, the King recommended him for an immediate award of the *Pour le Mérite* Cross, the Prussian equivalent of the V.C., which he had just founded. The ribbon was sent off at once. A few days later, when the officer turned up at the King's headquarters with dispatches, Frederick glanced at his neck and asked him why he wasn't wearing it. There had been a terrible mistake, the officer explained. The award had gone to a cousin in his regiment with the same rank and name. A look of deepening horror spread over the King's face, and when he had finished, the King jumped to his feet and drove him out, crying 'Weg! Geh' weg! Du hast kein Glück!' – 'Away! Go away! You've no luck!'

'Perhaps he said it in French,' Baron Pips said after a pause. 'He hated talking German.'

These walks carried us far afield. All trace of winter had vanished and the snow with it, except for a dwindling line here and there under a hedge or in the lee of a wall where the sun never

---

† 'It's *incroyable*, Princess! Your carriage seems quite *introuvable*.'
* He abdicated in 1919.

reached. Otherwise, the season had leaped forward into spring.
The grass, recovered from the lank pallor of its first re-emergence,
was bright green, and the banks and the roots of the trees were
thick with wild violets. Green lizards, freshly woken from their
winter torpor, scuttled electrically and froze in postures of alert
petrifaction. The hazel-spinneys and the elms and the poplars and
the willows and aspens along the streams were all putting out
new leaves. The universal white had vanished and an unseen
Europe was coming to the surface. The scores of larks and the
returning migrants reminded me that I had hardly seen any birds
except rooks, ravens and magpies, and an occasional robin or a
wren, for a quarter of a year. There was a fidgeting of wagtails and
the twittering that accompanied all the building and nest-repair
was almost an uproar. The peasants in the fields lifted fleece caps
and black hats with friendly greetings and Baron Pips would
answer with a wave of an old green felt with a cord round it, and
the ritual response in Slovak or Hungarian. The Váh,* the wide,
swift river that formed one of the estate boundaries, rose two hundred miles to the north-east, near the Polish frontier. The sides
were banked high against the danger of floods when the thaw
came to the Tatra mountains. The weather had changed so much,
we could lie on the grass there, talking and smoking cigars and
basking under a cloudless sky like the lizards, watching the water
flow past on its way to the Danube. One afternoon, carrying guns
so beautifully balanced that they seemed as light as feathers –
'relics of former splendour,' Baron Pips had said, filling his pockets
with cartridges in the hall – we went out after rabbits. We returned
through a vast warren as evening was coming on. They were
scampering about and sitting in groups and casting shadows
across the fields. I said, although I was carrying three of them,
that they looked so cheerful and decorative it was a shame to
shoot them. After a moment, I heard Baron Pips laugh quietly and
asked why. He said: 'You sound just like Count Sternberg.' He
was an ancient and rather simple-minded Austrian nobleman, he
explained. When he was on his death-bed his confessor said the
time had come to make a general confession. The Count, after

---

* Waag in German, Vár in Magyar.

racking his brains for a while, said he couldn't remember anything to confess. 'Come, come, Count!' the priest said, 'you must have committed *some* sins in your life. Do think again.' After a long and bewildered silence, the Count said, rather reluctantly, 'Habe Hasen geschossen' — 'I've shot hares' — and expired.

Just after sunset, six or seven log-rafts, bound for the Danube and the Balkans, floated by. The trunks had been felled in the Slovakian forests, then lashed together and laden with timber in neat criss-cross stacks. A hut was built on the stern of each of them and the fires for the raftsmen's suppers cast red reflections in the river. The lumberjacks in their leather knee-boots were turning into silhouettes in the failing light. They wished us good evening as they passed, and waved their fur caps. We waved back and Baron Pips called: 'God has brought you.' Except for the fires and their reflections, the rafts had melted into the dark by the time they slid out of sight among the distant trees.

One evening, after my temporary setback with Proust — though I enjoyed the passages that Baron Pips read out when he was particularly struck; for instance, the opinions of Charlus as he crossed Paris during an air-raid — I discovered a hoard of children's books and took them to bed. There were both *Alices*, several Coloured Fairy Books, *Struwwelpeter* in the original, which I'd never seen, and the illustrated couplets of Wilhelm Busch: *Max und Moritz, Hans Huckebein* and so on. There was plenty of French: Becassine, I remember, and the innumerable volumes of the *Bibliothèque Rose*. All these books were inscribed in childish writing with the names 'Minka' and 'Alix', and here and there the same hands had brushed in the outlines of the black-and-white illustrations with bold swirls of water-colour. They were my host's two beautiful daughters,* both by his first marriage, and already familiar from the photographs on his desk in the library. I was only to discover years later and long after the War, when we met in France and became friends, that I had an odd link with these girls — the addiction, that is, to saying things backwards. This habit is first engendered, I suspect, by the sight of the words TAM HTAꓭ rumpled across the bathroom floor when learning

_____
* Minka Strauss and Alix de Rothschild.

to read, and then by deciphering ЯTИAЯUATƧƎЯ and CAᖷƎ
while gazing out of the windows of restaurants and cafés. At first
single words are formed, then whole sentences and, by the time
they are spoken fast enough to sound like an unknown language,
this useless accomplishment has become an obsession. When I had
run out of material for recitation on the march I would often find
myself, almost without knowing it, reciting, say, the 'Ode to a
Nightingale' in this perverse way:

> Ym traeh sehca dna a ysword ssenbmun sniap
> Ym esnes, sa hguoht fo kcolmeh I dah knurd
> Ro deitpme emos llud etaipo ot eht sniard
> Eno etunim tsap dna Ehtelsdraw dah knus,

and so on. For the initiated, these utterances have an arcane and
unearthly beauty.

> Away! Away! For I will fly to thee!

becomes

> Yawa! Yawa! Rof I lliw ylf ot eeht!

and the transposition of

> Through verdurous glooms and winding mossy ways,

is

> Hguorht suorudrev smoolg dna gnidniw yssom syaw.

It seems almost to surpass the original in forest mystery.

I would have remembered most of the details of these days, even
without the re-discovery of my diary, but not all. The leaving-
present of a pocket-volume of Hölderlin would have outlasted
oblivion, and the old leather cigar-case filled with Regalia Media
cigars, but not the two-ounce tin of Capstan pipe tobacco* that

---

'* The diary lays a lot of stress on cigar- and pipe-smoking; I had
forgotten the latter. I think they were both slightly self-conscious
symbols of emancipation and maturity. I always seem to be 'puffing
away thoughtfully' or 'enjoying a quiet pipe', in these pages.

Baron Pips had discovered in a cupboard; nor the contents of the lunch parcel Sari had made up. Her name would have stuck, but not Anna's, the old housemaid, although I remember her face clearly.

Baron Pips kept me company across the fields till we said good-bye outside the little village of Kissujfalu. I looked back when I reached it. He waved when he saw I'd taken the right path, then turned and disappeared into his woods with the spaniel trotting behind.

'Pips Schey?' someone, a vague relation-in-law, said to me, years later in Paris. 'What a charming man! Magical company! And wonderful looking. But he never did anything, you know.' Well, he did in my case, as I have more than hinted. Though we never met again, we corresponded for years. He married soon afterwards, and, when things began to go wrong in Austria and Czechoslovakia, they left Kövecses and settled at Ascona, on the western shore of Lake Maggiore, just north of the Swiss-Italian frontier. He died in 1957 in his younger daughter's country house in Normandy – about twenty miles, in fact, from Cabourg, which is the main candidate for the Proustian town of Balbec. The literary coincidence completes a fortuitous literary circle in my mind. I wish we had met again. I thought of him often, and I still do.

I felt so buoyed up by these days, that even the vague speculation as to how I might have struck him failed to damp my elation: precocious, immature, restless, voluble, prone to show off, unreliably bookish perhaps ... it didn't seem to matter a damn. My journey had taken on a new dimension and all prospects glowed.

ELEVEN

The Marches of Hungary

THIS buoyancy carried me all the way across the flat country from Kissujfalu to the little town of Nové Zamky – Érsekujvár in Hungarian, and Neuhäusl in German – an hour or two after dark. I can't resist letting the diary take over for a few paragraphs:

'... attracted by a tinkle of music, I found my way to this coffee house. Village chaps are sitting round and talking, shouting and playing billiards or *skat*, smacking the cards down defiantly. The accoustics of the room are deafening and every now and then the older people trying to read their newspapers shout for less noise. For a moment everyone speaks in a whisper, than the crescendo increases to its former timbre, the same greybeards remonstrate again, *e poi da capo*. There is a very pretty, very made-up girl who sits behind a table laden with chocolates and strange Hungarian cakes. Her features are slightly Mongolian, with high cheekbones pushing up the corners of her enormous blue eyes. Her soft, heart-shaped mouth is painted crimson and her black velvet dress clings so tight it looks as though it might break. Blue-black hair falls over her brow in a fringe, and she keeps glancing over here. I can't quite make it out. When I look up from this diary she stares me full in the eyes, then turns coyly away. I'm going to sit on for a bit before finding a bed.'

Köbölkut. March 29
'I hadn't waited long last night before the waiter brought a slip of paper with the word *Mancsi* written on it and an address in a nearby street. I was a bit mystified, but the waiter (who, like many of the people there, spoke quite a lot of German) said Mancsi was very nice: would I like an interview? I twigged then and thanked him and said I didn't think I would. I saw him talking to her afterwards, both of them were looking at me and for the rest of the evening she looked no more my way but made

eyes at a small businessman or commercial traveller playing billiards. I felt a bit sad and rather an idiot, I don't know why. A chap was playing the violin accompanied by his wife on the piano and as he could speak some English he sat down to chat and drink cognac. He advised me not to have anything to do with Mancsi, she'd been with everyone in Nové Zamky; *qui-cumque vult*, in fact. But if I were going to Budapest, he told me to visit the Maison Frieda in the Kepiva utca, where, in his flowery words, everyone for five pengös can be a cavalier. This sort of advice is very frequent, ever since the beckonings from the windows of the Schlossberg and the headwaiter in the Astoria* asking Hans and me which of the ladies we would like. Hungarians are keen and direct about all this. I do like them. The violinist, after chatting with the owner, told me I could sleep in a room above the café for the equivalent of a shilling. So I did and set out early this morning.

'I crossed a bridge over the neck of a long marshy lake – part of the Nitra river and gentle hills began to rise. I fell in with three peasants and we kept each other company through the villages of Bajc and Perbete and at noon settled under a hazel-clump on the edge of a huge field. We shared the rest of the lunch Sari had put in my rucksack yesterday – a delicious whole roast chicken, like a tramp's dream – and they offered me great slices of bread with paprika-spiced bacon and afterwards we puffed at baronial cigars.

'The old man was called Ferenc. He talked in rather bad German about the troubles of the Hungarians hereabouts. I do sympathize. It must be terrible having one's country cut up like this and ending on the wrong side of the border. The Treaty of Trianon sounds a great mistake as all the local inhabitants, though Hungarians, are compulsory Czech citizens now. The children have to learn Czechoslovakian; the authorities hope to turn them into fervent Czechoslovaks in a couple of generations. The Hungarians hate the Czechs, and the Rumanians too, and on the same grounds – they feel less strongly about the Serbs, for some reason – and they mean to get back all their lost

---

* A Bratislava nightclub.

territory. This is why Hungary is a Kingdom still though it is governed by a regent. When a King is crowned on horseback with the old crown of St Stephen, he has to swear a most sacred oath to keep Hungary's ancient frontiers intact: so all Hungary's neighbours look askance on the monarchy. Attempts have been made to steal the actual diadem from the coronation church in Budapest, but it's impossible to get near it without electrocution. The Habsburgs are not very popular there, the old man said, as they have always looked on the Magyars as rebels. What a frightful problem.

'Under a broad-brimmed, flat-crowned hat which he wore at a rakish tilt, the old man's face was tanned and seamed like old wood and the skin, stretched taut over his cheekbones, made a fan of wrinkles at the corners of his eyes. He looked a bit like a Red Indian, except for the black moustache that jutted over a long, thin, brass-bound pipe-stem made out of bamboo or reed. He wore shiny knee-boots that creased softly like concertinas at the ankles, so did his wife and daughter. The red silk kerchiefs that were tied under their chins made them look like figures out of the Russian ballet especially the daughter, who was ravishing. Her bodice, sleeves, skirt and apron were all different colours and she had soft blue eyes and hair loosely tied in a thick plait. They called her Irinka, a lovely name, short for Irene.

'We had hardly said good-bye when a spectacled young man on a bike overtook me and dismounted, with a greeting in Slovak – 'Dobar den', I think, instead of 'jo nápot kivánok' – and asked where I was going.* He fell in step beside me. He was a schoolmaster and he enlarged on the past sorrows of Slovakia. It is true that the local villages are Hungarian, but further north they are pure Slovak as far as the Polish border. They had been under the Magyars for a thousand years and always treated as an inferior race, and when any Slovak rose in the world he was promptly seduced into the lesser Magyar nobility – with the result that all local leadership evaporated.

* Owing to my ignorance of both the local tongues, from now on all conversations were in German, unless stated otherwise.

Slovak children used to be taken away from their parents and brought up as Magyars. Even when they were fighting the Austrians in defence of their nationality and language, the Hungarians were busy oppressing and Magyarizing their own Slovak subjects. The schoolmaster didn't seem to like the Czechs much either, though this involved a different kind of resentment. The Czechs, it seems, regard the Slovaks as irredeemable bumpkins, while in Slovak eyes, the Czechs are bossy, petit bourgeois bureaucrats who take unfair advantage of their closeness to the government in Prague. The schoolmaster himself was from northern Slovakia, where – partly thanks to the Hussites, partly to the general spread of the Reformation in east Europe – much of the population is Protestant. I hadn't realized this. It was touch and go in the Dark Ages whether the Slavs of the North became Catholic or Orthodox. Under the proselytizing influence of SS. Cyril and Methodius – the Byzantine missionaries who invented the Cyrillic script and translated the sacred writings into Old Slavonic – it could easily have been the latter. When I asked why it hadn't, he laughed and said: '*The damned Magyars came!*' The link was severed, and the Czechs and Slovaks stuck to Rome and the West.

'When he reached his turning he asked me to stay in his village, but I had to press on. He pedalled away with a wave. A nice man.'

In these parts, SS. Cyril and Methodius, whose names are as inseparably joined as Swan is to Edgar, still enjoy great fame. In *The Good Soldier Švejk*, the hero's peculiar conduct lands him temporarily in a Prague lunatic asylum where he is surrounded by raving megalomaniacs. 'A chap can pass himself off as God Almighty there,' he said, 'or the Virgin Mary, the Pope, the King of England, His Imperial Majesty or St Wenceslas . . . One of them even pretended to be SS. Cyril and Methodius, just to get double rations.'

The dry paths had turned my boots and puttees white with dust. The empty sky was the clear blue of a bird's egg and I was walking in my shirt sleeves for the first time. Slower and slower however: a nail in one of my boots had mutinied. I limped into the thatched and whitewashed village of Köbölkut as it was getting dark. There was a crowd of villagers in the street and I drifted into the church with them and wedged myself into the standing congregation.

The women all had kerchiefs tied under the chin. The men, shod in knee-boots, or in raw-hide moccasins cross-gartered half-way up their shanks, had wide felt hats in their hands, or cones of fleece. Over the shoulders of a couple of shepherds were flung heavy white capes of stiff homespun frieze. In spite of the heat and the crush, one of them was wrapped in a cloak of matted and uncured sheepskin, shaggy-side out, that reached down to the flagstones. Things had become much wilder in the last hundred miles. The faces had a knobbly, untamed look: they were peasants and countrymen to the backbone.

The candles, spiked on a triangular grid, lit up these rustic masks and populated the nave behind them with a crowd of shadows. At a pause in the plainsong one of the tapers was put out. I realized, all at once, that it was Maundy Thursday. Tenebrae were being sung, and very well. The verses of the penitential psalms were answering each other across the choir and the slow recapitulations and re-phrasings of the responsories were unfolding the story of the Betrayal. So compelling was the atmosphere that the grim events might have been taking place that night. The sung words crept step by step through the phases of the drama. Every so often, another candle was lifted from its pricket on the triangle and blown out. It was pitch dark out of doors and with the extinction of each flame the interior shadows came closer. It heightened the chiaroscuro of these rough country faces and stressed the rapt gleam in innumerable eyes; and the church, as it grew hotter, was filled by the smell of melting wax and sheepskin and curds and sweat and massed breath. There was a ghost of old incense in the background and a reek of singeing as the wicks, snuffed one after the other, expired in ascending skeins of smoke. 'Seniores populi consilium fecerunt,' the voices sang, 'ut Jesum dolo tenerent et occiderent'; and a vision sprang up of evil and leering elders whispering in a corner through toothless gums and with beards wagging as they plotted treachery and

murder. 'Cum gladiis et fustibus exierunt tamquam ad latronem
...' Something in the half-lit faces and the flickering eyes gave a
sinister immediacy to the words. They conjured up hot dark
shadows under a town wall and the hoarse shouts of a lynch-mob;
there was a flicker of lanterns, oafish stumbling in the steep olive
groves and wild and wheeling shadows of torches through tree
trunks: a scuffle, words, blows, a flash, lights dropped and
trampled, a garment snatched, someone running off under the
branches. For a moment, we – the congregation – became the
roughs with the blades and the cudgels. Fast and ugly deeds were
following each other in the ambiguity of the timbered slope. It
was a split-second intimation! By the time the last of the candles
was borne away, it was so dark that hardly a feature could be
singled out. The feeling of shifted roles had evaporated; and we
poured out into the dust. Lights began to kindle in the windows of
the village and a hint of moonrise shone at the other end of the
plain.

I was looking for a barn for the night and a cobbler's shop – or,
linguistically more easily, a smithy – to get my boot-nail knocked
in. But as Smith – *Kovács* – is the commonest Hungarian sur-
name, just as it is in English, there was immediate confusion:
which Kovács? János? Zoltán? Imre? Géza? At last a voice in a
doorway said: 'Was wollen Sie?' It was a red-haired Jewish baker
and he not only hammered in the nail but put me up for the night
as well. 'We made a bed of straw and blankets on the stone floor of
the dark bakery,' my diary records, 'and here I am, writing this by
candlelight. Maundy Thursday is "Green Thursday" in German,
Gründonnerstag. I wonder why? Good Friday is *Karfreitag*.'
Next morning we talked in the sun outside the shop. There was
a bench under a tree. My host was from a Carpathian village
where quite a number of Jews, including his family, belonged to
the Hasidim, a sect which sprang up two centuries ago in the
province of Podolia – Russian then, Polish later – the other side of
the Carpathians. The sect represented a break with Talmudic
scholasticism and a plunge into mystic thought – the Cloud of
Unknowing *versus* the Tree of Knowledge – and the belief of the
Hasidim in a kind of all-englobing divine presence (a concept more

familiar to Christians than to Jews) was condemned by the orthodox, in particular by a famous scholar and rabbi in the Lithuanian
town of Vilna. But in spite of its heterodoxy and the anathema of
the Gaons, the sect multiplied. It prospered especially in Podolia,
Volhynia and the Ukraine and their tenets soon began to spread
from these flat and Cossack-harried provinces and found their way
south through the mountain passes. The baker himself was not a
zealot: the face under the carroty hair was plump, shrewd and
twinkling. I said I enjoyed reading the Bible. 'So do I,' he said;
then he added with a smile 'Especially the first part.' It took me a
further couple of seconds to get the point.

The church had lost its tenebrous mystery. But, by the end of
the service, a compelling aura of extinction, emptiness and
shrouded symbols pervaded the building. It spread through the
village and over the surrounding fields. I could feel it even after
Köbölkut had fallen below the horizon. The atmosphere of deso-
lation carries far beyond the range of a tolling bell.

When the low hills dropped, furrows fledged with young
wheat-blades ran symmetrically into the distance under scores of
larks. The footpath wandered through whitewashed farms and the
yards of low manor-houses and later through spinneys filled with
violets and primroses. Streams unwound under the willow
branches, dwindling and expanding again into pools that were
covered with watercress and duckweed and giant kingcups. The
tadpole season was over and the water-lily leaves were rafts for
little frogs. On a gregarious impulse, the shrill chorus would stop
suddenly for a few seconds and then strike up again, and my
advance touched off a mass of semicircular frog-trajectories and
plops while herons cruised low and settled among the rushes balanced watchfully on one leg. On a bank tufted with sedge and
reeds among mossy swamps a flock of sheep were tearing at the
rough grass and black pigs snouted after last year's acorns. The
herdsman lay smoking under an oak tree in his sheepskin and
there was no one else but scarecrows for miles. A fox trotted
across a clearing in a wood. The overhead blaze had reduced me to
shirt sleeves again and I was darkening like a piece of furniture.
About four in the afternoon I got to the little village of Karva.

The lane ended at the foot of a bank, and when I climbed it, there below – once again, long before I had expected it – the Danube was sweeping along.

Close to the bank, where reeds and willow-herb grew thick, the water gave off a gaseous tang of stagnation; but the ripples and the creases in midstream showed the speed of its flow. The plains which had expanded from Bratislava, with all their deviations and marshes and loops and islands, had yielded a few miles upstream to the enclosing advance of the hills. All strays had been gathered in and the higher ground on my bank was answered on the Hungarian shore by the undulations of the Bakony Forest; and, at long last, I was face to face with Hungary. It was only a river's width away. For a few miles it flowed unswerving between an escort of reflected woods and slid into the distance in either direction like a never-ending Champs Elysées of water.

I set off under the flickering poplar-leaves and I hadn't gone far before three villagers on horseback came trotting towards me upstream, one in loose white clothes and the others in black, with a chestnut foal scampering alongside. When we came level, we exchanged greetings and up went their three hats in a triple flourish. I knew the answer to the ritual question – 'Where do you come from?' – which always came first; it was: 'Angolországbol!' (England-from! Magyar is a language of suffixes.) And to the next question – 'Whither?' – the answer came equally pat: 'Konstantinópolybá!', Constantinople-ward. They smiled tolerantly. They hadn't the dimmest notion of the whereabouts of either. In dumb show, and with a questioning twiddle of the wrist, I asked where they were bound for. 'Komárombá!' they answered. Then straight as ninepins in their saddles, they put me in God's care and unlidded in concert once more. Touching their horses they headed Komárom-wards in a slow and stylish canter that lifted a long feather of dust along the towpath. The foal, taken by surprise, galloped anxiously to catch up until all four were out of sight many furlongs upstream. I wished I had had a hat to lift. These Hungarian salutes were magnificently ceremonious and hidalgo-like. (Komárom was an old town a few miles upstream at the mouth of the Váh. It disembogued in the Danube about thirty miles south of the point where Baron Pips and I had watched the rafts floating by. There was a bridge over the river there and some famous fortifications that the Hungarians defended through a long Austrian siege in 1848.)

The last sign of human habitation was a riverside hamlet called Čenke,* where crowds of rooks were noisily gathering for the night. Thereafter, the feeling of remoteness and solitude grew more pronounced with every step. It was getting darker too, but no colder: although it was the end of March, the air was as warm and as still as an evening in summer. Frog-time had come. Each pace, once more, unloosed a score of ragged parabolas and splashes. Flights of waterfowl detonated like spring-guns loosing off a whirr of missiles across the water. It was a world of scales and webbed feet and feathers and wet whiskers. Hundreds of new nests were joining the old ones in the damp green maze and soon there would be thousands of eggs and then wings beyond counting.

The meaning of the twin messages of the temperature and the wilderness took a moment or two to impinge. Then I understood, with sudden elation, that my first and longed-for night in the open had arrived. I found a hollow lined with leaves among the willow-trunks about three yards from the water and after a supper of Kövecses-remains and a new loaf from my baker friend and watercress from a stream, I stuck a candle on a stone to fill in my diary. It burned without a tremor. Then I lay, gazing upwards and smoking with my rucksack for a pillow, wrapped in my great-coat in case of cold later on.

The sky had changed. Flashing like a lozenge of icicle frag-

---

* Like a number of minor placenames in this chapter and the last, the name is part of the sudden rush of detail in the re-discovered journal; and, like many other names there, I can't find it on any map. Another of Baron Pips's parting presents was a set of pre-war large-scale maps, made by Freytags in Vienna – which disintegrated long ago, unfortunately – and perhaps this name was taken from one of them, or from a local signpost. As these maps were published in 1910, they had all the old Austro–Hungarian placenames and frontiers; though Čenke, with that diacritic over the C, giving it a 'tch' sound, looks Slovakian. The Hungarian form of the same sound would be 'Csénké'.

ments, Orion had reigned unchallenged all winter. Now it was already far down in the west and leading a retinue of constellations into decline and some of its wintry glitter had gone. The lower tip was growing dim in the vapour and dust that overhang horizons and soon the Pleiades were following the famous stars downhill. All the trees and reeds and flag-leaves and the river and the hills on the other bank glimmered insubstantially in the starlight. The fidgeting of moorhens and coots and of voles and water-rats doing the breast-stroke through the stems grew less frequent and every half-minute or so two bitterns – one quite near, the other perhaps a mile away – sounded across the vague amphibian world: loneliest of muffled cries, plainly to be heard above the shrill rise and fall of millions of frogs. This endless population, stretching upstream and down for leagues, made the night seem restlessly alive and expectant. I lay deep in one of those protracted moments of rapture which scatter this journey like asterisks. A little more, I felt, and I would have gone up like a rocket. The notion that I had walked twelve hundred miles since Rotterdam filled me with a legitimate feeling of something achieved. But why should the thought that nobody knew where I was, as though I were in flight from bloodhounds or from worshipping corybants bent on dismemberment, generate such a feeling of triumph? It always did.

The dimness of those dropping constellations was not all the fault of the vapours that haunt horizons. A rival pallor was spreading at the other end of the sky, and very fast. Behind a flutter of hills a rim of blood-red lunar segment was rising. It expended to its full diameter and then dwindled; and when the circumference was complete a tremendous crimson moon was casting loose. It changed to orange and then to yellow as it climbed and diminished until all the colour had ebbed away and left it to soar with the aloof and airy effulgence of silver. During the last hour's walking, twilight and darkness had masked the behaviour of the hills. Now the moon revealed that they had receded once more and left the Danube free to break loose. It was a week after the spring equinox and only a few hours short of the full moon, and as this is one of the few reaches where the river flows due east, the line of the moon's reflection lay amidstream where the current runs fastest and shivered and flashed there like quicksilver. The reefs and shoals and islands and the unravelling loops of water which had lain hidden till now were all laid bare. Wastes of fen spread from either shore and when the surfaces were broken by undergrowth or sedge or trees, they gleamed like fragments of flawed looking-glass. All was changed. The thin-shadowed light cast a spell of mineral illusion. The rushes and the flags were turned into thin metal; the poplar leaves became a kind of weightless coinage; the lightness of foil had infected the woods. This frosty radiance played tricks with levels and distances until I was surrounded by a dimensionless and inconcrete fiction which was growing paler every second. While the light was seeking out more and more liquid surfaces for reflection, the sky, where the moon was now sailing towards its zenith, seemed to have become an expanse of silvery powder too fine for the grain to be descried. Silence transcended the bitterns' notes and the industry of the frogs. Stillness and infinity were linked in a feeling of tension which, I felt sure, presaged hours of gazing watchfulness. But I was wrong. In a little while my eyes were closing under a shallow tide of sleep.

'Co tady děláte?' – 'I awoke with a start' – my diary says – 'someone was shaking me by the collar and shouting. As soon as I was fully awake, I made out two men in uniform. One of them, with an old-fashioned bull's-eye lantern on his belt, was keeping me covered with a rifle and his fixed bayonet was nearly touching my chest. Completely at a loss, I asked what was happening; but they spoke no German and only a word or two of Hungarian, so we were stuck. They made me get up and marched me along the path, one of them holding my arm in a ju-jitsu grip while the other, having slung his rifle, now carried an enormous automatic pistol. It was rather a comic scene; some mistake somewhere. Whenever I opened my mouth I was told to shut up, so I did, at least for a bit. After a while our little Švejk-like procession reached a wooden hut and I was put in a chair, still covered by the huge firearm. The pistol's owner had a bristling moustache; he fixed me with a bilious and bloodshot eye while the other began to search me from top to toe. He emptied every pocket and made me take my puttees and boots off. It was more and more mysterious. By the lamp in the hut I saw they were wearing the grey uniform of the Frontier Guard, which I had seen just before crossing to Bratislava. When he had finished with me, he untied the cord of my rucksack and turned it upside down so that everything tumbled on the floor in a disorderly heap. Then he began to unfold, or open and examine, every single item, feeling in the pockets of pyjamas and looking down the backs of books, even this wretched journal. This went on for some time until at last, as though realizing there was nothing to interest him, he knelt back in the middle of the floor, which was now littered with my ransacked belongings, and scratched his head in a mystified and baffled manner. The man with the pistol had also become a bit less fierce, and the two talked sadly, casting dubious glances at me from time to time. One of them picked up my passport, the only object that had attracted no notice during the search. When it emerged that I was English, it seemed to make a great difference. The man with the moustache laid down his automatic and I was offered a cigarette. We had been smoking for a minute or two when a third frontier-watchman turned up, a fat man who spoke German. He asked me what I was up to. I said I was on a walking tour across Europe. He kept looking from the photograph in the passport to me and back again, asked me my age and checked that it was nineteen. Suddenly he came to a decision: he smacked his hand hard on the table and burst out laughing. The others cheered up too. He told me I had been mistaken for a notorious saccharine smuggler called 'Černy Josef' – Black Joseph – 'Fekete Jozi', on the Magyar shore – who plied his trade from Čenke across the Danube into Hungary; the taxes on saccharine are so high there that it is an easy way of making a lot of money. I immediately thought of poor Konrad! But he'd promised me he was only going to take part on the business side.* Apparently Black Jo hides among the

---

* As we know from an earlier chapter, all went well. But this imbroglio on the Danube's banks made me anxious about him for some time to come.

trees and the reeds on this deserted reach of the river until a
boat rows across from the other side in the dark to pick him up;
so it had been rather a surprise to capture him – or someone like
him – on a night with a full moon; the trouble was, Jo was over
fifty ... We all laughed and the two men apologized for their
brusque treatment. In the end, they said they would fix quarters
for me. I'd have much rather slept out but didn't want to hurt
their feelings. We walked a mile or two inland across the water-
meadows and the moon was beginning to go down when we
reached a little farm. I am in the stable now on a soft heap of
straw with a hurricane lamp and catching up with the rest of
the night's doings before I forget them.

'Next day. The farm people were from Silesia. He was big and
tough and she very handsome, with jet black hair. There was a
stuffed otter on the wall – plenty of them lodge in the Danube's
banks. They gave me a lovely breakfast with coffee and black
bread and two boiled eggs and some hard white cheese sprinkled
with red paprika, and a swig of barack. Also, some things
wrapped up to eat on the way. I'm beginning to feel like Elijah,
fed by ravens.

'Dew covered the grass and a thin mist veiled the river, but
both were soon gone. The path still followed a grassy ridge
banked against flooding. I could see for miles, all last night's
scenery: strange and unbelievable then, calm and beautiful now,
rather like the woods and the polders seen from a dyke-road in
Holland. Poplars, willows and aspens sheltered the path – a
blessing, as it's been the hottest day of the year – and the
branches made a criss-cross of shade. I met nobody till I came on
some Gypsy boys who spend their time hunting weasels, stoats,
rats, field-mice and other humble fauna. The way they go
about this is very unsporting. They find their holes in the
banks, pour a bucket of water in the highest one and the
animals come scuttling half-drowned out of exits lower down
and the boys catch them and wring their necks. When I passed
them they waved bunches of dismal and draggled little corpses
at me, wanting me to buy some, as they eat them and expect
you to do the same – they eat anything. Baron Pips told me that
when his farm people bury a horse that has died of old age or

disease, Gypsies are sure to dig it up and eat it in the middle of the night ... '

There was a lull in the air. Holy Saturday, with its lamps out and shrines empty and the distant tolling over the fields, cast a spell of catalepsy and suspense. It was a time of sealed tombs and sleeping sentries with the Protagonist of the week's drama deep underground harrowing Hell ... There was not a fisherman on the river, not a peasant in the fields, nothing but those little vole-catchers and skimming wagtails, the waterbirds and the massed larks and the frogs, whose steady diurnal croak, though universal, seemed milder than the full-moon brekekekexing the night before. A thrown stick could silence an acre for several seconds. The flecks of dust on the current and the spinning fluff suggested mid-summer. I ate my bread and cheese on the shady side of a rick and fell asleep. (Hay-ricks are conical hereabouts, cleverly stacked round a centre pole and when most of the hay has been sliced away for fodder, the sun catches the shorn planes as if lopsided obelisks had been erected in the fields.) I awoke later than I had intended. The woods, full of rooks and wood-pigeons, were sending long shadows over the grass. I drank at a brook, sloshed some water on my face and tidied up. Civilization lay ahead.

Far away on the other bank I could see my destination; it had been growing steadily in size since my first glimpse that morning. A cliff loomed over a long sweep of the river and on this ledge was perched a white fane that resembled St Peter's in Rome. A light circle of pillars lifted a gleaming dome into the sky. It was dramatic, mysterious, as improbable as a mirage and unmistakable as a landmark for many miles across the desert of liquid and solid. The Basilica of Esztergom, I knew, was the Metropolitan Cathedral of all Hungary, the largest religious building in the Kingdom and the archiepiscopal See of the Cardinal-Prince-Arch-bishop: the Hungarian equivalent, that is, of Rheims, Canterbury, Toledo, Armagh and old Cracow. The Basilica, though spectacular and splendid, is not old: little in that part of Hungary was spared the ravages of the Tartars and the Turks; after the Reconquest everything had to begin again. But the town – the Latin Strigonium and the German Gran – is one of the oldest in the country. Ever since the first Apostolic King of Christian Hungary – the conquering Arpáds' descendant, St Stephen himself – was born and crowned in Esztergom, history has been accumulating here and entwining itself with myth. From my footpath, the Basilica was the only building in sight. The monasteries, the churches, the palaces and the libraries that encrust the steep little town were all in baulk. The great pile, with its twin cupola-topped belfries, its ring of pillars and its great nacreous dome, hovered above water and timber and fen as though upheld, like a celestial city in a painting, by a flurry of untiring wings.

The air was full of hints and signs. There was a flicker and a swishing along the river like the breezy snip-snap of barbers' scissors before they swoop and slice. It was the skimming and twirling of newly arrived swifts. A curve in the stream was re-arranging the landscape as I advanced, revealing some of the roofs of Esztergom and turning the Basilica to a new angle as though it were on a pivot. The rolling wooded range of the Bakony Forest had advanced north from the heart of Transdanubia, and the cor-responding promontory on the northern shore – the last low foot-hills of the Matra mountains, whose other extremity subsides in the northern-eastern tip of Hungary – jutted into the water under the little town of Parkan. Reaching for each other, the two head-lands coerced the rambling flood yet once more into a narrower and swifter flow and then spanned the ruffle with an iron bridge. Spidery at first, the structure grew more solid as the distance dwindled. (Twenty miles east of this bridge, the Danube reaches a most important point in its career: wheeling round the ultimate headland of the Bakony Forest and heading due south for the first time on its journey, it strings itself through Budapest like a thread through a bead and drops across the map of Europe plumb for a hundred and eighty miles, cutting Hungary clean in half. Then, reinforced by the Drava, it turns east again, invades Yugoslavia, swallows up the Sava under the battlements of Belgrade, and sweeps on imperturbably to storm the Iron Gates.)

In an hour, I had climbed the cliff-path into the main street of Parkan. A litle later my passport was stamped at the frontier post at the Czechoslovakian end of the bridge. The red, white and green barrier of the frontier post at the far end marked the beginning of Hungary. I lingered in the middle of the bridge, meditatively poised in no man's air.

The masonry of the piers below sent green Ophelia-like tresses of waterweed swaying down the current. Upstream, the water broke up the reflected turquoise of a sky full of dishevelled cirrus clouds. Pink and crimson threads were dispersed in conflicting drifts and then frozen in motionless turmoil; it was all the stranger as there had not been a breath of wind all day. Swifts were still skimming through the air and a heron flew across the river from wood to wood. A number of large and mysterious birds were floating high overhead and at first I thought they were herons too, but they carried their necks extended instead of coiled between their shoulders, and they were white. They were larger and more slender and less hurried than swans: the spread of wings scarcely moved as they revolved on the air-currents. There were about a dozen, snow-plumed except for black flight-feathers which ran along the inner edge of their wing like a senatorial stripe of mourning. They were storks! When they circled lower, the long beaks and the legs that trailed in the slipstream showed red as sealing wax. An old shepherd was leaning on the ramp close by and gazing up at them too. When some of the great birds floated lower, the draught of their feathers brushed our upturned faces, and he said something in Magyar – 'Nét, góbyuk!' and smiled. He hadn't a tooth in his head. Two of the birds glided upstream. One dropped on a haystack and fluttered to regain its balance. The second landed underneath in the meadow – becoming, as it folded its wings, a white bobbin with red lacquer stilts and bill – and paced to the water's edge. The others, meanwhile, were alighting on the tiles of the two little bridge-head towns and advancing with ungainly steps along the roofs to inspect the dishevelled nests that cumbered many of the chimneys. Two of them were even attempting, in defiance of the bells which were tolling there, to land in one of the Cathedral belfries – they remembered the harmless hazard from former incumbency. The bell-hampers were choked with tangles of last year's twigs.

Touching my arm, the shepherd pointed downstream at something in the dark-shadowed east high above the river and just discernible across the failing sky. Ragged and flocculent, fading to grey, scattered with specks of pink from the declining sun, varying in width as random fragments were dropping away and recohering and agitated with motion as though its whole length were turning on a single thread, a thick white line of crowding storks stretched from one side of the heavens to the other. Mounting Africa along the Nile, they had followed the coasts of Palestine and Asia Minor and entered Europe over the Bosphorus. Then, persevering along the Black Sea shore to the delta of the Danube, they had steered their flight along that shining highway until they had come to the great bend a few miles downstream. Defecting from the river, their journey was now following a westerly as well as a northern bias; they were bound for Poland, perhaps, and shedding contingents as they went at hundreds of remembered haunts. We gazed at them in wonder. It was a long time before the rearguard of that great sky-procession had vanished north. Before nightfall the whole armada would subside in a wood or settle all over some Slovakian hamlet – astonishing the villagers and delighting them, for storks are birds of good omen – like a giant snow storm; taking to the air again at first light. (Six months and hundreds of miles later, I halted on the southern slopes of the Great Balkan Range, and watched the same great migration in reverse. They were making for the Black Sea, retracing their spring journey before wintering beyond the Sahara.)

There was much going on: in the air and the sky, on the river, along the banks; almost too much. I was determined to linger, suspended there in a void, and let a few more hundred thousand tons of liquid rush under the girders before stepping across the remaining yards into Hungary. I might have been in the royal box opposite the milling *dramatis personae* as the curtain was going up.

A solitary bell, forerunner of the peals and scales that would come tumbling into the moonlight later on, had been joined by several others, but their summoning notes failed to hasten the ebb and flow under the trees: though the crowd, strolling and hobnobbing all along the waterfront, showed a slight tendency to veer towards a road that led uphill. There were hundreds of peasants from neighbouring villages. The men were mostly in black and white, but a burly figure in bandman's rig toiled through the crowd stooping under a big drum and the slanting sunbeams picked out a trombone here and a bassoon there, and three colleagues equipped with French horns who were drifting the same way. The clothes of the women and the girls, with their many-pleated skirts and their different-coloured bodices and aprons and kerchiefs, were enlivened here and there by clusters of ribbons and stiff bright panels of embroidery on billowing sleeves. As usual the brightest colours were at play in the flaring and flouncing of Gypsy women: violet and magenta and orange and yellow and shrill green. The hues were sprinkled like the flowers of an Indian temple-garland broken and scattered among the tamer European blooms. No rustic gathering was to be without them for the rest of the journey. On the plank of a rough cart outside an inn, a brown bear was seated as though he were about to pick up the reins; his dark-skinned master climbed beside him and they drove away. Creeping through the crowd and the village carts and pony-traps and the groups of horsemen, an anachronistic charabanc halted and discharged two nuns and a troop of schoolgirls and honked its way slowly offstage. A trio of tall Dominicans in shovel hats, as easy as magpies to pick out by their black and white markings, were gathered under a chestnut tree.

But it was a group of splendid figures, sauntering and halting along the flagstones of the quay that caught and held the eye. They were clad in dark, sumptuous and variously coloured doublets of heavy silk – or occasionally of velvet – fastened with chased buttons the size of gold hazelnuts and edged with brown fur at the cuffs and the throat and over the shoulders. Some wore knee-length over-tunics, furred likewise and open down the front and frogged with gold lace; others wore them slung across their backs with careful abandon, or askew over one shoulder like swinging dolmans. Tight breeches, stiff with embroidery, ended in Hessian boots which were black, scarlet, blue or rifle-green; gold braid edged their notched tops and gilt spurs were screwed into the heels. One or two had gold or silver chains about their necks and all of them wore kalpacks of light or dark fur. These were

shaped like hussars' busbies, tilted on their brows at challenging
slants and plumed with white aigrettes or herons' feathers that
burst from their jewelled clasps like escapes of steam. Carried non-
chalantly under their arms or in the crooks of their elbows or with
points touching the flagstones when stationary and hands resting
lightly on the cross-hilts, their nearly semi-circular scimitars were
sheathed in green or blue or plum-coloured velvet and mounted in
gold and adorned with jewels at intervals along the scabbards. The
splendour of princes in a legend stamped these magnates, and,
except for one, who was nearly spherical and rashly kalpacked in
white fur and booted in the same scarlet as his complexion, they
carried off all this bravery with accomplished ease: strolling, gossiping, glancing at their watches, leaning on their scimitars and
halting with one leg straight and the other Meredithianly bent.
As he talked and nodded, the monocle of a tall dandy flashed back
the sunset in dots and dashes like Morse code. A carriage halted,
three similarly-clad congeners alighted and there was a ceremonious doffing of bear's fur and egret and the clink of heels
politely joining. A magnificent old man remained inside; lame
perhaps, for his white-bearded chin rested on hands crossed on the
bone crook of a malacca cane. His scimitar was laid across his knee
as he bent forward, talking and laughing. The energy and humour
of the white-bristling face reminded me of Victor Hugo. Apart
from the brown fur and a gold chain round his shoulders and an
order at his throat, he was dressed entirely in black, and all the
more magnificent for this sobriety. (''Twould have made you
crazy' – the lines suddenly surfaced after years of oblivion – 'to see
Esterhazy/with jools from his jasey/to his dimond boots.'* Yes,
indeed.) Slowly this covey of grandees, with the carriage and its
white-bearded passenger driving alongside them at a walking pace,
strolled upstream under the sequin twinkle of the poplars.

Close behind me, girls in bright clothes were hastening excitedly across the bridge, all of them carrying bunches of water-
lilies, narcissi, daffodils and violets and those enormous kingcups
that grew in the streams. I waved as they dashed by, and one of
them turned and sent a string of good-tempered dactyls over her

---

* *Ingoldsby Legends.*

shoulder. If the Hungarians had not been monotheists, the impending Resurrection might have been followed by the ascent of Adonis and Prosperine.

I found it impossible to tear myself from my station and plunge into Hungary. I feel the same disability now: a momentary reluctance to lay hands on this particular fragment of the future; not out of fear but because, within arm's reach and still intact, this future seemed, and still seems, so full of promised marvels. The river below, meanwhile, was carrying the immediate past downstream and I was hung poised in mid-air between the two.

But today, with the clairvoyance of retrospect, I can fend off the fateful moment by assembling the data whose results the next few hours would reveal ... For I know now what must have been afoot. I can see the citizens of Esztergom aligning candles on their window-sills – wicks which, added to the tapers in the hands of a myriad watching peasants, were to surround the procession, later on, with a twinkling forest, and, peering up at the Basilica, I can float inside and along the vistas of acanthus-leaves and through the darkening criss-cross of mezzotint shading into the vast sacristy where the tiers of presses and the rows of treasure-chests have disgorged their silk and their brocade, all unfolded now, and their sacred instruments and their vessels. Mitres are clicked open, copes spread, the jewelled gloves and the pallium laid ready, candelabra and monstrances and crosiers set forth. In the Pannini-like emptiness under the dome, pale armfuls of new and unlit candles are pricked in tall palisades across the gloom. An unrolling carpet ascends the shallow steps under the Archbishop's canopy and the bell-ringers in their loft are getting thirsty.

In the stable-yard of the Archbishop's palace half-way up the hill, there is a clattering and a mutter of unseasonable oaths from the booted and busbied postillions and the grooms. Restive horseshoes strike sparks from the cobbles. The hindmost of the Cardinal's four greys, with a toss of mane and plume, is being backed between the shafts while the traces are run through. Half the size of the other postillions but identically frogged and plumed, a pink-cheeked tiger polishes the silver door-handle for the last time, then runs a rag over the varnished panel where a scarlet painted hat encloses a mitre-and-crown-topped escutcheon between its five-tiered pyramids of tassels, and slams it shut.

On the walls inside the Palace, meanwhile, Duccio's sombre Jeremiah and the shrivel-cheeked hermits and Doctors of Crivelli grow dim in their frames; likewise the Virgins and Child of Matteo di Giovanni and the Nativities of Giovanni di Paolo. The enthroned Madonna of Taddeo Gaddi and Lorenzo di Credi's *Assumption of the Magdalene* are losing their lustre and the sacred groups from Siena and Florence and Venice and Umbria and the Marches and the Low Countries and Spain are all on the brink of dissolution. Ambiguity ranges abroad! A Lombardic maiden has become one with the unicorn she clasps in her vermilion arms; and in a score of Martyrdoms, the gesso gleam of the haloes will outlive the incumbent saints. By assimilative collusion, the Danube School Temptations and Crucifixions have already swallowed up the shadows that are assembling along the valley. Evening gathers. Perhaps the Transylvanian visions of Thomas of Koloszvár – knights and bishops and St Giles in an ilex-glade shielding his pet hind from an archer – will be the last to succumb.

The other floors are astir with expectancy. There is a coming and going of staff, an anxious eye for the clocks that tick in the great rooms, an ear for the cathedral bells, a downward glance at the stables; but at the heart of all, in Monsignor Seredy, Cardinal Mindszenty's immediate predecessor, reigns imperturbable calm. A scarlet presence can be divined, a good-humoured face, a red skullcap, a ringed hand on a table beside a red biretta incandescent in the dusk. About his shoulders, instead of the customary lace, a white fur mantle is patterned with ermine: an ancient use makes the primate of Hungary a temporal prince as well as an archbishop and a Prince of the Church. All round his chair, the stiff, wide folds of his *cappa magna* cover the design of the carpet with yard upon yard of geranium-coloured watered silk. Pince-nez flashing, all cuff and Adam's apple, his chaplain and train-bearer flits attentively at his side. Anxiously at hand, punctiliously turned out in a dark magnate's splendour and with his hair neatly brushed, a youthful and newly-appointed gentleman-at-arms hovers. A plumed fur hat rests in the crook of his arm, a gloved hand grasps a scimitar in a black velvet scabbard at the point of balance. He is determined, come what may in the complexities of the long night ahead, to keep his spurs and his sword-point clear of that ocean of scarlet silk ... There is still time for a discreet cigarette at the far end of the room ... The Archbishop's chestnut-trees have opened a thousand fans under the tall windows, each to be pronged with a pink or white steeple before the month is out. An owl hoots! Beyond the poplars and the empty quay, the cobweb of the bridge looms across the Danube and somebody still lingers there. But beyond it, all turns dark. Upstream it is still daylight and the river glows wide and pale as it loiters west through the insubstantial green and silver foliage. As though in answer to the more urgent tolling, the voices of the frogs are suddenly louder.

I too heard the change in the bells and the croaking and the solitary owl's note. But it was getting too dim to descry a figure, let alone a struck match, at the windows of the Archbishopric. A little earlier, sunset had kindled them as if the Palace were on fire. Now the sulphur, the crocus, the bright pink and the crimson had left the panes and drained away from the tousled but still unmoving cirrus they had reflected. But the river, paler still by contrast with the sombre merging of the woods, had lightened to a milky hue. A jade-green radiance had not yet abandoned the sky. The air itself, the branches, the flag-leaves, the willow-herb and the rushes were held for a space, before the unifying shadows should dissolve them, in a vernal and marvellous light like the bloom on a greengage. Low on the flood and almost immaterialized by this luminous moment, a heron sculled upstream, detectable mainly by sound and by the darker and slowly dissolving rings that the tips of its flight-feathers left on the water. A collusion of shadows had begun and soon only the lighter colour of the river would survive. Downstream in the dark, meanwhile, there was no hint of the full moon that would transform the scene later on. No one else was left on the bridge and the few on the quay were all hastening the same way. Prised loose from the balustrade at last by a more compelling note from the belfries, I hastened to follow. I didn't want to be late.

TO BE CONTINUED

Index